BEYOND ALL HORIZONS

BEYOND ALL HORIZONS

Jesuits and the Missions

Edited by
Thomas J. M. Burke, S.J.

Preface by Anne Fremantle

Hanover House, Garden City, New York

Imprimi Potest: Very Reverend Thomas E. Henneberry, S.J.
Provincial, New York Province
Society of Jesus

Nihil Obstat: John A. Goodwine, J.C.D.
Censor Librorum

Imprimatur: ✠   Francis Cardinal Spellman
Archbishop of New York
February 18, 1957

BV2290
B8

Library of Congress Catalog Card Number 57–7378

Preface

Anne Fremantle

THE very word mission, in the technical sense in which it has been used during the past three hundred years, is probably a "Jesuit" word stemming from the Jesuit fourth vow, taken when a man finally becomes a full member of the Society of Jesus: the *votum de missionibus*. This vow, in the great edifice of the Church, stands, as it were, cater-cornered from the fourth Benedictine vow of stability (the first three being, of course, in both cases, poverty, chastity, and obedience). At first this fourth vow of the Jesuits referred not merely to foreign missions, but to any place to which their vow of obedience took the members of the Society, even in Catholic countries. Gradually, mainly owing to the use of the word in the documents emanating from the Sacred College of Propaganda, the term generally acquired its current connotation of *foreign missions*.

In the history of the missionary Church many of the most glorious pages have been written by the members of the Society of Jesus. The Church, although divinely guided, is a human society, and there have been, alas, all too many cases where her rightful missionary zeal was expressed and interpreted by all too human characters. Such horrors as the mass

5

baptisms of Clovis, or the arrival of the Crusaders in Hagia Sophia wading up to their horses' knees in Saracen blood, are infinitely more, not less, ghastly for having been perpetrated in "good faith" and in Christ's name. But the Jesuits have never, even by their bitterest enemies, been accused of brutality in their methods, nor of a lack of respect for the freedom of the human will to choose or to reject the Light for which it was created. If anything, their caution, and their almost meticulous desire to hold off the would-be convert until grace overwhelms him, has been dubbed dilatory. I remember the case of a member of a distinguished Alexandrian Jewish family, who was discouraged by his Jesuit schoolmasters from announcing his conversion while still in Egypt. He was the first convert in the history of the school, and his mentors were afraid parents would no longer send their children to this school for fear they might follow this bad example. I myself, at seventeen, surreptitiously at a kindly friend's house met Father Martindale, S.J. (my mother would not allow me to see a Catholic priest), and was told by him, "My dear child, never marry or become a Catholic unless you are quite sure you have to." It is this delicacy, this sensitivity, which Arnold Toynbee singles out for praise in two of his essays on the missionary work of the Jesuits. It is the long, slow ripening of the Jesuit novice which prepares him for the missions: the process of conversion must begin with the would-be converter, and can flow outward only after it has permeated inward.

There is a tendency, even among Catholics, to regard the Jesuits as hustlers and bustlers, men of action rather than of contemplation. One of the chief merits of this symposium is the emphasis it rightly places on the dual nature of the missionary activity. You can't give what you haven't got—and yet the Giver uses what human instrument He pleases and everything which the greatest of the saints, even Ignatius or Francis Xavier, had was not his, but was given. "Paul sows, and Apollo watereth, but it is God giveth the increase." So from the first, St. Ignatius envisaged the Society he founded as a living, breathing organism: breathe in, the work of sanctification, the Spiritual Exercises, the quest for perfection; breathe out, pour out, all the grace given; give until the hands are empty, and after the hands are empty praise the Giver, as the country priest did in George Bernanos' great novel, "for the mystery of the empty hands" that still have the power to bind, to heal, to loose. A Dominican, Father Jean de Menasce, has well put the Ignatian ideal:

"I am certain that contemplatives, when they become apostles, are more discerning than men supposedly practical, that they are more free and more judicious in their choice of instruments, more deeply anchored to their goal, have more freedom in their choice of means because they are aware of the relativity of all means, while respecting their real values as such. The hierarchy of values can only be established from above." ("Polarite de l'Activité Missionaire," article in *Nouvelle Revue de Science Missionaire*, 1945, p. 86.)

On 21 December 1924 His Holiness Pope Pius XI, opening the Vatican missionary exhibition, said, "We wish to emphasize the importance of the scientific, ethnographic, medical and literary aspect of missions, because it is always from the realm of ideas that the great directives of action proceed; also because the age in which we live is an age in which it becomes ever increasingly apparent that the greatest heroisms and all the sacrifices which accompany the missionary effort will not suffice if they are merely empirical. Science must be brought in to help, to illumine with her light the clearest way, the most direct paths; it is science that must suggest the most profitable combinations. As in industry, as in commerce, as in all the most practical and material manifestations of contemporary life, so also in the missions, this characteristic requirement of our era must not be evaded, but must be recognized and accepted."

This "new look" upon which the then Holy Father insisted so emphatically, this whole "new" orientation of the missionary activity of the Church, was originated by the Society of Jesus, and has gradually become the common property of the whole Church, and not only now is universally accepted but is—as this text shows—officially taught. For example, the insistence on the wearing of local costume, now so widespread (evidenced by the Little Brothers of de Foucauld, for example, or the contemplative Benedictine nuns in the U.S.A., or in India by the Benedictine author of *The Golden Thread,* now living there as a sannyasi), was pioneered notably by Father de Nobili, who became a Brahmin in India in the sixteenth century, and by Father Matthew Ricci, the famous priest mandarin of China.

Jesuits are imbued with a deep spirituality and a high vision, but their history shows that there is nothing of the doctrinaire about a real Jesuit. Whether in Europe or our own country or working in the smallest mission station the Jesuit is animated by a practical and profound love of God and men. The social works of missionaries, the extraordinary experiment of the South American Reductions, the weather stations of Asia, the numerous schools, the early and continued efforts to develop native-born priests and lay leaders are part of a concerted effort to enable men to live as sons of God in this world.

In this effort it is in education that the Jesuits have achieved their greatest reputation, and throughout the world since the foundation of the Society as many non-Catholics as Catholics, if not more, have extolled Jesuit pedagogy. "What is Beaumont?" the captain of the Eton cricket team contemptuously retorted to the Beaumont cricket team's captain when challenged to a match in the 1870s. And the reply of the cricket captain in the newly opened Jesuit school has become world-famous, a classic repartee wherever English is spoken. "Beaumont is what Eton once was, a school for the sons of Catholic gentlemen." The Jesuits believe that they exist to prepare the whole world to become what once it was, and what it must and can be again, a school for the sons (and daughters) of God.

It is a distinct pleasure to welcome in print this symposium, which is the first attempt in English to give a fairly comprehensive, yet thoroughly interesting, picture of what Jesuit missionaries in the past have done and what their not unworthy successors are doing today.

Grateful acknowledgment is made to the following publishers for permission to quote excerpts from the books listed below:

Farrar, Straus and Cudahy, Inc., *St. Francis Xavier,* by James Brodrick, S.J., copyright, 1952, by Pellegrini & Cudahy. E. P. Dutton & Co., Inc., *The Wise Man from the West,* by Vincent Cronin. Little, Brown & Company, *Edmund Campion,* by Evelyn Waugh. Hollis & Carter, Ltd., *Edmund Campion,* by Evelyn Waugh. Burns, Oates and Washbourne, Ltd., London, *Edmund Campion: Jesuit Protomartyr of England,* by Richard Simpson. America Press, *The Jesuits in History,* by Martin P. Harney, S.J. The Bruce Publishing Company, *St. Regis: A Social Crusader,* by Albert S. Foley, S.J. The Macmillan Company, *The Reformation in England,* Vol. III, by Philip Hughes; *Christians and Christianity in India and Pakistan,* by P. Thomas; *Bernardine Realino,* by Francis Sweeney, S.J. Oxford University Press, Inc., *The World and the West,* by Arnold Toynbee. University of California Press, *The Christian Century in Japan,* by C. R. Boxer. St. Joseph's Industrial School Press, Trichinopoly, S. India, *The Madura Catholic Mission,* by Fr. J. C. Houpert, S.J. Longmans, Green & Co., Inc., *The Progress of the Jesuits,* by James Brodrick, S.J., copyright, 1947; and *The Origin of the Jesuits,* by James Brodrick, S.J., copyright, 1940. B. Herder Book Co., *St. Francis Xavier, The Apostle of India and Japan,* by G. Schurhammer, S.J. The Vanguard Press, *The Jesuit Relations and Allied Documents,* edited by Edna Kenton, with a preface by Dr. George N. Shuster, copyright, 1954, by The Vanguard Press.

CONTENTS

Introduction

Thomas J. M. Burke, s.j.

JESUITS are commonly regarded as very shrewd men even though someone reading the *Jesuit Relations of North America* would find that such an eminent Jesuit missionary as St. Isaac Jogues had very poor insight into real estate values. At the time when many of the homes on Manhattan were made of a stucco of crushed oyster shells taken from the Hudson and East rivers, Jogues spent several days in the city. Later, in letters back to Europe, he revealed his belief that the land of New York was almost completely worthless since it was so rocky.

One might doubt the wisdom of the Jesuits if he had stood on the deck of the little *Santiago* as it sailed out of the harbor of Lisbon carrying St. Francis Xavier—it was his thirty-fifth birthday—who was going out with dreams of converting the Indies accompanied only by Camerino, an Italian Jesuit, and Mansilhas, a Portuguese scholastic.

At any time during a period of seventeen years one could have found the Italian Jesuit, Matthew Ricci—shortly after Xavier's time—living the life of a mandarin in a Chinese house in Nanking, Shiuchow, or Nanchang, astonishing the native mandarins—not only by his mathematical and astronomical knowledge, his expertness in making clocks and maps, but also by his extraordinary ability to memorize, at a single reading, the ideograms of a Chinese poem and then repeat them backwards. This might have seemed an extravagant waste of time on the part of one who had come to head the apostolate to China, even though one of the books he wrote at this period would introduce Christianity into Korea so effectively that over ten thousand fairly well-instructed Catholics greeted the first priest to arrive there.

For years the brilliant Father de Nobili—perhaps the first European to master Sanskrit—puttered about his little hut in India clad in ocher robes, wooden slippers on his feet, sandalwood paste on his forehead, sedulously avoiding alcohol or beef, living the difficult life of an upper-caste ascetic.

In recent years at the leper colony at Culion, as a simple chaplain, worked Father Rello, perhaps the most gifted linguist in the Philippines, at ease in all the major European languages as well as the languages and dialects of the islands. Somewhat like the Old Testament men, in his youth he had asked God for facility in languages, making a bargain that if he received that facility he would volunteer for work among lepers. Actually, though it might have seemed a waste of a most talented man, his appointment at Culion worked out excellently because he always could communicate easily in the dialects of patients from various sections.

Father Gherzi has worked in the observatory at Zikawei— now in Communist hands—for thirty-seven years trying to develop new techniques for predicting typhoons. In Micronesia in the South Pacific, Father Francis Cosgrove takes care of a parish stretching for thirteen hundred miles. Sailing day after day in a small boat, not much larger than a canoe, with a couple of broomstick masts and an outboard motor to be used only in case of major difficulty, he can visit his Stone Age people on different little islands perhaps every three or four months. Father D'Elia, an expert Sinologist after many years spent in China, teaches future missionaries in Rome. In the center of a Buddhist enclave at Kathmandu in Nepal, Father Marshall Moran opened in recent years a Jesuit school where the only thing approaching religion is a course in natural ethics. The school was requested because the son of a leading Nepal official spent so much time on his short-wave radio communicating with his former Jesuit teachers in Patna City that his father decided it would be easier to invite the Jesuits to open a school in the city. In the Belgian Congo the Jardin Gillet, named after its initiator, a Jesuit Brother who died about eleven years ago, is one of the most extensive tropical gardens in the world. On Taiwan (Formosa) a Hungarian Jesuit, Father Zsámár, and a French Jesuit, Father Deltour, are working with twenty-two other refugees from Red China under the direction of a Spanish Jesuit to prepare five Chinese dictionaries. Driving a twenty-ton trailer truck over the Alaska Highway is an American, Father Buchanan, S.J., bringing materials which he begged to build a boarding school on the Yukon River. Flying around his missionary diocese in Colombia, Bishop Aranga, a forty-five-year-old Jesuit, is collecting ten thousand coconut trees to plant around his newly founded minor seminary.

What are these men trying to accomplish? What are their hopes? Their ambitions? Why, for instance, did Father Schact in 1623 deck himself up as a seller of mousetraps in an attempt to enter Sweden? Why are Jesuits studying the Russian Rite and language year after year at Fordham University and at Rome?

This symposium tries in its modest way to supply the answer, to show the purpose which is common to these varied activities, to indicate what unites these men of highly diversified talents and intensive training who belong to the largest missionary order in the Catholic Church, to trace something of their achievements and their innovations, and their present work in the mission fields of the world.

A book on Jesuit missioners written, for the most part, by Jesuits may seem tinged with egotism, but one could always counter that the best informed about Jesuit work are Jesuits themselves. More profoundly, however, I think that since Jesuits are spread out on all the major missions of the Church and have been for four centuries, and are at the same time the largest single group working in missionary fields, their story of achievement, failure, and designs is fairly typical of what the Church is trying to accomplish. Rather than review the broad scope of all the Church's missionary activity, concentration on one highly active group makes possible—at least within a short book—a more unified and more intelligible account of missionary work. In addition Jesuits, although by no means the first missionaries, were the first order explicitly dedicated to the work of the missions. Polanco, first secretary of the Society of Jesus, wrote that "among the strongest of the natural bonds uniting the first companions (of St. Ignatius) was the hope of preaching to the infidel, or of dying among them for the faith of Christ." So also the Papal Bulls which approved the Society at its beginning, as well as the Constitutions written by Ignatius himself, suppose without any ambiguity that the Society was established for all kinds of missions, including those to infidels. This made the Society a new kind of religious order, the first in the Church where obedience to the rule implied for *all* the possibility of a missionary assignment. Missions are not, for a Jesuit, something extra, something laudable for volunteers only. A vocation to the Society includes a general vocation to the missions. The only exception made to the famous detachment and obedience of Jesuits as to various works is in favor of the missions. A man on entering may request to go to the missions; Superiors are to honor such a request. Modern Generals of the Society have insisted that in the choice of works missionary ones must be given preference.

Ignatius himself never went on the missions except for one romantic fling at converting the Moslems in the Holy Land. In Jerusalem he was forced to give the Turkish guards his only possessions, a penknife and a pair of scissors, to see the mount of the Ascension. The Franciscan Provincial worried about the impetuous Ignatius' safety, gently threatened excommunication unless he left the Holy Land immediately. It was not a very successful missionary trip.

Through the order he founded, however, Ignatius became one of the most influential missionaries in the history of the Church. Naturally speaking, he may have been influenced in his love of the frontiers of the Church by his older brothers, three of whom fought—two to death—in the wars between Spain and France to further their ambitions in the Mediterranean. Another brother sailed for the Americas when conquest and colonization were getting under way, only to die in the wars with the Indians, and still another brother perished in the Hungarian crusade against the Turks. But whatever the explanations on the natural plane might be, it is clear that Ignatius the saint, willing to do anything to spread the knowledge and love of Christ, envisioned his order as a special force to work, where this was most difficult, on the missions. His correspondence, so detailed, shows his great and unflagging concern with the problems and solutions of his followers in missionary lands. He set as a principle that only the best men should be sent to the missions. After Xavier died, Ignatius could not find a man of sufficient stature to succeed him. At last he named two men, one to be "the head," the other "the hand." For the introduction of Christianity to India he insisted on the necessity of education. He put first the instruction of youth and the foundation of schools and colleges, and then the instruction of adults. His whole mind, as frequently expressed, was this: Move fast but solidly; if you cannot move fast and solidly, move solidly.

Ignatius was not a solemn strategist any more than his followers today. Any man who loved roasted chestnuts as Ignatius did could not have been, I suspect, a truly solemn man. In the now completely authenticated anecdote we know that he at least once performed some of the songs and dances of his native Basque country to cheer up one of his spiritual clients who was overly depressed and melancholy. But Ignatius had an impressive respect for the power of various talents and creatures when organized in the service of men and of God.

His burning love for God begot an unfailing love for men. And Ignatius was a man of strong emotions. We know that a man who was admitted to the Society in 1551 was tempted, through love of one of his relatives, to give up his vocation. At that point Ignatius told him that when he, Ignatius, was reading a Book of Hours during the time of his conversion he was distracted by a picture in the book of the Blessed Mother. The picture looked a great deal like one of his relatives, and each time he saw it a surge of very human emotion swelled up within him. To avoid the distraction he had to keep the picture covered.

Purified by love of Christ and His Church, Ignatius retained a purified but powerful love of men. It was his strong charity for men which drew to him two of his earliest followers. Lainez, of Jewish descent, and Salmeron, twenty-one and eighteen respectively, abandoned their studies at Alcalá to seek out Ignatius at Paris because they had heard that this man, who had nothing, was the greatest friend and almoner of the poor in Salamanca, Alcalá, Barcelona, or wherever he might be. His charity had become a legend.

His followers in the past and today share something of his gaiety and his seriousness, his detachment and, therefore, his tremendous freedom in the use of creatures, his sincere and ever present love of men and of God. In the footsteps of Ignatius they try to love the Church and bring it to millions, because in the Church men can find Christ and the saving truth of God. No man can give anything more valuable to the world.

Christ Himself was on a mission to the world, sent by His Father, that men through Him might find redemption and be drawn to follow Him back to heaven. He established His Church to continue His presence and His teaching in the world for future generations. Thus the Church is essentially a missionary organization, continuing the mission of Christ. Divinity, which is at home to the whole world by Its presence, became localized, so to speak, in the Incarnation. Perhaps it could be said that the Church, which is at once a visible institution and the Mystical Body of Christ, also is at home to the whole world through the radiative grace of Christ. But the Church has the mission of continuing the work of God Incarnate to become localized in every corner of the world. The mission of the Church is, thus, at once supranational and national. It can never become entirely autonomous in any country, in the manner of some sect, because it is as world-wide as the coming of Christ. But it must become as localized as the native sky and climate.

The effort of missionaries, rather than primarily making converts, is to establish and make visible and at home in every nation the Church, the Mystical Body of Christ. This is why men go forth, this is what unites them no matter how different their backgrounds or talents, or the circumstances in which they exercise their apostolate. Love and intelligence in the pursuit of this goal which is of the greatest value to men was the theme of Ignatius' life; it is a tradition which his followers try to carry on today.

Many Jesuit missionaries have been and are today concerned with the expensive, lengthy drudgery of education. This has always been an important work, but today is a work of the utmost charity. Men cannot maintain their belief in God and the values which flow from that belief in the modern world, swept as it is by propaganda, unless they have more than a holy-picture notion of God. It is important for them, whether they be Buddhists or Hindus, to have a clear notion of why they believe in God and the truths which follow from such belief. If they believe in God, if they believe that they come from God and go with His help back to Him, it makes a difference in the way they regard themselves, the way they think, the way in which they act. It also colors their thoughts and actions towards others.

For the Christian it is of great importance that he be given the chance through mission schools, from kindergartens to graduate schools, to learn in his own language what it means to follow Christ. What difference does it make, or should it make, in this century if one believes in Christ? What did He teach? What does His presence in the world through the Church mean in one's life, the life of one's family, community, and nation? Education gives at least some people on the missions the chance to become fully intelligent followers of God, strong enough to withstand propaganda which would oftentimes destroy their beliefs, and ultimately destroy their regard for truth, their respect for themselves and for others. The more men know about God, the more they know about themselves. For ultimately a man's radical happiness, not merely in eternity but in this life, depends on his knowledge of, rapport with, and love of God which is found in its highest form only in the Church which the Son of God founded.

Through education on the missions, also, men and women are given the opportunity to gain the educational background necessary, given the grace of God and the courage to follow that grace, to become priests and nuns to take care of their own people. Unless there is a formation of native-born priests, a country will always depend upon priests from outside, will always be a missionary country. All missionaries are trying to so establish the Church in a country that it is self-sustaining and does not have to look elsewhere for reenforcements for the basic needs of religious life.

The Church has no mission to Europeanize the world. It

is true that, so far, the Church has reached its greatest expansion in association with Western culture, which it in turn helped to form. But the Church is tied to no particular set of cultural forms. Its mission is to Christianize.

Missionaries of the Church continue the all-embracing love of Christ, Who died for all men. That love stretches out without distinction of race or color or nationality. There is a continual interchange of life and grace and prayer among the various members of the Church, no matter how disparate their civilizations, for all are grafted on the One Vine. But to fulfill its essential mission the Church must, as it were, enter into the homes of men of every land, it must make visible the dwelling of Christ among the sons of men. Belonging to all the world, it can be a stranger to no man.

The great men of the missions have shown an intense respect for the local modalities of a civilization, the national customs and differences of temperament, excepting only that which would contradict the truth of Christ. The endeavor of men like Ricci or De Nobili or the great theorist of the missions, Valignano, was precisely to bring Christ and the Church to men while respecting the culture and the customs of the country. They knew that just as truly as Christ loved the world and spread out His arms on the cross for it, He also loved Bethlehem and the hilly paths of Nazareth and the local customs of His family's people. These might differ in value, and His love might differ in intensity, but one need not destroy the other. It makes no difference that the hymn of praise to the Godhead which rises from the living members of Christ is scored now in quarter tones instead of half-tones.

This problem of adapting Christianity as it is preached to various cultures is always a problem for missionaries when they come from a completely different culture. It is easy at times to confuse the natural adornments with the truth itself, which is in the long run disastrous. And to respect a culture is not merely to be careful that your churches have, say, in the Orient, an Oriental configuration, or your Madonnas have slanting eyes. In the present vast interchange going on in the world such mere external forms are no longer quite so important.

The missionary must carefully distill what is essential both as to the truth and its presentation. His problem is complicated by the fact that his beliefs are not merely a set of abstract truths that might be found in a book, but a living life handed down over the centuries, growing and unfolding under the guidance of the Holy Spirit.

In our time, perhaps, the area that must be respected most is the psychology of a people. Social scientists now maintain that the changes wrought by contact with an alien civilization affect the psychological pattern of a people last. Superficially a people may seem quite the same to a missionary, but deep in their way of looking at things even their way of thinking may be quite different.

The Japanese offer an example of what we are discussing. They have adopted many external forms of Western civilization. They have even modified their language in recent times, stressing the conceptual rather than the visual in Japanese. But their way of thinking remains quite different. In the center, so to speak, of the mind stands *jo* (feeling). This is the axis of their psychological life. Reason (*chi*) and will (*i*) hardly ever operate alone. *Jo* enters into them all the time, giving to Japanese thought a quality of intuition, providing the people with a high aesthetic perception and a stress in their lives, socially and morally, on such qualities as *ningenmi* (humaneness) or *ninjo* (compassion).

The scholastically trained mind may regard this as an unnecessary mixing of reason and sentiment, but will probably find that, since it is so—due perhaps to the history of the Japanese and the influence which China and India at one time had upon them—a catechetical approach in the presentation of truth is not the best.

The various chapters of this symposium will give a far more concrete and interesting presentation of the aims, work, and difficulties of the Church's missions as seen, for the most part, in the work of Jesuit missionaries. These essays cannot hope to be complete in the space of a single volume. The aim is a fairly intelligent, yet interesting, presentation of the important works of the past and the present. It seemed preferable to follow certain movements, representative works, and typical personalities in some detail rather than give an over-all, yet abstract, report. In this way the characteristic initiative of Jesuit missionaries and the fundamental purposes and methods of the Church's mission work are seen in sharper relief. Many interesting stories and activities of the past and the present of necessity were suppressed in the interests of concentration and a fairly brief presentation. There is enough to give the merely curious interesting reading matter, to give the casual observer of missionary news greater insight into the real purpose of missionaries, and those interested in the missions' inspiration a more profound and documented understanding.

The first half of the book deals with the past; the second half with the present.

The temperament and approach of the first missionaries, the men trained by Ignatius himself, form the subject of the opening essay by Father Ernest Burrus, S.J., an American Jesuit whose permanent work is the study of Jesuit history among the archives in Rome. In Father Burrus' work Xavier, the model of Jesuit missionaries, bulks large. Also included are the first men to reach South America and what is now the United States. In contrast with the first Jesuits to go out from Europe, Father Harold C. Gardiner, S.J., the literary editor of *America*, director of the Catholic Book Club, author and editor of several books, including *Norms for the Novel* and a life of Edmund Campion for the Vision Books series, treats of Jesuit missionaries to Europe itself. These were the men who faced a fairly modern problem, that of revitalizing the faith in nominally Catholic regions, or penetrating regions closed to Catholic priests. It is the same problem facing apostolic priests today in France, for instance, or South America; the same problem which faces heroic priests trying to penetrate the iron curtain. From these home missions in particular, as Father Gardiner shows, came the sometimes well-founded stories of the Jesuit in disguise.

So much for the very beginnings.

Three outstanding missionaries of Asia, who initiated the methods of missionary activity only recently adopted by the universal Church, form the subject of Jerome D'Souza—veteran member of the Indian delegation to the UN and director of the Jesuit Social Institute of India—regarded as the most successful of such run by the Society in the world. He sketches in some detail the career of De Nobili, who became a Brahmin in India and is the most spectacular example of the peculiarly emphasized adaptation of the Society in mission countries; Matthew Ricci, famous diarist of China, who showed the way to the Eastern mind; Valignano, successor to Xavier and one of the most competent of mission theorists.

Father Gustave Weigel, S.J., one of the better theological writers of our country, with a background of many years spent in the still-missionary country of South America, treats of some of the outstanding historical social works of Jesuit missionaries, with emphasis on the extraordinary Reductions of South America—those communal settlements for the natives which have intrigued philosophers and historians and were even in recent times the subject of a play on Broadway. The Reductions unfortunately died with the suppression of the Society, but they illustrate the keen interest which the Jesuit missionary must have in the social conditions of his people. It is very difficult for any poverty-ridden or exploited people to live a decent life.

Introduction

The work of the Society in education is fairly well known, so much so that many do not think of Jesuits as missionaries at all. Mr. George Shuster, the well-known author and long-time president of Hunter College, shows the educational work of missionaries in the past. He shows how keen the missionaries were to observe and record various cultures as found in the famed *Relations of North America* and the annual letters from other missions, their attempts at codification and even simplification of native tongues, the successful immersion in a culture so that men like Stephens and Beschi in India produced classics in the native languages. Missionaries spread the use of quinine, that first cure for malaria, originally called "Jesuit bark." They also popularized *maté*, which is still advertised as "Jesuit tea." Side by side with a general and original scientific approach to the various areas where they labored, the missionaries established schools in almost every country they reached. A college started by Xavier in Goa is still in existence.

Attached to missionary work has always been the threat of persecution either from the malicious or the bigoted. A French Jesuit, Jean Monsterleet, himself a veteran of persecution in modern China and the author of several books on the East now available in seven languages, provides perspective on the present by describing the devastating persecution of seventeenth-century Japan. This persecution, almost as subtle as the present ones under Communist governments, destroyed a most flourishing branch of the Church for centuries. There were far more Catholics in Japan then than there are today. If Christianity and the work of Jesuits had been allowed to continue, the modern history of Japan might have been quite different.

So much for the past. Father Clement Armitage, managing editor of *Jesuit Missions*, one-time missionary in Iraq, who has recently returned from a trip through the missions of Central America and the Caribbean, contributes a general survey of the present missionary work of the Society. Father Raymond Bernard, S.J., editor of *Social Order,* draws together some of the modern social works and shows why Jesuits are organizing co-operatives in the Fijis, establishing agricultural schools in various retarded countries, running housing programs and establishing new industries in areas like Jamaica, setting up social institutes in the Philippines or India. Barry Ulanov, professor at Barnard, more generally known for his jazz biographies, active in the lay apostolate in this country, shows that missionary educational effort is still as intense as ever. The flexibility of the Ratio Studiorum to meet educational problems on the missions today forms the bulk of his essay. Education today is of utmost importance, especially in mission countries, and is perhaps the most profoundly charitable work that can be done for the people of various nations. More emphasis on the varied individuals who are necessary for missionary work is supplied in the editor's own chapter. A major example of current persecution, that of the Jesuits in Red China, is supplied by an Irish Jesuit, Alan Birmingham, who, from his vantage point in Hong Kong, has been able to get a fine perspective on heroism pitted against subtle cruelty which produces twentieth-century martyrs of the missions.

The first American Doctor of Missiology, Father Edward Murphy, S.J., treats of tomorrow on the missions. What are the problems and the work cut out for missionaries just now departing or training to depart in the future? What is the stake of the Church in the world of the future? Are new emphases or new attitudes needed? What are the hopes for missionary work in a cold war world? What will be the place of the lay missionary?

My thanks are due to the contributors and several others who have been most generous and helpful in the writing and typing of this volume.

BEYOND ALL HORIZONS

1. First Missionaries

Ernest Burrus, s.j.

LIKE Pontius Pilate in the Creed, Diogo de Gouveia is to be
found in every biography of St. Ignatius. He is there because
Pedro Ribadeneira, that *enfant terrible* of the early Jesuits
and pioneer biographer of his hero Inigo or Ignatius, set the
pattern for all his successors.

Ignatius, the story runs, was not content to keep to his
notebooks, but determined on a practical reformation of his
fellow students at the University of Paris by putting them
through the all too exhilarating paces of the Spiritual Exercises.

So mighty a weapon in the hands of their creator proved
surprisingly effective—dangerously so on a trio of impression-
able students who must have had more of Don Quixote than
of Sancho Panza in them. The Spiritual Exercises of Ignatius
"transformed" them, if we may use Ribadeneira's uncopy-
righted verb, transformed them so completely that all things
earthly seemed vain and worthless to them—their books and
studies at the university included—a rather dangerous renunciation to make, especially in the eyes of college professors
and university authorities.

The stage is now set for the villain. Enter the villain—one

Diogo de Gouveia, principal of the College of St. Barbara and quondam rector of the University of Paris. Gouveia has ordered that Inigo, the dangerous innovator and spiritual anarchist, run the gauntlet of pedagogues in the humiliating presence of his fellow students. The whole scene is to be prefaced by a rebuke from Gouveia, more stinging than any lash.

Then comes the sudden, unexpected, and incredible denouement and strange climax. Ignatius, to save the apostolate he envisaged, speaks a few unrecorded words to Gouveia that have their well-known effect. The college principal, with Inigo at his side, then steps before the eager professors and impatient students and, to the amazement of the most callous and indifferent, speaks words of praise and commendation of his charge.

Such is the Gouveia of Ignatian biographies. Ribadeneira's authentic words have etched an unforgettable picture, historically not untrue nor inaccurate. And yet thus to remember the man whom Providence chose to change the whole course of the Society of Jesus and even that of the foreign missions is much like summing up the achievements of Julius Caesar by saying that he was bald-headed. For it was Gouveia who brought together the Jesuits with their desire for the missions and King John III, one of the two men who at that time controlled the personnel to be sent to the missions. Without the catalyst of Gouveia there might have been considerable delay before the early men of the Society of Jesus achieved their ambition of going on the missions. Xavier might never have sailed for India and the East to start the missionary work of the Society. And if Xavier had not fired others in the Society and outside of it with his pioneering missionary efforts, the course of the missions of the Church might have been different. Diogo de Gouveia had made the College of St. Barbara practically a Portuguese and Spanish enclave in the University of Paris. As a sort of roving ambassador for John III he tried to prevent Norman and Breton explorers from invading Portuguese spheres of influence in Brazil or in Guinea.

At the same time the principal and practically the owner of St. Barbara's dreamed, as he told his good friend the King, of being able to say Mass and preach in the great mosque of Fez, which was the second capital of Morocco. It was very important then that Ignatius impressed Gouveia because Gouveia had the friendship of John III. John had set up fifty scholarships at St. Barbara's as a token of his esteem for Gouveia. Simon Rodriguez, one of the early followers of Ignatius, was studying at the college on one of these grants. Towards the end of 1537 news reached Gouveia of the mass conversion of a tribe in India. In the middle of February 1538 Gouveia sent the report of the conversions to Simon Rodriguez, recommending to him and other members of the group formed by Ignatius the need of aiding in the conversion of India. Thus, two years before the Society of Jesus was approved by Paul III as a religious order, Gouveia pointed out to the Jesuits the boundless mission field of the Orient.

But Gouveia not only wrote to the Jesuits and urged them to turn their zeal to the foreign missions, he appealed directly to the one man who could open up both the East and the West to these spiritual conquistadores. This man was John III, King of Portugal, whose fleets sailed the seas westward to Brazil or rounded the Cape of Good Hope to the mysterious and enchanting Orient to hold sway over half a world. There was much truth in the saying, "The Portuguese have a small country in which to be born, but a vast world in which to die."

Like the mighty Spanish monarch Charles V, so, too, the Portuguese ruler John III exercised not only temporal power over his dominions, but held them in spiritual patronage.

Today John Kenneth Smythe founds a college or William Quincy Browne leaves his millions to endow a hospital. In earlier centuries both would have been called "patrons" of these institutions. Multiply such benefactions many times over; make the sovereign of the nation their source; have the burden and the privileges linked with such patronage handed down from the royal ruler to his descendants; and the concept of royal patronage has been formed in its broader outlines.

The Portuguese called such a relationship *padroado* and the Spaniards *patronato*. Countless volumes and studies have been written to explain, defend, or defame an institution which was born when kings believed in their God-given faith and considered themselves its promoters and its crusading protectors; they did not see anything really illogical in making even the Church subservient to their ever widening absolutism.

The sovereigns presented to the Popes the names of those whom they wanted consecrated bishops in their dominions; they determined what churches and schools were to be erected, what mission fields were to be opened up, what missionaries were acceptable for the new apostolate; papal and other ecclesiastical documents were passed upon by royal officials, crown treasurers paid the passage of missionaries to the overseas dominions and, when once the missionaries were there, they received a modest yearly salary of about three hundred dollars.

The Church and state were thus closely bound for weal and for woe. The rapid and extensive evangelization of the Spanish and Portuguese empires, the most extensive the world has ever known, was made possible only through such royal patronage.

The subsequent history of attempted control of the Church even in its spiritual ministration, of hostile interference, of governmental oppression, and of open persecution, is intelligible only in the light of this earlier institution. Let both nations be credited for their noble intentions and for their high ideals as well as their unstinted generosity, which has brought entire continents into the fold of Christ. All the world knows only too well their mistakes, both factual and fictional.

John III, as patron of the Church in the Portuguese dominions of the East and West, instructed his Ambassador at Rome, Pedro Mascarenhas, to make investigations about the character, virtues, and abilities of the men whom Gouveia commended so enthusiastically. If they seemed satisfactory for so high and arduous a mission as the evangelizing of his dominions across the seas, Mascarenhas was to obtain an order, if necessary, from His Holiness to secure some of them for this apostolate.

Paul III praised the intentions and plans of the Portuguese King and added his own commendation to that of Gouveia, but declined to put the Jesuits under any formal order because, in his own words, "a voyage so long and perilous ought to be undertaken voluntarily."

This put the next move up to the Ambassador to deal directly with Ignatius. "In this matter," he wrote John III, "I had little trouble, for with great content they agreed to the mission, although they could offer me only two men for it, as they are scarcely six in Rome now and two others are to go on a papal mission to Ireland and Scotland."

The two chosen in 1540 for the mission to the Orient were the Spaniard Francis Xavier and the Portuguese Simon Rodriguez. The latter was detained in Portugal, of which he became the first Jesuit Superior.

Xavier was destined for a more glorious but also vastly more arduous apostolate in the limitless lands of the rising sun. On April 7, 1541, the East India fleet, which lay in the harbor of Lisbon, gateway to the Orient, weighed anchor for its thirteen-month voyage.

Xavier was sailing to the Orient as Papal Legate, but of its title and dignity there was little show or evidence. When the King's gentleman, Count Castanheda, urged him to take at least a personal servant to do his washing and cooking, since such employments would diminish his ambassadorial dignity, Francis replied, "Senhor Conde, it is precisely such dignity and authority of yours which has reduced the Church of God to her present plight . . . and the best means to acquire true dignity is to wash one's own clothing and cook one's own food, without being beholden to anyone." Of all King John's generous gifts Xavier accepted "a few books necessary in the Indies and a cloak or two of rough material against the cold of the Cape of Good Hope."

As Xavier stood on deck with the two Jesuits who were to accompany him to the Orient, Father Paul of Camerino, an Italian priest, and Francisco Mansilhas, a Portuguese scholastic in his studies leading to the priesthood, the city receded from their sight, the coast line grew dimmer and the water ever darker as the high sea was reached. Xavier was generous in all things except words, and so when he sums up the sufferings of the voyage in such terms as, "for myself, the hardships of the voyage were of such a kind that except for God's sake alone I would not have faced them during a *single day* for the whole world," we can well consider his generalization as the most fearful and frightening of all comments on the voyage to India.

As Francis watched the Europe that he knew fade from his sight, did he recall that the very day he sailed marked his thirty-fifth birthday? Was he even dimly aware what that day would mean in the annals of the Church? And yet the day was more memorable than the birthday of the greatest apostle of modern times, more important than the beginning of the intense activity of a second St. Paul: it was the birth of the Society of Jesus as a missionary order, the largest the Church was to know through the centuries.

The external apostolate of Xavier spans some eleven years, from 1541 to his death in 1552. Scenes change rapidly: the interminable sea voyage that carried him across the Atlantic within a hundred miles of the Brazilian coast, back to Africa, up to Mozambique, then northeastward to the dotlike island of Socotra, a Christian outpost in a Mohammedan world. The heart of Xavier was as tender as it was strong, the very soul of pity and understanding. Touched by the misery and utter neglect of these followers of Christ, endangered by their Mohammedan overlords, he pleaded with the admiral of the fleet, Martim Afonso de Sousa, to remain as the spiritual guide of the Socotrans.

But a vaster world needed his charity and his zeal. First, Goa, on the west coast of India, emporium of a hundred ports and kingdoms, and a Christian city in a limitless pagan world, would witness his apostolate of faith and love.

Xavier was not the first missionary to Goa: diocesan priests had preceded him; some thirty Franciscans carried on their effective ministry; a new college, named after the Apostle of the Gentiles, had been founded to train some sixty seminarians; guiding the spiritual activity of this Christian oasis was the aged Franciscan bishop Joao de Albuquerque.

For five months the strange varieties of Western and Oriental humanity that made up Goa beheld the persevering charity of Xavier. In the streets he gathered the children about him to sing or recite the catechism; in the hospital he went from patient to patient to speak his encouraging words of strength and consolation and to ease the end of life and the beginning of eternity. He was the tactful, courteous, and cheerful guest of government officials to raise them out of a life of religious indifference and utter neglect.

But the world Xavier longed to conquer for Christ was not confined to the city limits of Goa, nor was he the meticulous organizer and administrator to remain in any one place; above all, he was a pathfinder, a spiritual explorer, a tireless adventurer for souls.

Before the year 1542 was out, Francis left for Cape

Comorin, several hundred miles from Goa, along the southern shores of India. The region was called the Fishery Coast and its inhabitants were known as Paravas. The Portuguese had bravely saved them from annihilation or the crueler fate of slavery at the hands of the Mohammedans.

Xavier's native language was Basque, for which he had precious little use in the missions, for there was as much chance of Basque meeting Basque in this Oriental world as of two planets colliding. With the Portuguese he could employ his own version of their difficult language, a strongly Hispanicized Portuguese. But once he was among the natives, his worst trouble was their numerous languages, one differing from the other more than Chinese from English. His comparatively brief stay in any one place kept him from mastering a single native language. Xavier did learn isolated words and snatches of phrases; he even memorized bits of Tamil, Japanese, and other languages; but he possessed no gift of tongues, no pentecostal miracle flashed the meaning of his words to that variegated Oriental humanity. For the consolation of his countless successors through the centuries, no missionary ever worked harder with poorer results.

And yet Xavier did understand all and readily made himself understood by all. Without interpreter he quickly comprehended the misery of the Paravas, their fear of the persecutor, their ignorance and debasing superstition. He spoke a language grasped by all without difficulty—the light of pity and goodness in his eyes, the cheering smile of his countenance, his untiring hands and feet, the charity of his deeds, his unfailing courtesy and generous kindness; his whole being spoke a language that none could fail to understand. This was his miracle of tongues.

After a year on the Fishery Coast, Xavier returned to Goa. He came for helpers to reap the abundant harvest. Father Paul of Camerino and the seminarian Mansilhas, who two years earlier had stood with Xavier on the deck of the *Santiago* as Lisbon slipped behind the horizon, would now be enlisted for this fruitful spiritual expedition as were also several lay catechists.

Xavier penned hurried letters to the Queen of Portugal and to his Jesuit Brothers in Rome begging for money to pay his catechists and for reinforcements to win the battle of Christ.

Early in 1544 Xavier was back on the Fishery Coast with his new contingent of helpers. Xavier's baptisms, mathematically minded historians inform us, add up to about thirty thousand for the ten years of his mission activity in the Orient. His baptisms were not more numerous because he wished this sacrament to be understood by his converts, esteemed and treasured by them as the expression of God's generous gift of the true faith to them. For this reason he thoroughly catechized and carefully instructed his charges whenever possible.

But during his second visit to the Fishery Coast he decided to depart from his more cautious procedure. The fishers of Macua, related to the Paravas, inhabited some fourteen villages along the Travancore coast. Oppressed by both Mohammedan marauders and native tyrants, they expressed the desire to embrace Christianity. This was a providential opportunity not to be lost. More thorough instruction could follow. In one intense month the waters of baptism made some ten thousand partakers of the true faith. If anyone think Xavier imprudent, let him at least remember that despite the countless vicissitudes the Macuas are Catholic to this day.

But Francis was not one to spend much time rejoicing over success. While still in Travancore, Mansilhas sent an urgent message to inform him that the steadfast faith of the Christians of northern Ceylon and the tyranny of their King had given the infant Church there some six hundred martyrs. To insure the future of Christianity, Xavier hastened to set out for the island.

To hear of a new land where Christ's name was not yet known was for Xavier an order to go there. The year 1545 saw him cross the Bay of Bengal past the northern point of Sumatra to Malacca, the colorful market place of India and the Far East. Here his charity went out to all: neglected Portuguese, contemptuous Mohammedans, slaves of every hue, and their haughty masters.

But again the El Dorado of the spiritual empire he would conquer lay still farther beyond—the extreme limit of the Orient known at that time, the Molucca Islands. By the spring of 1546 this saint, ever in a hurry, set sail again, this time to the southeast until he reached the island of Amboina, rich in spices. It had been once evangelized, but was now shepherdless. Xavier had brought with him João d'Eiro, a veteran Portuguese soldier and ex-merchant, now turned restless catechist with much of Xavier's zeal. D'Eiro remained in Amboina while Xavier hurried on to the islands of Ternate and Moro and back to Malacca.

By early 1548 he returned to Goa after stopping off in Cape Comorin to instruct the newly arrived Jesuit missionaries, the Italian Father Antonio Criminale, the first martyr of the Society of Jesus, among them.

Encouraging reinforcements had also reached Goa: Xavier was no longer a leader without an army. His recent recruits were few for so vast a world, but their charity and zeal made each count for many.

The relative quiet of Goa was interrupted by yet another dream. Xavier's new Quivira was Japan, to which he would be the first to proclaim the teaching of Christ. The people, he heard from Pablo, a repentant Japanese murderer, were intelligent, thirsting for knowledge and the true faith. Pablo's own life was hardly a warrant for the truth of his statements, but Xavier saw only goodness where others suspected fraud and deceit. To Japan would he go then, even if he had to sail in a pirate's junk.

It was on August 15, 1549, the fifteenth anniversary of his vows in the presence of Ignatius at Montmartre, when Xavier reached the land where all was different. These islands of the rising sun were to be his home and the scene of his heartbreaking efforts for nearly two and a half years.

With enough charity in his heart to make saints of headhunters Xavier battled heroically against superstition, prejudice, fear of the common people, the overweening power and pride of the rulers, sensuality in its most disgusting forms. To the most impoverished of peasants; to the mighty samurai, all too conscious of their nobility and military eminence; to the depraved bonzes, who contemned the uninitiated; to dukes, princes, and even to the King of Japan, to all Xavier brought the message of salvation, of purity, of charity, of forgiveness.

There is boundless zeal for truth and not a little humor in the Dai Nichi incident. Xavier had sought an apt Japanese translation for God. He was misled by the Shingon bonzes into believing that their god Dai Nichi was the Supreme Being. He then tirelessly cried aloud along the streets to all who could hear him, "Pray to Dai Nichi, pray to Dai Nichi," believing all the while that he was encouraging men to turn to their Creator. But when he learned that Dai Nichi was no personal god, much less omnipotent, he hastened to repair his unwitting mistake by going through the streets accompanied by his catechist Fernandez crying even more zealously than before, "Do *not* pray to Dai Nichi, do *not* pray to Dai Nichi."

And yet, for all his seeming lack of success, the message of Christ had been brought to Japan and His Church planted there. Not all the persecution that the enemies of His Name could devise would ever be able to destroy it.

Xavier provided for the future of the faith in Japan by

leaving missionaries and catechists there when he had to return to Goa in early 1552, and would soon send others to extend this arduous apostolate. He had sown in tears; others would soon reap in joy and in abundance, and still others would reap the martyr's crown.

The Portuguese Jesuit Luis Frois, who was in Goa when Xavier arrived, wrote this enthusiastic account to his Brothers in far-off Coimbra: "He came when we were least expecting him, the elect of God, our Father in Christ dear beyond all others, Master Francis . . . Soon he will be steering towards China. The satisfaction, the transports of spiritual joy expressed by all of the Society and by the entire people at his coming, so eagerly awaited, is something I know not how to convey . . . Since his arrival at this College of St. Paul in Goa great things have been done for the glory of God which give a halo and lustre to the Society. The flowers have appeared in our land, the time of pruning is come, the voice of the turtledove is heard, the fig tree hath not put forth her green leaves, the vines in flower yield their sweet perfume . . ."

But Xavier took out little time to feast his eyes on the flowers, inhale their perfume, or listen to the cooing of the turtledove. Other lands called to him. He revisited Malacca before setting out on his last adventure—China—in the late autumn and early winter of 1552, a sea voyage of some two thousand miles.

The ship, aptly named the *Holy Cross* (*Santa Cruz*), carried Xavier and his two helpers to the small island of Sancian off the coast of China. Here he waited in vain for the junk to smuggle him into the mainland. The death sentence against foreigners who dared trespass Chinese soil held no terrors for Francis. He would boldly proclaim himself to the Chinese Emperor the Ambassador of the Portuguese King; he would free the Christians rotting in Cantonese dungeons and fearlessly preach the message of Christ.

But these were dreams never to be realized. Sickness, the sister of death, kept inexorable watch over him in his lonely hut on Sancian until her sterner brother, mightier than all Xavier's zeal and love for his fellow men, could take over. In the early morning of December 3, 1552, Francis' earthly adventure ended to begin his apostolate from heaven that will close only with time.

And this is the greatness of Xavier. Not what he accomplished while on earth, but what from heaven he has inspired others to do. His earthly life was quickly over: 1506–1552. His apostolate in the Orient spans only a small fraction of those years: 1542–1552. His second apostolate, however, has but begun.

Regardless of the country from which the missionaries hailed, the century when they lived, or the mission field where they toiled, they had one trait in common: they were other Xaviers, his ideals and motives were theirs, even his methods of evangelization.

By setting out for the Orient in 1541 Francis was, of course, the first Jesuit missionary. During the fifteen years that from that time remained to the life of St. Ignatius, countless were the pleas from those of his sons who longed to follow in the footsteps of the Apostle of the Indies.

The letters that reached Europe from Xavier and his fellow workers found a responsive echo during an age of spiritual no less than of temporal adventure. Should a Cortes or a Pizarro prove more daring or braver than these missionaries?

More than three years before Francis Xavier died on Sancian, Jesuits had volunteered for the missions in the Western Hemisphere, had crossed the Atlantic to Brazil, and had founded there the first province in the Americas.

In the Orient, Gaspar Barzaeus and Cosme de Torres; in Brazil, Nóbrega and Anchieta; in Florida, Pedro Martínez and Juan Bautista Segura; in Mexico, Pedro Sánchez; in the Philippines, Alonso Sánchez: these were the successors and even contemporaries of Francis and close imitators of his zeal and virtues, and rivals in the best sense of the term of his heroism and true success.

With the passage of time we meet such incomparable explorers of North America as Salvatierra, Piccolo, Marquette, Consag, and Kino. The last explored Lower California and proved for all time that it is a peninsula; he founded the rosary of missions in northern Mexico and crossed into the present United States, establishing the first permanent mission of our Far West; he wrote as well as made mission history and drew the most exact maps of his century. Kino's heart was set on the Orient, scene of the apostolic work of his patron, Francis Xavier. But Kino's fellow Tirolese Jesuit, Anton Kerschpamer, also preferred the missions of the East, and Kino was not one to be selfish even in heroism. They agreed to cast lots. Kerschpamer drew the Philippines, gateway to the Orient; Kino drew Mexico, and thus the course of their lives was fixed by a bit of pious gambling.

Many years later Kino was to write: "These new American missions of this unknown North America are superior to and more fruitful in conversions than the Asiatic missions and Great China." This enthusiastic exclamation is not to be relegated to the category of sour grapes, but was the conviction of a seasoned missionary that his pious gamble with Kerschpamer did not turn out so badly after all.

Kino's words are recalled as indicative of the realization that the good effected in the New World was far more extensive, permanent, and far-reaching than in the Orient, and should remind the modern reader that today one half of all Catholics are to be found in the Western Hemisphere.

Juan María Salvatierra was the first to succeed in colonizing Lower California and in founding missions there after nearly two centuries of defeat and disaster. His countryman, Francesco María Piccolo, arrived there at the crucial moment to save the beachhead established by Salvatierra.

Diego Luis de Sanvitores was the first to bring Christianity to the Marianas Islands, erected the first churches and schools there, and sealed his apostolate with his own blood.

When foreigners were admitted into the missions of Spanish and Portuguese dominions, it was with the proviso that they work among the infidel natives, not in the schools and parishes of the cities. This explains why we find Anton Benz and Jakob Sedelmayr on the rim of our southwestern missions, Benno Ducrue and Jakob Baegert in Lower California, Matthias Strobel, Lazlo Cross, Martin Dobrizhoffer, and Bernhard Nussdorffer in the Reductions of Paraguay.

With his sons no longer gathered about him in Rome or within relatively easy summons from some European country, but scattered in the Orient and in the New World, St. Ignatius insisted that the family spirit that once animated his first companions be maintained through frequent letters to and from Rome. These letters, in turn, fired many with the desire to enter the Society and devote their lives to the missions.

But soon even more numerous than the letters of the missionaries in the field were the petitions of those who begged to be accepted for the missions rapidly opening up in both the Spanish and Portuguese empires. Goa, the Fishery Coast, Japan, Macao, China, Ethiopia, Ormuz, Congo, Morocco, Angola, these and other regions came within a few years into the widening sphere of Jesuit missionary activity.

Across the world their fellow Jesuits had consolidated their position in Brazil, they had attempted to establish a beachhead in Spanish Florida, and had founded the province of Peru and Mexico, as well as the mission of the Philippines, dependent upon Mexico.

Such intense missionary activity set off among the youth of Europe an extraordinary chain reaction of generosity, inspiring many to enter the Society of Jesus and firing others already in the order with the desire to volunteer for the foreign missions. Time has spared only a small portion of their heroic pleas. In one deposit of fifteen thousand such requests no less than two thousand assign as the impelling motive of their mission vocation the example of St. Francis Xavier.

Nor has it been only Jesuits whom Xavier has inspired to follow in his footsteps. Diocesan priests who have volunteered for the missions, men and women of every religious order and congregation have caught the fire of his apostolic spirit. Francis Xavier is not the patron of only Jesuit missions but of all foreign missions.

The good he accomplished has thus become as enduring as heaven itself and his apostolate successful beyond his most daring dreams.

Saints are sincere and practical, none more so than Xavier. Hence he has a word to say to us today: gratitude in our hearts, esteem and abiding love for the faith he so treasured; prudent but ardent zeal to share Christ's message with others. He reminds Catholics that they have a heavy debt to repay. Xavier pleads with all Christians of good will to enlighten and strengthen the faith of millions already in the fold of Christ, not to bring doubt and confusion and disbelief into their lives, not to strive to undo the work of centuries.

Only the unabridged edition of the book of life contains the full story of Xavier's influence on other missionaries. But we may nevertheless be permitted to glance at a few marginal notes on three of his closest and earliest imitators: Manoel da Nóbrega in Brazil, Pedro Martínez in Florida, and Pedro Sánchez in Mexico.

When the King of Portugal wished to bring the word of Christ to his limitless domain in the West, he again turned to Ignatius. The founder of the Jesuits chose Manoel da Nóbrega to be the trail blazer for his sons in the New World. Like so many of the early Jesuits, Nóbrega was a university man. He studied first at Salamanca in Spain and then at Coimbra in Portugal, from which he graduated with honors.

Writers who love picturesque details in preference to sober history have made of Nóbrega a stutterer and of Anchieta a hunchback. Out of deference, no doubt, to the limping Ignatius, two of his sons are colorfully sketched with their own variety of physical defects! True, Nóbrega did have a speech defect, but as one of the most effective orators in the entire history of the missions he cannot have suffered from a very serious impediment. Anchieta's slight stoop has been arched into a hunchback!

The apostolate of Nóbrega is not merely a bit of domestic history of the Jesuits, but forms a large part of the general history, both civil and ecclesiastical, of early colonial Brazil; and, because of its far-reaching effects, inseparable from the history of the nation. Nor let it be forgotten that today Brazil has grown into the world's largest Catholic population—over fifty million.

Unlike in Mexico, Peru, and the vast regions of the Orient, other missionaries had not preceded the Jesuits in the greater part of Brazil. Nearly everywhere in these boundless and unmapped regions the sons of Ignatius pioneered among the natives and opened the first schools, built the first churches and wrote the first grammars, dictionaries, and catechisms in the Brazilian languages. They founded the towns that are today the nation's teeming metropolises.

With five Jesuit companions Nóbrega set sail from Portugal on February 1, 1549. Fast and furious winds filled the sails of the little armada wafting them safely to land in eight quick weeks, a pleasant excursion compared with Xavier's thirteen trying months.

Ignatius appointed Nóbrega Superior of all the Jesuit missions in the Western Hemisphere. For seven formative and decisive years he guided the zealous missionary in his vast apostolate; for twenty-one years Nóbrega was to be the soul of a missionary activity that has few equals in the annals of the Church.

Nowhere on earth had a Christless humanity sunk lower than in tropical Brazil. The highest concept of happiness was to kill one's enemy and devour him. Cannibalism was so much a part of the Indians' way of life that some Portuguese, clergy included, held that it was useless to attempt to change their dietary habits of so many centuries. Others thought it a welcome means for Indian to get rid of Indian and make way for the white man. Such a debased portion of humanity, they held, was neither rational nor capable and worthy of Christianity.

Nóbrega saved both conquered and conquerors and helped to found a great nation by tirelessly crusading against cannibalism, by defending with vigorous pen and eloquent words the conversion of the Indians and their basic ability and worthiness to receive the word of Christ.

He built schools for the colonists in Baía, Pernambuco, São Paulo, Rio de Janeiro—to mention but a few of the key centers—in order to form an enlightened Catholic laity. He made use from the start of lay helpers, even children, to teach the Indians. He founded mission stations and schools for them. He encouraged his fellow Jesuits to follow his example in learning the native languages and early saw the vital importance of an educated and morally fit native clergy; nor did his conviction remain a dead letter, he both admitted such into the Society and, through the schools and colleges he established, prepared worthy candidates for the secular and regular clergy.

In the 1553 expedition of Jesuits to Brazil was a Spanish novice, José Anchieta by name, born in the Canary Islands, who later was to walk in the footsteps of Nóbrega as the Provincial Superior of the rapidly expanding mission. Both as administrator and exceptional writer he helped make permanent the good effected by Nóbrega.

During the last years of Nóbrega's Brazilian apostolate the second Jesuit mission in the New World was founded. Several thousand miles to the northwest of Brazil, within the limits of the present United States, Father Pedro Martínez opened up the first mission field in the vast overseas dominions of Philip II of Spain. Father Martínez was sent by St. Francis Borgia, third General of the Society of Jesus.

Pedro Martínez's entrance into the Jesuit order was unorthodox, to say the least. At the University of Valencia in Spain he had divided his time between the lecture hall and the fencing field. He carried off first honors in philosophy and became so skilled with the sword that there was rarely a challenge or a duel in that quick-tempered city in which he was not principal, second, or promoter.

History has not preserved for us what event made Pedro entertain a fierce hatred for the Jesuits, but has recorded the unusual circumstances of his entrance into the Society of Jesus. On a sweltering summer day of 1553, out of a mixture of courtesy and curiosity, he accompanied to the Valencian Jesuit College some of his comrades who had decided on entering the new order. With the seeming fickleness and impetuosity of youth he changed his hatred for the Jesuits in general to an enthusiastic liking for those he met at the college and joined his comrades in petitioning entrance into the Society.

But if Pedro was impetuous, that prudent appraiser of men, Jerome Nadal, was not. He calmly told Pedro to reflect upon his unexpected decision and to report back after eight days. An indifferent motion of the head scarcely hid Pedro's anger and humiliation at what he held to be an unjust delay. He left the college determined never to return; he would continue his comforting hatred of the innovating Jesuits!

But Pedro did not need to brood very long over the unpleasant incident, for word got around quickly that another challenge to a duel had been given in Valencia and accepted; Pedro, of course, was chosen as arbiter. Time and place were agreed upon. Pedro was the first on the scene, then the friends of the challenging parties took their places. The appointed time passed; anxious moments went by.

Elsewhere both principals of the duel had come to their better senses, patched up their differences, but did not even bother to inform Pedro. After waiting over an hour for them he turned homeward in an angry but also reflective mood. First, he mentally berated the cowardice of the principals, then he fiercely condemned their lack of honor in keeping to the appointed hour. The latter reflection, by an evident association of ideas, evoked his own failure to keep an appointment—that very day—to report back to Father Nadal. He hastened to his room, bundled up what he thought he might need, and hastened to the Jesuit College before its large gate was barred for the night. Angels must have smiled to see our dapper dueling dandy and elegant arbiter of every quarrel pleading eloquently with Father Nadal to become a Jesuit.

And a Jesuit he did become—the only one accepted from among all those who had applied at the college—even if his impetuosity was not checked in a day, not even in his first year of noviceship. On a walk from the novitiate in Gandía he was attracted by the excited shouts at a bullfight. No Don Quixote ever tilted his lance more vehemently against windmills than did our young Pedro fling himself into the arena, determined to stop both astonished bullfighters and their intended victim. A sight not to be forgotten: the young novice with cassock flying in the breeze, arms waving violently, quivering voice exhorting and condemning, altogether unconscious of the danger. The narrative does not fill in the colorful details we would like to have, but merely adds dryly that His Excellency the Duke of Gandía succeeded in rescuing the anti-bullfight crusader and then banned the performance.

As a second-year novice he preached to Jews and Moors. Ordained a priest in 1558, he crossed over to northern Africa, as one of the chaplains to some twelve hundred soldiers, in the disastrous Spanish expedition against Oran.

In 1565 St. Augustine, our oldest city, was founded. That same year Pedro Menéndez, Governor of the almost limitless Spanish Florida, resolved to consolidate his tenuous hold on that vast region by converting its native inhabitants. To do so he pleaded with Philip II for Jesuits to aid him. Philip, in turn, wrote his intimate friend, St. Francis Borgia, for missionaries.

In the annals of Christianity there are seeming disasters and defeats that are decisive victories with far-reaching consequences. This was strikingly true of Father Martínez's expedition to Spanish Florida and his martyrdom on Cumberland Island, just off the coast of the present state of Georgia. In late September or early October of 1566, only a few days after our missionary landed, a tomahawk put an end to his earthly existence. If it deprived the New World of a Francis Xavier, it gave North America its first Jesuit martyr.

Pedro Martínez learned no Indian language, he built no mission school or church, he did not even preach a single sermon to the natives. But his courage and heroism inspired hundreds of eager volunteers to take his place. From his blood sprang the Jesuit province of Mexico, the largest and most important beyond the boundaries of Europe.

Culturally Mexico—or New Spain, as the country was then commonly called—ranked first among Spain's overseas dominions. The Aztecs and Mayas had raised its native civilization far above that of any other region in the New World.

For fifty years before the coming of the first Jesuits the Franciscans, Dominicans, Augustinians, and secular priests had extended the word of Christ farther than the bravest of the conquistadores had dared venture. It would be hard to find any other nation in history which had accepted Christianity so readily. But there was real danger that not only the millions of baptized Indians but even their European overlords and their descendants, so absorbed in things material, would retain but a tenuous hold on their faith.

This was the 1572 mission of the Jesuits to Mexico: to confirm and consolidate the faith imparted by their pioneering predecessors. Hence the extensive network of schools, first in Mexico City for Spaniards, Mestizos, and Indians; then in Michoacán, among the Tarascans, the devoted charges of that amazing organizer and saintly bishop, Vasco de Quiroga. In Oaxaca, far to the south of Mexico City; in Veracruz, the gateway to Mexico and the emporium of two hemispheres; in Puebla, the second-largest city in New Spain; in Guadalajara, center for the northwestern advance into new territories; in Tepotzotlán, headquarters for Aztec and Otomian ministry—here and elsewhere throughout New Spain schools were opened to form an educated clergy and laity.

Soon began the mission march northward among the pagan Indians who had not yet heard the word of Christ: Sinaloa, Sonora, Pimería, Arizona, and Lower California; northwestward among the Tepehuanes and Tarahumares. Each mission had its school for the Indians to learn to read, write, and take part in divine services.

Churches in cities, towns, and mission stations ministered to the spiritual and temporal needs of hundreds of thousands. Social work was carried on effectively with the help of the laity in behalf of the poor and the imprisoned, as also of homeless orphans.

The man chosen by St. Francis Borgia to inaugurate this extraordinary ministry was Father Pedro Sánchez, brilliant doctor of the University of Salamanca and its distinguished rector. He headed the 1572 expedition of fifteen Jesuits to Mexico and summoned to his assistance the survivors of the Florida Mission.

For eight decisive years he guided and inspired the varied apostolic activity of the new province. From Mexico City he sent out his eager soldiers of Christ over a territory more extensive than Europe. Native vocations proved surprisingly numerous. Danger and hardship were but a spur to his European Brothers.

In 1580, when he turned over his command to his successor, Juan de la Plaza, the number of Jesuits had risen to 107. In all truth, the province of New Spain had taken root.

Such is in brief the story of Manoel da Nóbrega, Pedro Martínez, and Pedro Sánchez, three missionaries who walked in the footsteps of St. Francis Xavier. He would be proud to call them his brothers. One attained to the glory of martyrdom and the other two preached the word of Christ in regions where today there are some one hundred million Catholics. All four helped establish that tradition and spirit which has made the Society of Jesus great as a missionary order.

2. *Missionaries to Europe*

Harold C. Gardiner, s.j.

I

On March 29, 1565, a famous lawsuit began in Paris. The University of Paris opened suit against the Jesuits. The real matter under dispute, beneath all the superficial contentions, was the issue of Gallicanism, that movement, particularly strong among the French clergy and hierarchy, which held, among other things, that a Council of the Church ranked, in decisions on faith and morals, higher than the Pope. The Jesuits of the College of Clermont, Paris, were on the side of the Pope; the university backed the Gallicans. The trial was to determine whether the college should be suppressed.

It is not the purpose of this historical note to introduce a long discussion of the trial and its outcome. But it is the purpose of the note to introduce the reader to one Etienne Pasquier, the lawyer hired by the university to prosecute the Society. For M. Pasquier was indeed a unique character. In addition to being a brilliant, if somewhat shady, lawyer he achieved fame as the inventor of the "secret, disguised" Jesuit. In his account of the trial and of the character of M. Pasquier, Reverend James Brodrick, S.J. (*The Progress of the Jesuits*, 1556–1579, New York, Longmans, Green, 1946,

p. 64), remarks what a boon this invention has been to novelists, and quotes in a footnote a silly passage from Thomas Mann's *The Magic Mountain* to illustrate his point. Father Brodrick concludes his delightful footnote—his notes are generally spiced with a wry and whimsical sense of humor—by saying, "Herr Thomas Mann, evidently a believer in the existence of such wildfowl, disposes of his disguised Jesuit, who for good measure is also an atheist, by means of a dramatic suicide in the snow."

There is, however, something to be said for M. Pasquier's invention. The "secret, disguised" Jesuit he conjured up for the shuddering contemplation of the populace and for the long manipulation of novelists was, to be sure, a sinister figure, in intent if not in appearance, and the wily lawyer paraded his creation before the world out of no feeling of love for the Society. But, at the time he was launching his attack, there actually were "secret, disguised" Jesuits making their way into dozens of towns, cities, and countrysides all over Europe, and from the days of St. Ignatius up to our own times the sons of St. Ignatius have had not too infrequently to go secretly and in disguise if the Gospel of Christ was to make its way to ears longing to hear.

In fact, there seems to have been, especially in the early Society, rather a fondness for disguises. This is not to say that masquerades were adopted when and where they were not needed, but it does seem that once the need was evident the Jesuits entered into the game with particular zest and daring. This was perhaps because the order was, after all, a young foundation and possessed the verve and adventuresome spirit with which we usually credit the young. But there was another factor, too, if it does not seem too farfetched to adduce it as a complementary reason for the rather widespread taking to disguises. From its very earliest days the Society of Jesus had realized the vivid and impressive apologetic value of the drama. Plays were adopted as a regular feature of Jesuit education from the beginning. The comedies and tragedies acted were not for mere amusement or diversion, but had a severely practical intent. The purposes of them, as one of the most prolific Jesuit dramatists, Father Luis da Cruz, expressed it, was "to promote studies, to give authority and renown to the school, and to foster piety and good conduct among the scholars."

It may be of interest to note that such dramatic representations were regularly part of the Society's missionary apostolate wherever schools were established. So, for example, in India there are records of plays as early as 1602 at Tranquebar and at Goa in 1609, and "such dramatic performances were very frequent . . . all over India." (H. Heras, S.J., *The Conversion Policy of the Jesuits in India*, Bombay, Indian Historical Research Institute, 1933, pp. 30, 33). Again, when the Jesuits penetrated into the Kingdom of Akbar and finally established a school at Lahore (this was their third mission), sure enough, on the Christmas Day of 1600 a miracle play, in which one scene was a "discussion between Mercy and Divine Justice," was presented (Pierre du Jarric, S.J., *Akbar and the Jesuits*, New York, Harper, 1926, p. 128).

At any rate, the familiarity of the Jesuits with the trappings of stagecraft may have "conditioned" them, as we would say today, to the stratagems of disguise used in the service of Christ in missionary activities.

When we confine ourselves to Europe alone, however—and this will be the sole theater of operations dealt with in this chapter—we have to distinguish between the two types of missionary activity. One type was the missions to neglected, overlooked, practically undiscovered people living in countries still Catholic. Such was the task that faced heroic missioners in France, Italy, and parts of Germany. Their labors, as we shall see through specific examples, were no less herculean than the more immediately dangerous toil of missionaries who penetrated into countries in Europe where the heretics were in control and where a Catholic, and especially a Jesuit priest, ran the imminent danger of imprisonment, banishment, or torture and death, often without benefit of even the semblance of a trial.

To keep the distinction clear, then, this first section will treat of Jesuit missionaries to the European faithful—to those nominal Catholics, namely, who lived in Catholic countries, but whose ignorance, debased morals, or almost complete lack of contact with priests and the Sacraments had reduced them to such a level that they offered virtually a virgin field for true missionary activity.

Here is an example of the type of apostolate waiting for the Jesuit missionaries in rural France at the end of the sixteenth century. Every four months local Jesuit Superiors in Europe had to send reports to the Father General. A report from Périgueux contains the following statement and appeal:

"Would to God that Father Ignatius might be inspired to send hither some of his brethren. They would achieve far more for the glory of God in these parts than in India itself . . . In matters of religion our people are more ignorant than many savage tribes. There is a forest near Bordeaux thirty leagues in depth whose denizens live like the beasts in the fields. Persons of fifty years and more are to be found who have never heard Mass in their lives, nor learned a single syllable of the faith."

One reason for these appalling conditions was, as Father Brodrick indicates, that "about forty of the French bishops lived permanently in Paris, leaving their dioceses to be governed or misgoverned by surrogates. Father Broet (one of the Jesuit missionaries who preached in this region with great fruit) expressed a wish that they might all be excommunicated if they did not return to their flocks."

It was to meet such needs that men like St. John Francis Regis (1597–1640) were raised up by the providence of God. St. Regis was allowed only nine short years of missionary

activity, all of them devoted to "popular" missions. Calvinism
had penetrated deeply even into the sections of southern
France which were his mission field, irreligion was even more
widespread than devotion to heretical sects, and brigandage,
rapine, murder, and revolt occupied the time of many of the
inhabitants. Speaking of the saint's missionary work in the
diocese of Vivarais, one biographer remarks that the locale
in which he toiled was a "nest of vipers, among whom was to
be preached a religion of love." St. Francis had, early in his
Jesuit life, entertained the holy ambition to join his brethren
laboring in New France (Canada), but had been refused
permission because he was not thought robust enough. He
found all the privations of the foreign mission field, however,
right there in his native France.

He was allowed by superiors to devote six months in a year
to missions in the mountain valleys and, in order to share the
danger and privations of his Brothers in the New World, he
chose the winter months for his journeys. For the last seven
years of his life he covered on foot more than fifty villages
in Vivarais, Forez, and Velay, preaching, instructing, consoling, bringing Mass and the Sacraments to people sunk in the
indifference engendered by long neglect. When the winter
journeys were over, the hot and humid summers were spent
in the narrow, fetid streets of the towns. The poor, the prisoners, and those stricken by the plague received his most
fervent ministry, but it seems that the children of the poor
were those to whom his great apostolic heart went out most
lovingly—and, true to the practice of his Jesuit confreres, he
early hit upon the device of religious "plays" to bring home
to all the truths of the faith. His reputation for sanctity took
root early, grew consistently, and blossomed into universal
acknowledgment immediately before and after death. He
was beatified in 1716 and canonized in 1737.

The year St. John Francis Regis died was the year Julien
Maunoir began his forty-three-year period of missionary

work among the Bretons. He had been born in 1606 in the diocese of Rennes, but the plight of the peasants in Brittany had early attracted his sympathy and zeal. Before his ordination he set himself to the task of mastering their difficult dialect, realizing that one great reason for their ignorance of religion was not their fault so much as the fault of the local clergy, the great percentage of whom did not even bother to learn the language of the people to whom they were presumably ministering.

Father Maunoir's long apostolate was crowned with enduring success, and one great factor in this was that he early devoted much of his labors to reforming the clergy. It speaks volumes for his charm and tact that this delicate work roused little resentment; it was so well received by his fellow priests that he finally had more than a thousand priests in the region ready to assist him in missionary work. He was able to dispatch as many as forty at a time to remote villages and hamlets, where they put to good use the catechism, the hymns, and the books of devotion which he himself had translated into Breton. Julien Maunoir was beatified in 1955.

These two "home missionaries" working in their native France were by no means unique, though St. John Francis Regis seems, from all human estimates, to have been the giant among those devoting their lives to such apostolates. Back in the days of the order's very foundation the work of the home missions had been marvelously carried on by such men as Silvestro Landini, who toiled among the peasants of Abruzzi, Calabria, and Apulia in Italy before going to the even worse physical conditions and more appalling religious ignorance and misery of the poverty-stricken island of Corsica, where he died in 1554, two years before St. Ignatius, spent by his labors and privations.

Later such missionaries as Blessed Anthony Baldinucci (1665–1717) had great success among the citizens of Italy's Frascati and Viterbo and in the surrounding countryside.

Again, this apostle devoted no little part of his work to the reformation of the clergy, and his esteem among the people was so great that often, when he drew near a city to begin his preaching, the walls would be black with people who had climbed to this vantage point to catch an early glimpse of the fervent missionary. Then there was St. Francis de Geronimo (1642–1716), the Apostle of Naples. For the forty years from 1676 till his death this city was the center of his incredible work, which was most remarkable for the great crowds he led to the reception of the Blessed Eucharist on the third Sunday of each month. It was estimated that as many as fifteen thousand men regularly frequented these celebrations. Though the fetid and squalid quarters of Naples were his main battleground, he journeyed throughout the countryside, often in a single day passing through forty hamlets, in every one of which he preached. Finally, mention might be made of Father Pedro de Calatayud (1689–1773), famous throughout Spain and especially around Bilbao for his preaching, as well as for his writings, which were particularly numerous for a man who led such a busy missionary life. The type of mission he gave may be estimated from the appelation of *"portentosa"* given to a mission he preached in Bilbao.

Up to the suppression of the Society in 1773 the apostolate of the home missions was a special love of the Society, and it would be difficult to estimate in human values whether the preservation of the faith in Europe through this apostolate did not do as much for the total health and well-being of the Church as did work on the foreign missions. Certainly, in one sense, the work of a Regis, of a Landini, was even more heroic than that of a Xavier or a Jogues, in that there was on the domestic front very little of the glamour that inevitably surrounded the missionary who was leaving Europe for presumably exotic and exciting lands. The martyrdom lived in rural France or Italy or Germany was a humdrum affair; the rewinning of sluggish, indifferent, loutish, and bored Catholics did not, humanly speaking, have about it the dash and challenge that cast an aura about the conversion of Chinese, Red Indians, Ethiopians, and Tartars.

It is to be remarked, too, that the Jesuits who engaged in the work of the home missions were, so to speak, consistently "talking themselves out of a job." One of the greatest services the Society of Jesus rendered to the Church was not merely the part such men as Canisius, Salmeron, and Lainez played in the deliberations of the Council of Trent, but also the zeal with which men like Regis carried the reforms inaugurated at Trent into practice in their apostolate. Now, one of the great tonics Trent administered to the clergy of the day was the forceful reminder that preaching and the teaching of catechism was a cardinal duty of bishops and priests. When men like Maunoir, accordingly, recruited the secular priests of Brittany as adjutants, they were laying the foundations for the day when each European diocese would do its own mission work and religious orders would not have to send shock troops or relief forces to fill the breach left yawningly open by the too long neglect of bishops and clergy.

Such work among the clergy, which was little by little to render the work of the Jesuit missionaries unnecessary, can be illustrated by the example of Regis. "We have had occasion in the course of this sketch," states Father Foley in *St. Regis: A Social Crusader*, p. 258, "to note his dealings with the priests and religious who heard him at Le Puy and with the country pastors with whom he lived during his missions. In 1636 or 1637 that great force in the movement for sacerdotal renewal, M. Jean-Jacques Olier, had passed through Le Puy and observed there a congregation of ecclesiastics, mostly canons, among whom the fiery words of the 'holy Francis Regis' had rekindled into new flame their spark of priestly zeal. Later in that year, Olier . . . described in a letter to friends in Paris the work of this congregation: 'These priests give examples of virtues that delight the whole province. Catechism classes are conducted by them in many places about the city; visits to prisons and hospitals are frequent here, and at present they are preparing to give missions in all the places that depend on their chapter.'"

Another example of this type of work for the renovation of the clergy can be found in striking detail in the work of St. Bernardine Realino (1530–1616). The sodality for priests which he founded in the Italian city of Lecce in 1583 was, in the words of his latest biographer, "the heart of his work for the reform of the religious and the parish clergy . . . it was his sling and pebbles against the mailed and roaring Goliath of clerical incompetence."

For it must be remembered that this was the situation. Europe, from the days of the foundation of the Society until its suppression, did not labor from a shortage of priests as much as it did from the evil of absentee bishops, an inadequately educated clergy, and the inroads of all the religious confusion that had sprung from the Pandora's box of the Reformation. Following the decrees of Trent the Jesuits (by a coincidence of history or, better, under God's providence) injected something new into the religious life of Europe by the type of home missionary work they spearheaded. First of all, the very fact of sermons in rural districts was new— or rather, a renewal of an apostolate that had flourished earlier under the Franciscans and Dominicans. But, above all, the manner of the sermons was new. It was, as we would say today, down to earth. The Jesuit missioners would have none of the florid, oratorical, spread-eagle style of the popular court and big-city preachers. In this they were but following the constant reminders and exhortations of the Fathers General of the Society, who, in season and out, recalled to preachers that they must not think that they fulfilled the demands of the Institute of the Society with regard to preaching and catechizing by preaching "customary sermons —rhetorical and bombastic sermons after the onetime fashion." So spoke Father General Mutius Vitelleschi in a letter of March 1625, directed to the French Assistancy, and his reminder is typical of the Society's care to reach the real needs of the people. This directness and simplicity of approach were especially valuable because of the fact that most of the Jesuit missionaries were called on to combat the new doctrines of the various sects that sprang up in the wake of the Reformation. This aspect of the work gave a particular cachet to Jesuit missionary sermons.

This directness, simplicity, and tremendously moving sincerity are qualities that are emphasized time and again in the words of the biographers of St. John Francis Regis, to take him as an instance. One who was a famous preacher of the times, Father Guillaume Pascal, and whose sermons are said to have "wrung pity from the most hardened hearts, and money for alms from the most miserly," himself paid tribute to the preaching of Regis in 1632, exclaiming, "How futile are our preoccupations with polishing and adorning our sermons! Look at the crowds that rush to the simple catechism lessons of this man, and the conversions he produces, while our affected eloquence obtains results of no consequence."

Several special fields of home missionary activity seem to have exercised a peculiar attraction for the sons of Ignatius. Prisoners and slaves were among their first loves. St. Bernardine, for instance, shortly after his arrival at Lecce, became "the apostle to the prisons," among whom "his greatest service was his devotion to the condemned." "Before long," writes Father Francis Sweeney in *Bernardine Realino: Renaissance Man*, New York, Macmillan, 1951, p. 106, "it was he who went with every convict sentenced to death and remained with him until the state had exacted its barbarous toll."

Records are most abundant of the work of the home missionaries for the galley slaves, who were such a frequent and disgraceful feature of the social scene of the period, and the number of Jesuits in this age of the Society who gave their lives while attending the plague-stricken is, relatively speaking, enormous. In 1558, for example, twenty Jesuits died in Aragon alone while caring for the sick; in the following year eighteen made the same sacrifice in Lisbon. Again, many of the Fathers acted as chaplains for armies and navies, and, to take but one instance, there were four Jesuit priests serving as chaplains in the fleet of Don Juan at the battle of Lepanto (October 7, 1571) and, together with their Franciscan, Dominican, and Capuchin brethren, they tended the wounded, consoled the dying, and inspired the champions of Christendom all through the five hours of the fight. It is stated that "not a single sailor, soldier or galley-slave died that memorable October evening without the comfort of the sacraments." (Brodrick, *Origin of the Jesuits,* p. 269, who adds the quaint footnote that the Sicilian Jesuits made a modest contribution to the fighting forces of Christendom in the shape of three hundred indigenous bandits whom they had converted and persuaded to turn their murderous abilities against the Turks.)

In the generations between the foundation of the Society and its suppression so much of the work of the Fathers was devoted to the apostolate of the classroom and the foreign missions that a modern viewer of the history of the Society may get the impression that these were the main apostolates of the order. As a matter of fact, as these few examples may have shown, the amount of missionary work done in the home fields is astonishing. One will find that wherever human misery cried out for understanding and alleviation, wherever ignorance of religion and depraved morals, injustice inflicted by the civil governments, or turmoil stirred up by civil strife existed, there the Jesuit home missionaries were to be found. This humble and unglamorous work can be followed in great detail in *Les Jesuites et les humbles,* by A. Belanger, Paris, 1900.

After the restoration of the Society in 1814 there was, comparatively speaking, not the crying need for home missionaries that had existed in the old days when the clergy were too ill prepared to cope with the ignorance of the people. Accordingly, relatively little is heard in Europe of the extensive mission tours into rural regions after the mode of a John Francis Regis or a Landini. "Missions" in Catholic lands today generally means the course of sermons preached during a parish mission, and we tend to restrict the word to apply to foreign missions. But in the old Society the missions in Europe were just as hazardous, just as demanding and, thanks to the zeal of the men and the grace of God, often just as bountiful in their harvest of souls as the missions of fellow Jesuits in India, Canada, and all the world that was opening up to the crusaders of Christ far out in the front lines.

If the work of extensive missionary journeys within the countries of Europe has now to a great extent been superseded by the growth of the secular clergy, with the consequent withdrawal of the Society from the work, it is still true that arduous missionary activity on the home front is still one of the works the members of the Society devote themselves to when the need is crying. We may mention, as a striking example of this apostolate which is carried on even in more recent times, the work of Father Fleury among the gypsies of Spain and Provence (Walter Starkie, *In Sara's Tents,* New York, Dutton, 1953) and the traditional evangelizing of the jugglers in the market places of France, which was carried on consistently until 1880 (Alexandre Brou, S.J., *The Ignatian Way to God,* Milwaukee, Bruce, 1952, p. 82 and note).

II

It is time now to embark in the short space available on something like a brief summary of the work of the "secret, disguised" Jesuits in Europe. The missionary work we have been sketching up to now was work in which the toilers were known to be priests. It was precisely because they were priests or religious (for many a lay brother shared in the apostolic work) and known to be acting as such that their ministry was effective. But there were in the Europe of post-Reformation times regions and countries wherein to be known as priest or Jesuit meant speedy arrest, expulsion, or imprisonment and death. It was in these regions that the Jesuits employed to the full the flair for acting and disguising that seems, as we have already mentioned, to have been one of the characteristics of the young order.

Some of the roles to which Jesuit missionaries were assigned seem to manifest that many of the missionaries were indeed having a good deal of fun along with their toil and danger. It may not be too wide of the mark to feel that many a hunted Jesuit, in England, in Russia, in Poland, the Scandinavian countries, and elsewhere, was playing, for the glory of God and the winning of souls, the game of an apostolic Scarlet Pimpernel. We know, for example, that Blessed Edmund Campion (1540–1581) and Father Robert Persons (1546–1610) enjoyed a hearty laugh at one another's appearance (Campion disguised as a jewel merchant, Persons as a soldier) when they were showing off their borrowed finery while preparing to steal back into England. Blessed Edmund, to quote but one allusion, wrote to the then Father General in Rome, Everard Mercurian, and humorously described Father Persons in his disguise as "'such a peacock, such a swaggerer, that a man needs must have very sharp eyes to catch a glimpse of any holiness and modesty

shrouded beneath such a garb, such a look, such a strut.'"
(Richard Simpson, *Edmund Campion: Jesuit Protomartyr of England,* London, Burns and Oates, 1907, pp. 174–175.) The spirit with which Campion and Persons literally galvanized Catholic life in the England of Elizabeth and struck terror to the hearts of the sectaries has been sensitively limned by Evelyn Waugh:

"They came with gaiety among a people where hope was dead. The past held only regret and the future apprehension; they brought with them, besides their priestly dignity and the ancient and indestructible creed, an entirely new spirit of which Campion is the type; the chivalry of Lepanto and the poetry of La Mancha, light, tender, generous and ardent. . . . Campion's generation . . . surrendered themselves to their destiny without calculation or reserve . . . though it led them through bitter ways to poverty, disgrace, exile, imprisonment and death, (they) followed it gaily." (Evelyn Waugh, *Edmund Campion,* Boston, Little, Brown & Company, 1946, pp. 22–123.)

If this was the spirit of Campion, it can be said, too, that it was the spirit of the Society in general. How else account for the almost exuberant prodigality with which missionaries donned their disguises and set out in their perilous ways? In Sweden in 1623, for example, Father H. Schacht (d. 1654) decked himself up as a seller of mousetraps (what could the garb for *that* have been?) to effect entrance for the purpose of consoling persecuted Catholics. He himself was caught, however, and after seven months in prison, during which he was tortured three times, was expelled from the country. In 1558 again Father Nicholas Gaudan, disguised as a peddler, despite the fact that he came as Papal Nuncio, made his entry into Edinburgh to bring consolation to Mary Queen of Scots. Father C. M. Dufour (d. 1698), determined to live among the rabid Calvinists at Geneva so as to bring aid to the cowed Catholic minority, apprenticed himself to a cobbler; Fathers Frederick Schwabenski (d. 1634) and Adam

Krawarski (d. 1660), having been driven out of Prague by the heretics, blackened their faces to look like coal peddlers and returned to the city driving an oxcart (Brou, op. cit., p. 80 and notes).

Others were disguised more impressively and regally. Many of the truly missionary activities of the Jesuits before the suppression were carried out on a high diplomatic level. Perhaps the most remarkable personage in this respect was Antonio Possevino, who, "at the age of twenty-seven, had begun in the Maritime Alps his extra-ordinary career of roving Papal ambassador, which culminated at the court of Ivan the Terrible as peacemaker between Poland and Russia." (Brodrick, *The Progress of the Jesuits*, pp. 54–55.)

This remarkable man (1533–1611) who had been a "home missionary" of the caliber of a Regis or a Jerome—he spent ten years of incessant battling with the Huguenots at Paris, Avignon, Bayonne, Rouen, Dieppe, and other French places —penetrated into Sweden in 1577 (two other Jesuits had preceded him, Father Warszewski, a Pole, in 1573, and Father Nilsson, a Norwegian convert, in 1576), dressed in lay clothes and proceeded to work for the conversion of King John III and the re-Christianization of the country. The King was baptized but proved to be a very unstable Catholic, and Possevino's mission resulted in failure. He did much for the future of the Church in Poland, however, by his insistence that the country would never become Catholic until it was evangelized by local clergy, and he brought back to Rome with him a number of Swedes and Finns to be trained as missionaries. In 1581 Possevino was chosen by Pope Gregory XIII to mediate peace between Poland and Russia, as a preliminary step to winning the Russian schismatics back to Rome.

Not only was Possevino appointed to the position of Secretary to the Father General (Everard Mercurian, who was responsible for the dispatch of the Jesuits back into England), but he was entrusted with other diplomatic missions as well. He returned to Poland as Nuncio and twice visited the court of the Emperor Rudolph II in an endeavor to ameliorate conditions between the Emperor and Poland. During his protracted stay in the north he was not only the diplomat, but the missionary as well, preaching extensively throughout Saxony, Livonia, Bohemia, and Transylvania.

These diplomatic missions were not an infrequent apostolate in the early Society. As far back as 1542 Father Nicholas Broet and Alphonsus Salmeron had been sent as Nuncios to the persecuted Church in Ireland. Their task was to "confirm the bishops and chieftains in the faith, bring about reforms, open Latin schools, find suitable candidates for the episcopacy and care for the poor" (Harney, *The Jesuits in History*, p. 88)—certainly an apostolate varied enough to keep the good men more than busy. It is interesting to note that St. Ignatius gave them explicit instructions to adapt themselves to the Irish customs—good mission practice that was to become the standard and often heroic *modus agendi* of men like De Nobili in India and Ricci in China. After visiting James V at the Scottish court the two Jesuits made their way into Ireland, though persuaded by all not to risk their lives in a useless venture. They spent exactly thirty-four days in Ireland, most of the time fleeing before the troops hot on their trail. Father Salmeron was later (1555) sent on a similar mission to Poland which surpassed anything in his wide experience of suffering and frustration.

One of the most fascinating of the Jesuit missionary-diplomats was the Dutch Father Nicholas Gaudan (his family name was Floris, but he was called, after the fashion of the times, after his native town Gauda). The plight of Catholics in Scotland and especially the tribulations of Mary Queen of Scots seem to have exercised a peculiar fascination for the early Jesuits (is this another indication of the Scarlet-Pimpernel-for-God motif?), and this humble man was dispatched as Papal Nuncio in 1562. At this time Scotland was the most dangerous country in the world for a Jesuit to enter, and Father Gaudan enjoyed the singular privilege of being fulminated against by John Knox. Nothing much came of the mission save that a group of young Scotsmen were recruited for the Society, but the interesting aspect of Gaudan's venture, for the purposes of this paper, is that he assumed no less than four different disguises: first "in court finery, with top-boots, a plumed hat and a sword swinging at his girdle," second, in order to visit some of the bishops of the country, successively as a serving man and a banker's clerk, and finally, in order to make his escape from the country, as a sailor. If Father Gaudan's mission was not prolific of fruit—as indeed many of the Jesuits' diplomatic endeavors ended in apparent failure—perhaps the ultimate evaluation of all these apostolic efforts can be summed up in Father Brodrick's words about the venture in Scotland: "But though the good priest brought no light into the darkness of Scotland, he shines in his own right and gives the dignity of one faithful selfless heart to a story wherein all else is folly, treachery, black bigotry and meanness." (*The Progress of the Jesuits,* p. 199.)

Lest it be thought that these apostolic forays in disguise—whether the disguise was mean and humble or gay and ostentatious—were merely impulsive and thoughtless outbursts of the chivalry and daring of a Lepanto, it may be well to emphasize that there was always behind them the cool calculation and the objective weighing of hopes and probabilities that we would expect from the sons of Ignatius, himself noted for his practical zeal. It cannot be maintained that every missionary venture was as well thought out ahead of time as was the daring and attention-catching penetration of Fathers Edmund Campion and Robert Persons into Elizabethan England. It does remain true, however, that their mission was quite typical of the sense of strategy that characterized Jesuit mission work.

An eminent historian, Philip Hughes, has summarized the work of Campion and Persons, and the thought that went into its inauguration, in the following words:

"The Jesuit superiors thought the whole thing out very carefully. There was not a single chance or misfortune that came to pass as the years went by that they did not anticipate as possible . . . In the apostolate of Persons and Campion, we have, for once, the spectacle of the right idea brilliantly carried out: understanding of the first need, namely to know the position exactly; the organized, rapid tour, next, to survey the whole country; the "national mission" by two preachers of genius which this becomes; a work of reconciliations and conversions over an area so extensive, and covered so speedily, that the two Jesuits seem simultaneously everywhere; a work whose kind and whose effects cannot be kept secret—all the Catholics of England, it seems, knew of it, half expected (we feel) to meet the famous priests sooner or later; and they knew of course, as did all England, of the elaborate hunt to capture them." (Philip Hughes, *The Reformation in England*, Vol. III, *True Religion Now Established*, New York, Macmillan, 1954, pp. 306–307. In the extended note on p. 305 Father Hughes gives some rather amusing instances of how the Jesuit-in-disguise motif threw the sectaries of the day into shudders and still influences the writings of the not too careful historians.)

The thrilling story of the whirlwind campaign of these two priests for the recapturing of England to allegiance to the ancient faith is perhaps too well known and certainly much more expertly told elsewhere (by Simpson and Waugh, for example) to warrant a retelling here. Suffice it to say that in a brief thirteen months of active ministry (June 1580–July 1581), new courage was instilled into the hearts of Catholics who had remained faithful but whose spirits were drooping under the vision of unending repressions and persecution; that the defenders of the new heretical doctrines were put on a defensive from which they never quite recovered; and the existence of the faith, under whatever difficulties, was assured. Evelyn Waugh has summed it all up in the concluding sentences of his memoir of Campion:

"The Catholic cause was very near to extinction in England [when Campion and Persons began their crusade]. Families who had resisted the onslaught of persecution were quietly conforming under neglect. The Church survived here and there in scattered households, regarded by the world as, at the best, something Gothic and slightly absurd, like a ghost or a family curse. Emancipation still lay in the distant future; no career was open to the Catholics; their only ambition was to live quietly in their homes, send their children to school abroad, pay the double land taxes, and, as best they could, avoid antagonizing their neighbors. It was then, when the whole gallant sacrifice appeared to have been prodigal and vain, that the story of the martyrs lent them strength. We are the heirs of their conquest, and enjoy, at our ease, the plenty which they died to win." (Op. cit., pp. 214–215.)

Another facet of Jesuit missionary work in Europe itself which is highlighted in the apostolate of Campion and Persons, but which is quite typical of the work in general, is the insistence that only the men best qualified in intellectual stature be assigned to such work. This conviction that missionary work demanded more than merely a strong body and a deep zeal was characteristic of St. Ignatius from the beginning, and is nowhere more strikingly manifest than in the fact that missionaries to the American Indians often were men who had held positions as professors of theology in the European universities. But for the missions in Europe itself intellectual excellence was most imperative, because the Jesuits in particular were called on to combat the theological errors of the times. Accordingly, we find that the missionaries were almost invariably men who could wield a pen as well as preach a rousing sermon and stand the rigors of exhausting journeys. So, for example, the one thing above all that set the heretics in a rage to capture Father Campion was his little booklet, *Ten Reasons,* which set forth a decade of arguments to show that the Church of which the Pope was the visible head was the only Church founded by Jesus Christ. It is typical, too, to note that the title Campion originally wanted to give to this trenchant little work was *De Heresi Desperata—On Heresy in Despair*. At the very moment when the heretics seem to be sweeping all before them, Campion rose with a gallant laugh and challenge, telling them that they were losing. One is reminded of "My right wing is crushed, my left is collapsing, my center is threatened—I attack," of Marshal Joffre at the Marne in World War I.

To return to the matter of men intellectually eminent as missionaries. Perhaps no better example of this realistic passion to apply really top-notch men to positions where their very lives might soon be snuffed out is more evident than in the letters Father Persons kept sending back to the Father General in Rome. So, explaining the needs of the English Mission to Father Rudolph Aquaviva in October 1581, he writes, "*Iterum atque iterum vestram Paternitatem rogo ut non mittantur huc nisi homines valde idonei* [Again and again I beseech your Paternity to send hither only men who are extraordinarily fitted]." And Father Persons set his sights very high, indeed. Though there is a note of resignation in his phrase in the same letter, "*Patrem Bellarminum non audeo postulare* [I don't dare to request Father Bellarmine]," there is also the wistful hope peeping out that perhaps the General *will* send the noted theologian.

Scant justice has been done to Blessed Edmund and Father Persons in this brief summary of their work and the sense of strategy that underlaid it. Certainly for English-speaking Catholics the world over their brief, glorious, gay, buoyant apostolate sets up a thrill along the spine and a sparkle of love and pride in the eye. Theirs was the spirit of irrepressible youth dedicated to the cause of Christ, and it distilled in purest essence the spirit of the young Society.

But we must hurry along. No more than an allusion can be made, as this chapter comes to its conclusion, to the missionaries—most of them martyrs—who followed the steps of Campion and in his spirit. A Southwell, a Garnet, a Gerard, a Weston—these are names of English brothers of Regis, Baldinucci, Possevino, Gaudan—and brothers of Xavier, De Nobili, Ricci, Jogues as well. All, whether laboring for Christ their King in the missions among the Indians or the Japanese or among fellow Europeans, crystallized the youthful eagerness, the noble eagerness, the chivalric spirit of the young Society of Jesus, and still ran their apostolic path with a maturity of planning, a sober appreciation of scholarship that reflected the practical zeal of St. Ignatius and the Fathers General who followed him.

This account of Jesuit missionary activity does not, as will have been apparent, pretend to follow that work very widely into the activities of the restored Society. Anticlericalism in France and Spain, especially, after the Society had resumed its corporate existence and its influence, gave many an opportunity for the "secret, disguised Jesuit" to play his dangerous game of "dressing up for Christ." There is perhaps no better example of the fun—but what deadly serious, and gloriously apostolic fun!—the members of the Society have always found in masking and mumming for the advancement of God's kingdom than was furnished in our own times by Father Miguel Augustin Pro in the Mexican persecutions of the 1920s. Europe was not the field of his action, but the spirit of a Campion or a Regis lived in this martyr of our day. He had been a superb little mimic as a boy, and after his ordination in Europe and his return to a Mexico that was grinding the Church into the dust (it thought), Miguel Pro turned his histrionics to good use, indeed. Dressed as a taxi driver, as a mechanic, as a peon, he eluded the persecutors for many a month. Under his shabby jacket or serape he brought the Body of Christ to thousands hungering for It and, in his laboring man's hands, the absolution and blessing which were God's pledge of companionship with the Mexican Catholics in their dark days.

When Father Pro extended his arms to bare the full expanse of his breast to the bullets of the firing squad on November 23, 1927, and shouted in triumph, "*Viva Cristo Rey* [Live Christ the King]!" before he crumpled into heaven, his cry must have found glad echo in the ranks of all the Jesuit home missionaries, canonized and uncanonized, who waited to welcome him. And all the Jesuit missionaries who had spent their lives in foreign fields also recognized the paean of victory, too, for all, whether at home or abroad, had worked that Christ might live and that all the world might at last be at home with Him.

3. *Giants of Asia*

Jerome D'Souza, s.j.

THE physical immensity of Asia, the vastness of her population, the variety and complexity of her many civilizations should be a deterrent to anyone inclined to generalize about the continent as a whole. Nevertheless, in this vastness and complexity there is a certain underlying unity, particularly in what pertains to religion, culture, and social ideals, which also should not be ignored.

It is precisely this unity—and if that seems too strong a word, let us say similarity between the component parts—which comes into evidence when we examine the history of Catholic missionary effort in Asia, whether we consider the difficulties which confronted the missionaries or the remedies with which they attempted to solve them. Therefore let me say at once that the choice of certain outstanding personalities among the earlier Jesuit missionaries of Asia has not been made in a haphazard way but in the belief that, notwithstanding considerable differences among them, their ideas and careers fall into a certain recognizable pattern. The writer of these brief sketches hopes that this pattern may emerge in the course of the following pages.

The impression of unity to which I have referred is reinforced by the purely accidental fact that the first and the greatest missionary of Asia, St. Francis Xavier, is not merely Apostle of India but Apostle of "the Indies," a term which stood in older parlance for the entire Far East. He labored, and set hearts aflame, "burning a trail" in the deepest sense of the term, on the west and east coasts of India, in the Malaya Archipelago as far as the Moluccas, and then back again and northwards in Japan. He died at the gateway of China, *"tendentesque manus ripae ulteriori amore* [and stretching forth his hands in longing for the farther shore]," as a Protestant writer said in one of the most eloquent passages ever written on this "canonized saint of universal Christendom." (J. K. Prothero, *The Psalms in Human Life.*) So from that day to now no missionary and no student of the missions can ever break up the Asian scene and think of each country, however great, in isolation. From Ormuz to the Moluccas, from Cape Comorin to the Great Wall, it is one immense field of action, and those who played the greatest roles there were the children of Ignatius Loyola, Brothers of Francis Xavier, not unworthy to walk in even his footsteps.

I. ALESSANDRO VALIGNANO (1539–1606)

Of those successors of St. Francis one of the most remarkable was Alessandro Valignano, also called, inaccurately, Valignani. Father Alessandro's character and achievements, though they have been more justly estimated in recent times by Protestants and Catholics alike, have never received the full measure of recognition due to them. As Visitor to the Indies and Envoy of the Viceroy of Goa he had an official position similar to that of St. Francis. He had, like him, the Asia-wide vision, and he spent his long years of stay in Asia developing all the Asian Missions, the Indian, the Japanese, and the Chinese. Like Xavier, he came to be called the Apostle of the East, and he deserved that title because his farsighted work of organizing and consolidating the Asian Missions was as important as the original work of St. Francis Xavier. Xavier was the conqueror, Valignano was the organizer and administrator.

Alessandro Valignano was born in Chieti in 1539, member of a distinguished family which was on terms of close friendship with the archbishop who later became Pope Paul IV. He studied law and took his doctorate in Padua. He then went to Rome to seek preferment since his brilliant talent and commanding personality ensured high success. But in Padua itself a fight in which he was involved brought him under the rigor of the law, and he was banished from the city. Four years later, a changed man, he entered the Society of Jesus, where his great ability was quickly recognized. In 1574, at the age of thirty-five, he was sent to the Indies as Visitor, with thirty-two missionaries and with authorization to gather eight more, in India and elsewhere, wherever he could find them.

The evangelization of the Indies had been placed under the patronage of the Portuguese monarchy by the Holy See, and all missionaries had to come East by way of Lisbon and Goa, as St. Francis had done. Valignano had to follow the same route and make the same perilous voyage. Since the dangers had to be undergone by all the missionaries to the East, it is best to give an idea of them in the words of Valignano himself. He describes them, in his *Memoir of St. Francis Xavier,* in the following words:

"The perils and hardships suffered in this expedition are very extensive and terrifying. The first hardship is the lack of accommodation. True, the ships are large and powerful, but so packed with passengers, merchandise, and provisions, that there is little room left for anyone to move about, and the ordinary people aboard, for whose comfort there is no arrangement whatever, must stand all day on deck in the blazing sun, and sleep somehow all night in the cold. On the other hand the berths put at the disposal of noble or wealthy persons are so low, so narrow, so confined, that it is all a man can do to fit himself into them. The second hardship has to do with food and drink. Though His Highness the King provides daily rations of biscuits, meat, fish, water and wine, sufficient to keep the passengers alive, the meat and fish are so salty, and the provision of utensils to collect the rations so inadequate, that the suffering on this account specially among the soldiers beggars description. The third hardship among the general run of the voyagers is due to their being poor and happy-go-lucky. They set out with little or no clothing, the little they bring soon rots on their backs, and they suffer dreadfully in lower latitudes, both from the cold and from the stench of their rags. The fourth hardship is caused by the calms off the Guinea Coast, which may last for forty, fifty or sixty days. During that time, the passengers almost sweat their souls out and suffer torments from the heat beyond the power of my pen to set forth. The fifth hardship, and the worst of any, is lack of water. During much of the voyage, the water doled out in the daily ration is so foul and malodorous that it is impossible to bear the stench of it, and the passengers have to put a cloth before their mouths to filter off the corruption. This liquid is distributed only once a day, and many fail to get their portion through having no jugs in which to collect it. Others drink their entire ration at one gulp, the result being that large numbers die of thirst. The sixth hardship results from diseases of every description among the passengers, who suffer a thousand miseries before dying or recovering. The King appoints a surgeon to each ship, but he and his remedies soon cease to be of any use. . . .

"It often happens that the majority of the passengers die, sometimes five hundred, sometimes four or three hundred, on a single ship, and it is a most heart-rending thing to watch each day the poor inflated bodies being committed to the sea. With all these and other perils, it is extraordinary that so many Portuguese should seek to come to India every year . . . yet they do." (James Brodrick, S.J., *St. Francis Xavier*, pp. 98–99.)

I have quoted this long passage, though the substance of it must be known to many, and placed it here, as it were, on the lintel of the gate of the East, so that the reader may judge whether the hundreds of men who braved these dangers in the course of centuries were not men of heroic resolve, fired by the most ardent love of Our Lord.

Valignano spent four years in Goa before going to the Japanese Mission. I shall not enter into the details of his work in India because he is in a special way the organizer of the Japanese Mission, and it is there that he did his most significant and lasting work. It is enough to say that in India he saw at once the defect of the missions, the excessive confusing of conversion to Christianity with the adoption of European manners and ways of living. As the example given by the Portuguese soldiers and officials was far from edifying, the harm to the Catholic apostolate can be easily imagined. But ampler treatment of this aspect of mission work in India will be given at a later stage. Valignano did all he could to encourage the work of education in Goa, the training of catechists, and the study of the Indian languages. He founded a school for Indian languages in Goa, for studying Konkani, Marathi, and Tamil. He was distressed to find that even the missionaries made no attempt to learn these languages and expected their Indian converts to confess to them in Portuguese.

In 1578 he went to Macao, the Portuguese settlement in the estuary of the Canton River which the Portuguese were permitted to hold for the sake of the Japanese and Indian trade. This place was to be the headquarters whence he was to sail for Japan three times in the course of the next twenty-five years, entering there at crucial moments in the history of the evangelization of the country and at each visit ensuring a period of progress and prosperity for the missions. It was from Macao, too, that he organized, as we shall see, the great mission of Ruggieri and Ricci to China. But for the moment our concern is with the Japanese Mission.

St. Francis Xavier had landed in Japan in 1549 on Assumption Day. He had gone there in his usual poor garb and quickly found that this made no impression on the Japanese. Soon he appeared in the splendid robes of his office as Papal Envoy and gained contact with some of the daimyo or feudatory rulers of the various principalities into which Japan was divided. This brought immediate results. His disputes with the Buddhist monks or bonzes also gave him prestige. There was opposition to the bonzes in Japan itself, and to the power and wealth they had acquired. St. Francis left Japan in November, appointing Fathers Torres and Fernandez to carry on his work. By the time he left, there already were over a thousand converts.

This group multiplied rapidly under the successors of St. Francis. The method of securing the conversion of the leading men in the small principalities gave considerable success. It reached its highest point with the emergence of Oda Nobunaga as the Shogun in 1568. This man, one of the most forcible leaders Japan has produced, disliked the bonzes intensely and, being the real ruler of the country rather than the Emperor at Kyoto, whose authority was only nominal, favored the missionaries. A succession of able men, Fernandez, Froes, Vilela, gained great influence over him. Their friendship was agreeable to him not only because of their opposition to the bonzes and their frequent triumphs over them in disputes, but also, let it be admitted, because it enabled him to promote the China trade which was carried through the intermediary of the Portuguese in Macao. When Valignano arrived in Japan in 1579, there were many thousands of Christians, but only twenty missionaries. He was received with enthusiasm at Nagasaki and led in triumph to the church. He stayed in Japan for three years and during that time introduced several farsighted reforms.

From the first he realized the peculiar position of the missionaries in Japan. They were not there as in India, with the political power of the Portuguese to enforce discipline and to exercise pressure to make conversions. He realized the strength and sensitiveness of the Japanese character. His judgment on them should be read in his own words.

"The people are all white, courteous, and highly civilized, so much so that they surpass all other known races of the world. They are naturally very intelligent although they have no knowledge of sciences, because they are the most warlike and bellicose race yet discovered on the earth. From the age of fifteen onwards, all youths and men, rich and poor, in all walks of life, wear a sword and dagger at their side. . . . They are absolute lords of their land, although the chiefest among them frequently league together for defense against their suzerains who are thus often prevented from doing what they wish. They think nothing more of killing a man than they do an animal. . . . Many men kill themselves by cutting their intestines with a dagger.

"They are the most affable people, and a race more given to outward marks of affection than any yet known. They have such control over their anger and impatience that it is almost a miracle to witness any quarrel or insulting words in Japan. . . .

"They are likewise so poor that it is an amazing thing to see with how little even lords and kings can sustain themselves. . . . On the other hand, every one in general and the nobles in particular, are served and treated so cleanly and honourably that it is a marvel to see how despite so much poverty they can keep such cleanliness and good breeding, although their dress, food, ceremonies and all else they have or do, are so different from those of Europe and all other known races that it seems as if they purposely contrive to do everything clean contrary to every one else. Thus we who come hither from Europe find ourselves as veritable children who have to learn how to eat, sit and converse, dress, act politely, and so on. Many things which are regarded as courteous and honourable in Europe are here resented as great insults and injuries." (C. R. Boxer, *The Christian Century in Japan*, pp. 74–76.)

It must not be thought that Valignano was blind to the faults of the Japanese. He speaks frankly of their cruelty, their duplicity, and the mask with which they hide their thoughts. He speaks of "many iniquitous practices and horrible sins which they regard as positive virtues." However,

"when they become Christians, they leave off cultivating these vices and are much addicted to religion and the celebration of the divine cult. Thus they frequent the churches and the sacraments and treat holy things with great reverence and outward humility. Finally since this people is the best and the most civilized of all the East, with the exception of the Chinese, so it is likewise the most apt to be taught and to adopt our holy law and to produce the finest Christianity in all the East, as in fact it already is." (Ibid.)

Very quickly Valignano realized that Christianity could not be firmly established and developed in Japan by the force and prestige of European nations. He saw that in Japan and in China such position as the Europeans had or were likely to have was bound to be temporary, based on the commercial interests of these countries. He decided that the Church in these lands should be built on the foundations natural to the country, with a clergy recruited from among the people, and, further, religious practices and customs must be developed consistent with the traditions of these ancient civilizations. His first preoccupation, therefore, was to have seminaries and novitiates opened for the Japanese, and centers for the study of the Japanese language and arts. The Superior of the Japanese Mission, Father Francisco Cabral, did not believe in this policy. So Valignano, exercising his authority as Visitor, had Father Cabral transferred and in his place appointed Father Gaspar Coelho, who was more amenable to these new ideas. Seminaries were then established in Arima and Adsuchi, and a novitiate for the Society in Usuki. The daimyo of these places were Christians, and Christian influence among the nobles was strong. He founded a college for their children at Funai. A press was also established for the publication of devotional works, grammars of the Japanese language, and texts (suitably "bowdlerized," be it said, in conformity with the Jesuit system in Europe!) for the lay students. The use among Christians and missionaries of Japanese art was encouraged. While steel engraving was introduced to Japan, screen painting and other traditional crafts of the Japanese were promoted.

Valignano did not hide his initial surprise at some of the artistic tastes and preferences of the Japanese. He was astonished at the prices paid for little teacups "small enough for birds in a cage . . . in the same way, they are ready to pay three, four or ten thousand ducats for a little bird or a small tree painted in black on a sheet of rice paper by the hand of an ancient master, a thing which we would regard as worthless." This sentence gives us an idea of the incisiveness of Padre Alessandro's style in his *Memoirs and Letters*. Father Brodrick's comment on the last sentence is worth reproducing:

"What a Philistine! we may think, but the matter is not so simple as that. The Padre was an Italian, used to the well filled canvases of his native land, and could not fairly be expected to have appreciated the exquisite economy of the Kakemono in which so much of the space is left blank. . . . [But] Valignano learned fast. One of his missionaries wrote to Rome in 1594 that 'God had given the Father an incredible love for the Japanese.' He became the great apostle of conformity and accommodation, and ruled that his Jesuits, insofar as possible and compatible with their religious profession, should 'Nipponize' themselves. They must build their churches and houses in the Japanese style . . . diligently study and acquire all the intricacies of [Japanese] etiquette [particularly the etiquette] observed by Buddhist monks who were to be the Jesuits' models in . . . etiquette." (Brodrick, *St. Francis Xavier*, pp. 365–366.)

One important decision which Valignano made in Japan has been subject to much controversy and attack by adversaries both within and without the Church. The Japanese Mission was always hard-pressed to procure the minimum sum of money necessary for its maintenance. It needed at least twelve thousand ducats a year; yet it could count on only eight thousand from various sources in Europe and India. The remaining four thousand was always uncertain. Now Nagasaki, where the Great Ship of the Portuguese made its annual stop coming from China with Chinese silk, was almost a fief of the Jesuit Mission, having been granted this privilege, subject to non-interference from the local authority, by a Christian daimyo. For services rendered to the Portuguese traders the Jesuits agreed to accept a certain quantity of silk as a gift which they could sell as their own property. The General, Father Aquaviva, acquiesced in this arrangement somewhat reluctantly, preferring that other methods should be found for aiding the missions. Occasionally the Jesuits also acted as intermediaries, brokers, if the term is preferred, but with no profit to themselves, between Christian daimyo and the Chinese who wanted Japanese silver in return for Chinese gold. It is easy to say at this distance of time that the Society should have avoided even the appearance of trade. But it is difficult to condemn a Superior who, hard-pressed by the needs of the mission, accepted a gift in kind instead of in money and was at no time guilty of "buying and selling for profit."

In the course of this visit to Japan, Valignano met Oda Nobunaga, the most powerful man in Japan, who had reduced to complete helplessness the last of the Ashikaga Shoguns. By the most skillful diplomatic and military measures, in which the support of the Christian daimyo had been an important element, he had established his authority over twenty of the sixty-odd principalities of Japan. He was to extend this power steadily till his assassination some years later. This encounter between two strong men and born leaders made a great impression on each of them. However, in spite of favorable appearances, Nobunaga never became a Christian; he was, in fact, an agnostic at heart. But Valignano confirmed him in his dispositions of friendliness towards the Christians.

He also arranged for the sending of a mission of important Christian samurai from Bungo, Arima, and Omura to Europe. By this means Valignano wanted, in the first place, to impress the Japanese by the evidence of Christian power and culture in Europe. At the same time he wished to foster sentiments of friendliness and admiration for the people and civilization of Japan among the Catholics of Europe. This was the only means of securing the support he needed for the maintenance of the Japanese Mission and the pursuance of his pro-Japan policy. Valignano left Japan in the company of these cultured samurai and accompanied them as far as Goa. Their visit to Europe was a triumphal march. They were received with honor in the courts of Spain and in the cities of the Papal States, and in Rome itself, where the aged Pontiff, the munificent patron of the Jesuit order, Pope Gregory XIII, gave them every mark of honor and heaped dignities upon them. Everyone was charmed by the dignity of their bearing, the exquisite courtesy of their manner, and the quickness with which they learned the ways and etiquette of high life in Europe. During this time Valignano remained in Goa. He returned to Japan again in the company of the returning samurai, and in conditions very different from those of his first visit.

Nobunaga was assassinated soon after the departure of Valignano and in the confused wars that ensued, a masterful ruler named Toyotomi Hideyoshi (the Taicosamo of our Martyrologies), became master of Japan. He is the second of the architects of Japanese political unity. He, too, began by being very friendly to the Christians though, unlike Nobunaga, he was a Buddhist himself. But some of his trusted lieutenants and generals were Christians, and he realized that the Christian missionaries with their influence over these daimyo, and their importance in ensuring a continuation of the Portuguese trade, were powerful people whose friendship was necessary for him. Hence in the first years of his rule the number of converts and churches increased rapidly. When Valignano left Japan, there were 150,000 Christians. Soon there were a quarter of a million. Hideyoshi was on good terms with Father Gaspar Coelho. He invited him to the castle at Osaka and showed him every mark of respect. He, however, cleverly secured from Coelho the promise to exercise his influence over the Christian daimyo to be faithful to Hideyoshi, and to support him in his plan for a war against China for the conquest of Korea. Coelho even promised the help of the Portuguese to the dictator in this Chinese war.

This promise to help him politically, although gratifying to Hideyoshi, was most imprudent. He was severely blamed by Valignano, because the Visitor did not want interference by the missionaries in political affairs. The readiness of Coelho must have helped to sow seeds of mistrust in the suspicious mind of Hideyoshi. There were also powerful daimyo in the immediate entourage of Hideyoshi who filled the mind of the ruler with exaggerated notions of the power and designs of the European missionaries. From being a friend he suddenly turned against the missionaries, and in 1587 promulgated an edict against them ordering churches to be destroyed, missionaries to be banished, and Christians forced to give up their religion. Coelho reacted to this very imprudently. He stirred up the Christian daimyo to resist the order, and even organized an armed revolt, and sought the help of the Portuguese. Valignano, who had at this time reached Macao with the samurai back from Europe, was horrified by the way Coelho had handled the crisis. He wrote to Hideyoshi asking for an audience. The all-powerful ruler agreed, but said he was receiving Valignano not as a missionary but as the Envoy of the Viceroy of Goa. Valignano's tactful negotiations with Hideyoshi had the desired result. Without the edict's being formally revoked, the persecution ceased and Christians had everywhere the appearance of being restored to favor.

But though the number of Christians continued to increase rapidly, the lull in the persecution was only temporary. A new and ultimately fatal danger had to be confronted. The rivalry between the European powers, and the effort of each of them to gain a part of the profit of the China and Japan trade, led to these difficulties. Unfortunately the first manifestation of this rivalry was between the Spaniards and the Portuguese, and it had a serious repercussion on the fortunes of the Jesuit missions. In spite of the celebrated decision of Pope Alexander VI that the evangelization of the East was the responsibility of the Portuguese, the Spaniards, too, were anxious to play their role in the political and commercial activity of the East. They were well established on the Philippines and from there made repeated attempts to get a hand in the China-Japan trade. Moreover, the Franciscans were anxious to take part in missionary work, and they made no secret of their objection to many of the methods of the Jesuits, particularly what they considered to be their partiality for work among the rich.

Valignano realized that the entry of new missionaries with new ideas of evangelizing the Japanese, animated also by a certain degree of national rivalry against the predominantly Portuguese element among the Jesuits, would be a danger to the prosperity of the Japanese Mission. He saw that new and intemperately zealous men, without the long experience of the Jesuits, were sure to commit mistakes and provoke the scarcely pacified minds of the suspicious Japanese rulers. He appealed to Rome not to permit the entry of missionaries other than the Jesuits into Japan. He did secure a decree from the Holy See that all missionaries to Japan should pass through Goa, and it would have been surprising if the Portuguese had permitted Spaniards to go to the Japanese Mission. But the Spanish Friars had no intention of obeying this order. Circumstances, moreover, helped them to get a foothold in the country. It was the beginning of a series of events which led to the total undoing of the flourishing Japanese Mission.

A great Spanish trading vessel, the *San Felipe,* was wrecked off the coast of Japan, but the costly cargo and the treasures in it were saved. The question was to decide whether or not the ruler of the country was the master of the booty. The Spanish sent Franciscan emissaries to the court of Hideyoshi to plead for the Spanish owners. While this discussion dragged on, the Spanish Friars began missionary activity in the country in a manner irritating to the Japanese, exactly as Valignano had foreseen. To crown these blunders a Spanish pilot captain, De Olandia, told the Japanese authorities, in order the better to impress on their minds the power of the Spanish monarchy, how many countries they had conquered and how their missionaries were the precursors of the conquering soldiers. All the smoldering suspicions and jealousies of the Japanese ruler flared into flame again. The edict of 1587 was revived and reinforced, and a number of Spanish Franciscans and some Jesuits were arrested, tortured, and crucified.

This was in 1597. Valignano was in Macao. He had remained there after his return from Japan in 1590. The news of this outburst confirmed his worst fears regarding the consequences of the entry of Franciscans and Spaniards into the Japanese mission field. He returned to the country and once again sought to allay the fears of Hideyoshi. His "magic touch" succeeded yet again in calming the ruler and mitigating the force of the persecution.

In the following year Hideyoshi died. Valignano had the greatest admiration for the courage and sagacity of this man. He noted the skill with which he had tried to secure the succession for his young son Hideyori to the shogunate, and the appointment of a council of five generals to rule during his minority. One of these five, the most powerful among them, Tokugawa Ieyasu, known as Daifusama in Europe, soon became dominant among them and won over almost all the supporters of Hideyori. He continued and completed the work begun by Nobunaga and Hideyoshi of consolidating the central power in Japan and reducing the numerous feudatory rulers to unity and subordination. He was the founder of the Tokugawa shogunate, which ruled the country for more than two hundred years, until, in fact, it opened its doors to Europe and modern progress in the nineteenth century.

Valignano sought an interview with Ieyasu and was well received. He persuaded the new ruler that his best interests lay not in antagonizing but in conciliating the Christian daimyo and the numerous Christians. In truth the number of the Christians had gone on increasing steadily. The martyrdoms of 1587 and 1597 had stirred up an incredible zeal for the faith among the Japanese. The numbers were now well over three hundred thousand. Contrary to what has been generally believed regarding the attitude of Ieyasu to the Christians, it is certain that during the first years of his rule he was favorably inclined towards them. He was greatly attached to Rodriguez, the Portuguese Jesuit interpreter at his court, known as Tcugu to the Japanese. He was practically Ieyasu's adviser on foreign affairs. Matters being satisfactorily composed, Valignano returned to Macao in 1603. While carefully supervising the work of the Japanese Mission he gave more and more of his time to the Chinese Mission, where, as we shall see, Ricci was carrying on his remarkable apostolate. Valignano died at Macao in 1606. He had spent thirty-two years in the Eastern Missions.

The full stature of this man has been realized only in recent times. Pastor, among the great Catholic historians, was perhaps the first to estimate his real greatness. He states that he deserves, along with St. Francis Xavier, the title of "Apostle of the East." Latourette, in his great work, *A History of the Expansion of Christianity*, describes him as "a man of energy, breadth of vision, imagination, and the gift of leadership." Father Brodrick says that he was "the greatest organizer of missions the Jesuits have produced." Yet the Catholic Encyclopedia did not think it worth while consecrating even a few lines to him! Beyond doubt he was the one who, among the early missionaries, understood best the problem of evangelizing countries of ancient civilization, saw furthest into the future, and indicated once and for all the lines of action in dealing with them. Circumstances did not permit the full efflorescence of the movements which he had initiated, directly or indirectly, in Japan, in China, and in India. In Japan in particular, which he loved with a quite exceptional love, the glorious work of the early missions was all but utterly destroyed in the course of the succeeding years.

It is beyond the scope of this sketch to enter into the story of the Japanese persecution and the destruction of the missions. Ieyasu, who began in such friendly wise, became the most implacable enemy of the Catholics. By 1614 their numbers increased to nearly a million. These numbers frightened him. Stirred by a Protestant English Adviser, Will Adams, who had replaced the Jesuit Rodriguez, he promulgated the decree that sent, in the course of a few years, two hundred thousand Japanese Catholics to the stake and the gibbet. The persecution was one of unimaginable cruelty, that cruelty which Valignano had noted in the Japanese character from the first. But the entire Church was not destroyed. From the remnants of those Christians, so dramatically discovered by Father Petitjean in the nineteenth century, the Japanese Church, rising like a phoenix from its ashes, bids fair to regain the prosperity of ancient days. Tried in the fire of humiliation, the great Japanese nation is opening its heart once again to the message of the Gospel. We may be sure that from heaven Alessandro Valignano watches over this Japanese second spring and, along with the host of Japanese martyrs, intercedes mightily for his beloved people.

II. MATTEO RICCI (1552–1610)

When Alessandro Valignano was in the Roman College acting for the Master of Novices in 1571, a noble youth from

Macerata named Matteo Ricci knocked at the door for admission into the Society. Valignano welcomed him, little dreaming that the careers of both of them would take them to the Far East, and that the young applicant would be one of the most brilliant and most successful executors of his own farsighted policy in regard to work in the Eastern Missions. For Matteo, under the guidance of Valignano, and following his spirit, was destined to be the first modern missionary to enter into the sealed Empire of China, to master its ancient learning and open the hearts of its people to the teaching of Our Lord.

He was born in 1552, the year of the death of St. Francis Xavier, at Macerata, a town in the Papal States, son of a prominent noble of the place, who had ambitions for his gifted boy. But the young Matteo had already come into contact with the Fathers of the Society of Jesus in the college at Macerata, and when he went to Rome in 1568 at the age of sixteen he came to know them better still. In 1571 he asked for admission to the novitiate. Strongly opposed by his father, he finally got his way. On finishing his novitiate he began the study of philosophy, and of mathematics, in which he had the famous Father Clavius as master.

Life in the Society brought Ricci into contact with members of every nationality in Europe, and from these early years his curiosity regarding ways of life other than his own was stirred. With this curiosity went a remarkable capacity for the understanding and assimilation of varying ideas and manners of living, and an affectionate and generous disposition. It was impossible that a man of that kind should not be moved by the call of the missions. St. Francis Xavier's marvelous achievements were still fresh in the minds of people in Europe. Young Jesuits in Rome were kept well informed of the progress of the missions in India and Japan, and they saw each year groups of the best and most promising among their numbers leaving for Lisbon to sail for the distant East.

Matteo Ricci earnestly asked for the missions and secured the permission of the General in 1577. The following year, in September 1578, he was in Goa. In the same boat there was Michael Ruggieri, a companion from the Roman College, destined for China. The very day that he arrived in Goa another boat brought there Rudolph Aquaviva, destined to go to the Mogul court and gain the friendship of Akbar, and die a martyr in Salsette, and also Francisco Pasio, who, along with Ruggieri, had been appointed to the enterprise of entering China.

Goa did not please Ricci. The period of successful missionary work and conversion by preaching had come to an end, and now it was the rigor of the Inquisition which brought in unwilling conversions. After some time spent in teaching in St. Paul's College, Ricci was sent to Cochin, also to teach. There in 1579 he was ordained a priest. He had not completed his theology, and for this purpose was sent back to Goa. The warm enthusiastic temperament of Ricci was subject to moments of depression. He asked himself whether he was destined to spend his missionary life in this uncongenial atmosphere teaching classics to the Indian boys. Suddenly the prospect changed. Ruggieri, whom Valignano had asked to prepare for entry into China by learning the Chinese language, requested that Ricci might be given as companion to him. By the end of 1583 Ricci was in Macao.

Valignano, who had chosen Ricci for this mission, was the mastermind who organized the missionary work in Japan and planned the entry into hitherto closed China. He had a great admiration for the Chinese, whom, in spite of his love for the Japanese, he considered even more civilized and more suited to learn the Christian message. He admired the industry of the Chinese people, the wealth of the country, and the order which reigned there. Above all, he was struck by the fact that, unique in the history of the world, China was governed not by soldiers but by learned men, by philosophers whose title to authority was their knowledge of the classics and their success in the examinations by which that knowledge was tested. He realized also that the conversion of the Chinese, like that of the Japanese—even more than that of the Japanese—depended on the thorough understanding of their culture and the mastery of their language. He had entrusted to Ruggieri the task of learning the language and, from the Portuguese enclave of Macao, of securing an entry into the mainland. Ruggieri was not making too great progress in the study of Chinese. Valignano thought of Ricci because he believed that not only would his unrivaled memory make it easier for him to learn Chinese, but also, as a brilliant mathematician and student of astronomy (which he had studied under the great Clavius), he would be able to impress the Chinese by his learning.

The hopes of Valignano were not belied. In three months Ricci had learned more Chinese than Ruggieri had in three years. The fame of his knowledge of the sciences had reached the mainland, and sometime in 1583 a messenger from the Governor of Kwangtung, Wan P'an, came to Macao inviting Ricci and Ruggieri to Shiuhing. The missionaries were overjoyed. Carefully and discreetly they sailed up the West River and reached Shiuhing. There they donned the robes of the Buddhist monks, a measure recommended by Valignano, who believed that this would ensure greater respect. They were summoned before the Governor, who received them kindly. He was fascinated by the properties of the prism which they presented to him, "glass which imprisons the rainbow" was the way the Chinese so magnificently described it. Wan P'an was thrilled by a picture of Our Lady because, differently from Chinese and indeed Asian painting, knowledge of perspective had given depth to European painting, and so, to the dazzled eyes of the Chinese, the picture looked lifelike. As the Emperor Wan Li was to say many years later about a similar picture, it was a "living idol."

When these preliminaries were over, the Governor asked them what their purpose was in coming to China. To this Ruggieri replied in terms which they had carefully rehearsed, words of supreme significance as expressing the aim of missionary work not only in China, as they faced their host on this crucial occasion, but in all countries and at all times. "'We are religious who serve the King of Heaven, and come from the farthest parts of the West, that is from India. Our journey has taken three or four years. We have heard of the good government of the Middle Kingdom and all we ask is a piece of land away from the commercial distractions of Macao, where we can build a small house and pagoda. There we will remain serving Heaven until we die. We beg Your Excellency to help us. We shall give no trouble. We intend to seek alms for our food and clothing, and shall remain indebted to Your Excellency for the rest of our lives.'" (Vincent Cronin, *Wise Man from the West*, p. 43.)

The Governor needed time to decide the question whether there was any ground for permitting the permanent residence of strangers within the Middle Kingdom, whether any exception could be made to the ruling of the Emperors that foreigners were not to be allowed to settle in China. So he dismissed them for the time, arranging for their temporary stay. Ricci and his companions looked around them, and little by little the utter strangeness of their surroundings broke in upon them. Here was a world very different from all that they had been accustomed to and they were proposing to be citizens of it. Ricci walked through the little town observing "the low wooden dwellings, their roofs windswept waves of a brown river, verandahs landscaped with miniature rock gardens and dwarf cedars, past the flat round faces, eyes set obliquely, black hair worn shoulder length, voices high-pitched and nasal. There were children playing, a single tuft on their shaven heads,—but not a woman to be seen. . . . Beyond the town gate, hung with edicts, vertical columns of sabre-slashing characters, Ricci found more at which to wonder: banyans with vast rooting branches and mulberry trees, their shadows splashed as though with blood; the silt laden river, where black cormorants, throats fastened with cords below the pouch, darted under water and returned to disgorge fish at their master's feet; rich men, androgynous creatures dressed like women in ankle-long colored silk, carried in sedans like holy statues to and from town. Gryphons and headless creatures might have startled him more, but for a short while only. Because they could be dismissed as another species, their monstrosity was not reciprocal. These were men, his own sort, yet their totally different ways bewildered and challenged. He had been prepared for the marvelous, the unique—and these he had found,—but not for this all pervading music in an alien mode, setting all things within him off-key. It was his own accepted truths which began to appear curiosities, and he himself a creature outlandish in body and mind." (Ibid., pp. 44–45.)

After some time they were again summoned by Wan P'an. He had consulted learned mandarins who had found a means of authorizing them to stay in China. But the price was not a light one. It implied an almost total break from their European ways and a complete adoption of the Chinese manner of life. "You must promise," said the Governor, "to fulfill certain conditions. You must not be joined by other barbarians; you must continue to wear our dress; you must promise to conform to our habits; you must obey our magistrates; if you marry, you must choose a woman of our country. You will become, in all save your physical appearance, men of the Middle Kingdom, subject to the Son of Heaven." With all their generosity Ricci and his companion must have paused before this renunciation. Surely they must have thought of their colleagues in India, where to become Christian meant not only the acceptance of the Gospel, but Portuguese names and dress and ways of life. But Ricci knew, as indeed the hundreds of his successors of all nationalities at the present day know, that a missionary vocation demands not only departure from home and country, but the deeper sacrifice of social amenities and cultural ties and the adoption of an alien people and alien modes of thought in an all-embracing charity. Matteo Ricci and Ruggieri made the promises.

They were soon allotted a piece of land for a dwelling, and another for a church, near a tower which the graduates of Shiuhing were building in order to serve as a center of recreation and also to protect the town from ill luck. There were objections on the part of the graduates, the extent of whose influence in Chinese life Ricci soon discovered. A compromise was made, the house and chapel were built, and Ricci settled down in Shiuhing for the next six years.

Making rapid advance in the study of Chinese, Ricci began by translating the Ten Commandments, the Pater, the Ave, and the Credo. He also quickly noted the religious situation in China. Confucianism was the basic belief of the Chinese. The classics of Confucius were the texts for the examinations which the graduates had to pass. It was the official philosophy on which the social system and the government of the country were based. He saw that fundamentally it was a pure natural religion based on respect for heaven and the fulfillment of social duties. It lacked a metaphysic and a doctrine of life after death. It sought happiness in man himself and in the creation of earthly conditions intended for perfect happiness. Buddhism, next in importance to Confucianism, had a pantheistic metaphysic which seemed to Ricci to be less consistent with Christianity than Confucianism. Taoism, the third of the popular religions of China, seemed to have an animistic base, and there were many superstitions and magical ceremonies connected with its practice. However, in most cases the daily religion of the Chinese consisted of a mixture of all three. Ricci decided that the best way for the introduction of Christianity was to show its consistency with the fundamental beliefs of Confucianism, and present Christianity as the crown and fulfillment of the ancient religion of China.

Soon after they settled down in Shiuhing, Ruggieri returned to Macao and was not sent back to the Chinese Mission. In his place Antonio de Almeida, a young, fervent, ascetical Portuguese Jesuit, was sent as companion to Ricci. They stayed in Shiuhing six years, and at the end of that period they had seventy converts. In 1589 a new Viceroy was appointed. He coveted the house of the missionaries to convert it into a pagoda in his own honor. After painful negotiations with him Ricci decided to settle down in Shiuchow, in the same province of Kwangtung, to the north of Shiuhing.

The stay in Shiuchow from 1589 to 1595 marked yet one more stage in the intellectual and spiritual evolution of Ricci. Although they secured land for a house and church there they realized that the bonzes and the graduates were not friendly to them. Many looked upon them as sorcerers, as men who knew alchemy and could transform base material into silver. Ricci suspected that his dress of a Buddhist monk was not calculated to bring him honor. However, he proceeded deeper and deeper into the adoption of Chinese ways. He built his house and chapel in Chinese style and not European. He came to be known as Li Matou, the nearest Chinese transliteration of his name Ricci Matteo. After some time he received the son of a mandarin, Ch'u T'aisu, as a disciple, and the young man, astonished at the scientific and geographical knowledge of Ricci, paid him all the respect which the Chinese students were wont to give to their masters. Ricci loved the Chinese life that he led, the food that agreed with him better than his own European food, the scenery, the lights and sights of the festivals, the courtesy of the people.

But the place did not suit him. It was situated in a low humid area. Malaria struck down Almeida and soon carried him off. Ricci himself was attacked more than once and was reduced to much weakness. At a time when he was feeling particularly depressed, it happened that the Vice-President of the Ministry of War from Peking came to Shiuchow. He approached Ricci, of whose skill and learning he had heard from learned mandarins, to cure his son, who was suffering from melancholia. Ricci saw in this a chance of going to Peking. He offered to accompany the Minister in his boat to the capital and treat the boy in the course of the voyage. Shih Hsing agreed, though not without fears about introducing a foreigner into the capital.

The voyage was not a happy one. One of the boats capsized. Baradas, the companion of Ricci, was drowned. Ricci himself was in danger and saved himself by great bravery. Shih then reconsidered his decision to take Ricci to Peking, gave him some letters to the Governor of Nanking, and advised him to land and seek a residence there.

It was in Nanking that Ricci made one of the crucial decisions of his life. Having realized that the dress of the Buddhist monks brought him no respect, he decided to don the silk garb of the graduate, and to practice the manners proper to that all-powerful and respected fraternity. Dressed in these robes, he paid a visit to Liu, the son of a friendly Governor he had known. Not without trepidation he repeated the formulas of courtesy proper to a graduate calling on a mandarin and felt that he had played his part correctly. Liu himself was surprised and showed by his behavior that his foreign friend had succeeded in assuming the character of literatus both by his learning and his politeness. Indeed, Ricci now knew more Chinese ideograms out of a total of fifty thousand than most of the mandarins, while his knowledge of mathematics and astronomy, his skill in constructing clocks and globes, his mastery of map making, placed him high above the others and made him a person of authority compelling respect from the most learned of the Chinese.

But the Governor of Nanking was not at all disposed to permit Ricci to stay in the city which was the second capital of the Empire. The letter of Shih had no effect on him. Very soon Ricci had to think of another city for his residence. He decided to go to Nanchang, down south, about halfway between Shiuchow and Nanking. He reached the place, once again in a mood of great discouragement, fearing that twelve years of study and prayer had availed him nothing, and that the Celestial Empire would never open its doors to the Gospel. But he was nearer success than he suspected, though it was not before another five years had elapsed that he attained his cherished goal of securing residence in Peking with access to the Emperor.

At Nanchang life opened out far more joyfully than he had expected. In the first place, when he fell very seriously sick his disciple Ch'u tended him with a devotion and love which seemed, at last, an answer to the deep affection which Ricci felt for the Chinese people. Moreover, here the mandarin class showed him no distrust. His new garment and his being a "graduate theologian," one of the recognized learned classes of China, gave him entry into the houses of the noblest and most learned among them. His astonishing memory became the talk of the town. By a single reading he could memorize the ideograms of a poem and repeat them backwards. He was invited to the long banquets where the "feast of reason and the flow of soul" prolonged themselves for over eight hours. Here in Nanchang, Ricci wrote his treatise on friendship, which had a great vogue among the Chinese literati.

It was in Nanchang, too, that he received news that Valignano had appointed him Superior of the Chinese Mission. This was a challenge to him; it also gave him authority to decide with greater confidence the method of apostolate in China. He had understood already in Shiuhing that the honor given to the dead and even the offering of food to them was not necessarily a superstitious practice. The same inclinations of the head were made before living persons who received the honors of a pagoda like Wan P'an, the Governor of Shiuhing. He thought that the Christians should be permitted to give these customary honors to their ancestors, so that they might not be accused of waning in loyalty to the social traditions of China. He had translated into Latin some of the Chinese classics and ensured the correct knowledge of China and a growing enthusiasm for Chinese culture in several circles in Europe. His weapons were therefore polished and ready, and he waited for an opportunity to try them in the capital.

A friend of the name of Wang was to travel to Peking. Ricci secured permission to travel with him and, sailing up the Imperial River, reached Peking for the first time in 1595. But on reaching there he found it impossible to get into touch with the Emperor. The preoccupation with the war with Japan which Hideyoshi had begun by his invasion of Korea made it difficult for any foreigner to get a hearing. The Son of Heaven, hidden in the inaccessible secret chambers of his thrice-walled palace, was surrounded by courtiers and eunuchs. Ricci found it was easier to reach Peking from Macao than to gain access to the Emperor within the palace. Sadly he returned to Nanking and settled there for the next six years. There was much less objection to his doing so than when he had first gone there in 1589. At Nanking he resumed the life he had lived in Nanchang. He bought an excellent house, frequently met the learned circles of the great city, studied more closely the conditions in China and the state of scholarship, and discovered that the knowledge of astronomy had declined from what it had been some centuries before.

From Nanking he awaited a second opportunity to go to Peking.

That opportunity came in 1601. The war with Japan had ended and there was less suspicion of visitors to the Celestial Capital. With his possessions and all the presents which he had prepared for the Emperor, clocks, prisms, globes, maps, paintings, he sailed up the Imperial River once again. At Lintsing he fell into the hands of a rapacious eunuch who was tax collector and one who had influence with the Emperor. This man, Ma T'ang, was a cruel and avaricious man who would have liked to take the presents himself and offer some of them to the Emperor as his own. However, Ricci refused to part with them and Ma T'ang wrote a letter to the Emperor stating that Li Matou wanted to come to Peking to offer presents of clocks and other objects to the Emperor. For some time there was no reply. But the letter had been placed before the august Lord of the Flowery Kingdom, and the mention of the clocks had interested him. He sent an order stating that the barbarian Li Matou might be permitted to go to Peking and offer his presents.

Ricci was then at long last within the precincts of the palace and enabled to offer his presents. But the Emperor was not accustomed to see any stranger personally. The presents were taken before him. The pictures and the clock were acceptable to him. He permitted the visitor to stay in the city as imperial guest.

But Ricci's troubles had not ended. There were dangers caused by the jealousy of the eunuchs and the opposition of the bonzes. The Ministry of Rites, resenting the entry of the foreigner through the influence of Ma T'ang, practically imprisoned him and his companion in the Castle of the Barbarians. But the need the Emperor had to repair or rewind the clocks, his interest in the maps he had asked Ricci to make, the keenness of the court musicians to learn to play the clavichord, all these ensured for him the continued protection of the court. But Ricci never succeeded in seeing personally the Emperor Wan Li. The interviews and exchange of ideas about life in Europe and the conditions in the rest of the world were always through intermediaries. Finally he secured a decree authorizing him to buy a house and settle down permanently in Peking and preach his doctrine.

In his preaching Christianity to the learned in Peking the opposition of the bonzes, instead of being a source of weakness, soon became an element in his favor. The accepted philosophy of the court was Confucianism. Ricci showed in his books that the Christian religion was more in harmony with Confucianism than was Buddhism. The attacks of the Buddhists on Confucian doctrines, and also a pasquinade against the Emperor which was suspected to have been written by a Buddhist, turned many of the mandarins against the bonzes and inclined them to be sympathetic to Ricci.

Ricci's work of conversion now attained considerable success. He gained several noblemen whose dismissal of their concubines and refusal to practice astrology and geomancy impressed the learned world. From Valignano, Ricci obtained formal permission to allow the honors to the dead customary among the Chinese because he was convinced, and he convinced his superiors that those were civic honors only. Even the offering of food to them was only a symbolic gesture. But he refused to permit Chinese funeral customs which were definitely religious in character. He wrote his best-known Chinese works during this period—improved and fuller catechisms than the ones he had in Shiuchow, a "Disputation about God" against the Buddhists, "Twenty-five Sentences," an exposition of the Christian doctrine, and finally "Ten Paradoxes," an indirect teaching of the Christian faith in the form of moral sayings.

These last years were consoling and laborious. Ricci had devoted Chinese disciples and colleagues. Foremost among them was Paul Hsu, whom he had first met in Nanking and who, helped by Ricci, passed the highest examination and became a member of the Imperial Academy. Ricci had the consolation of hearing that Bento de Goes had succeeded in reaching Soochow by the overland route to China, starting from Lahore and passing through Kabul and the mountain barriers of the northwest, on through the Taklamakan Desert. From the diary of Goes, Ricci learned that he, too, had come to the conclusion which Ricci himself had reached for some time, that fabled Cathay was not a realm different from China but only another name for the Middle Kingdom, that Cambaluc was Peking, and that the Christians of Cathay were the few survivors of the early Nestorians or possibly the converts made at the time of Monte Corvino.

Success brought to Ricci not only converts but an intolerable burden of visits and the exhausting formalities of Chinese courtesy. His strength began to fail. Valignano had died in 1606. Hardly any one of the companions who were given to him had been able to offer him the intimate friendship and comfort which his lonely spirit needed, except perhaps De Ursis. Fearing that after his death erroneous accounts of his journeys and activities would be given, he had written in the last months of his life a detailed account of all his doings in the mission of China. These journals constitute the most accurate and most authoritative source of his life in China. (Translated from a Latin version by Father Louis Gallagher, S.J., and published by Random House, New York. No English translation of the original Italian has been made.)

When he felt that the end was approaching he made a general confession to De Ursis and gave clear instructions regarding his funeral. Then with deep sorrow for his sins and shortcomings, in humility and confidence, while the prayers for the dying were being recited over him, he rendered his heroic soul to his Maker. It was May 11, 1610, the fifty-eighth year of his life, the twenty-eighth since his entry into China.

The mere recounting of the events of this life is enough to

show the stature of this extraordinary man—the brilliance of his mind, the strength of his will, and the warmth of his heart, his capacity for love and devotion, his courage, his religious zeal and fervor. Speaking of his intellectual achievement, Arnold Toynbee says that his work of infusing Chinese philosophy into Christianity is comparable to the work of Origen and Clement of Alexandria of infusing Greek philosophy into Christianity. He calls him "one of the greatest of modern missionaries and modern scholars." (*Civilization on Trial*, p. 239.) But the most moving of all the tributes which Li Matou received was the one that his favorite disciple, Paul Hsu, wrote in the preface to the "Twenty-five Sentences."

"I found him by chance at Nanking, and after a short conversation realized that he was the most learned man in the whole world. . . . Later he arrived in Peking and his fame spread throughout the Middle Kingdom, and the wisest and the most famous men went to visit him. Amidst troubles and adversity, during conversation or at dinner, it is impossible to find in a thousand million of his words a single one contrary to the great principles of loyalty to the Emperor and filial piety, not one which does not bring peace of mind and strengthen the moral code. In ancient times, the kiosk where the phoenixes built their nests was considered by the Court a precious object, ensuring peace and stability in the Empire. Today we have the True Man, learned and great, who brings our moral code to completion and protects our Court; is he not even more precious? Let us praise him to the heights." (Cronin, op. cit., p. 219.)

A few words only need be said of the fate of the glorious mission which Ricci founded. Notwithstanding many vicissitudes it continued to flourish, and under such successors as Adam Schall and Andrew Verbiest attained extraordinary success and prestige. Its chief adversary came from within. The controversy of the Chinese Rites raged all through the seventeenth century until the decree of Cardinal de Tournon decided against many of the practices permitted by Ricci.

From that day the influence of Christianity waned. But the

missions, Catholic and Protestant, started afresh in the nineteenth century under new auspices and under other conditions. In many instances they gave the impression of being linked up with foreign domination, the danger which Valignano and Ricci had tried to avoid. The tragic developments within China after the second world war have led to the establishment of the Communist regime. The faith is once again proscribed, and foreign missionaries expelled with pitiless severity. The Church in China is undergoing its baptism of blood.

The wisdom of Ricci has been amply vindicated. Even the honors to the spirits of the ancestors which he allowed and which the decree of De Tournon had forbidden are now permitted once again. Catholics do not doubt that when the storm will have passed, and China emerges once again with freedom for religion and respect for the Christian religion, the pioneer work of Ricci will at last bear the amplest fruit. Once again the best minds of China will see in Christianity a doctrine that completes their moral code, protects their culture, and brings them peace of mind.

III. ROBERT DE NOBILI (1577–1656)

India is par excellence the land of diversities and contrasts. Though today it is a single nation with equality for all citizens, and a strong central government, it is a nation quite unlike all other nations in the multiplicity of its races, languages, and cultures. It might have been thought that the Catholic section of India at least would show the uniformity which characterizes it in other lands, but even among Indian Catholics there are diversities of external form and ways which reflect the complexity of India as a whole. There are three groups among the Catholics of India. There are first the descendants of the converts of St. Thomas the Apostle, a very distinctive section, inhabiting the Malabar Coast, speaking Malayalam, and following the Syriac and Malankara Rites in their worship. There is next a section which, without being of European descent, at least not for the most part, have Portuguese surnames and have been Europeanized to some extent in their ways and habits. They are to be found in Bombay, Goa, Mangalore, and the Fishery Coast, on the western shores of India. Finally there is a large group of Christians, mainly in Tamilnad or the Tamil-speaking parts of the Madras State, who have names which are very similar to Hindu names, who dress like Hindus, and observe many social customs peculiar to the Hindus. To Christians bearing Portuguese names and easily distinguishable from their Hindu compatriots the existence of other Christians who externally resemble Hindus sometimes comes as a surprise. It seems odd to them that there should be Christians with tufts on their heads, males wearing earrings, and with names like Swaminathan, Rajendram, Gnanapragasam instead of Portuguese or English names. What is the origin of these differences? Why this divergence among Catholics of the same country who should have inherited the same culture? Which of the two represents the true spirit and traditions of the missionary Church? Which method is likely to make the convert happier and the message of the Gospel more acceptable to the vast masses of Hindus around them?

First as to the origin. The converts of St. Thomas were numerous but, faithful as they were to their religion in the course of long centuries, they remained isolated in their corner of India, indifferent to preaching the Gospel and to bringing their countrymen to their own faith. The stagnation in missionary effort was ended in the sixteenth century by the coming of the Europeans, and particularly by the zeal of the Portuguese. This second period of the missionary expansion in India owes a vast debt of gratitude to the Portuguese. But it was marked also by certain peculiarities which few would approve at the present day.

The sixteenth-century missionaries came to India at a time of great religious intolerance, when the doctrine of the freedom of conscience was not fully understood, when violence against those who did not agree with one was the order of the day in Europe: Christian versus Moslem, Catholic versus Protestant. Moreover, it was a time of rising nationalism, of growing European dominance, of the sense of racial and cultural superiority of those who braved the seas and overcame those who resented their intrusion and set up their power in distant lands. Consequently there was hardly any question of studying with sympathy and understanding the culture and religion of the conquered people. They regarded those people as barbarians and their religion as a debased superstition.

Even so great and enlightened a statesman as Albuquerque showed himself, in regard to the Moslems, ruthless and cruel to a degree that astonishes us. For Hindus there was more tolerance at the beginning. The prestige of the conquerors led to many early conversions. Then came the marvelous apostolate of St. Francis Xavier, whose burning zeal and manifest holiness brought thousands of genuine converts. After him the flow of conversions thinned. Then coercive measures were introduced, and many forcible conversions were made on the principle of *Compelle intrare,* and on the accepted European maxim, *Cujus regio illius et religio.* But even this did not make any serious impression on the vast Hindu mass. By the end of the sixteenth century conversions in the Indian Missions had practically stopped. Vincent Cronin in his *Wise Man from the West,* from which I have already cited excerpts, gives the following description of the situation (p. 29):

"Those who could not be bribed were coerced. Nominal rolls of all Hindus were made, a hundred on each list being compelled on alternate Sundays to hear sermons on the benefits of Christianity, sermons delivered through interpreters. These laws were rigorously enforced by the Inquisition. If an Indian dissuaded another from becoming a Christian he was liable to death. Denounced by a child he might spend two or three years in prison without knowing the cause, before being sentenced and taken, on a great feast day, to execution. Prisoners were paraded through the torrid streets in shirts steeped in sulphur, and painted in lurid colors with flames of fire pointing upwards in the case of those to be burned at the stake."

Robert de Nobili was the great pioneer who disapproved the use of force, developed the method of sympathetic approach and persuasion, and by this means broke the deadlock in the missionary activity of India. He was born in Montepulciano in September 1577, son of Pier Francesco de Nobili, Count of Civitelle, a brave warrior who became a general in the Papal Army. The De Nobilis were related to the great families of the Buoncompagnis and the Sforzas. Robert's uncle was the pious Cardinal Robert de Nobili, who had been raised to the purple at the age of thirteen by his uncle, Pope Julius III. Robert's father had high ambitions for his gifted son. But Robert had early made up his mind to join the Society. The striking achievements of the Society in India and Japan were stirring the minds of all the noble youth of Italy. Facing the opposition of the family, Robert ran away to Naples and lived for some time unknown in the family of the Duchess of Nocera. Permitted finally to join the Society, he entered the novitiate at Naples under Father Orlandini. He had always desired the missions, India at first, then for a while under the influence of Father Orlandini, Japan, but again and definitely, before long, India, which was to be his abiding love.

Soon after joining the Society, Robert renounced his title and claim to the countship and, a little against his will, surrendered his other property also to his family. He studied theology in Rome under the very best masters, Bellarmine, Vasquez, Gregory of Valentia, and others. Ordained priest, he asked for the Indian Mission and in spite of the opposition of his family he obtained permission to join it. In 1604 he left for Goa. The voyage was eventful, involving a shipwreck in which the Viceroy, who was sailing with them, lost his life and a halt of nearly six months at Mozambique. He arrived in Goa in 1605 and had been so badly shaken by the voyage that he had to spend some months there to recuperate his health. He was then sent to Cochin.

It took very little time for Father de Nobili to note the sterility of mission work in India and to understand the causes of it. The great mistake had been to impose on the neophytes Portuguese names and ways of life. In particular the converts were forbidden to preserve any of the distinctive marks and customs by which they were recognized to belong to one or other of the castes of India. Now while the observance of caste and the external marks by which men were recognized as members of a particular caste were closely connected with religious practices, caste itself was a social institution not necessarily bound up with religion. The Christian missionaries, without making any attempt to disengage the social or civil observances, insisted on their converts' giving up every mark of their appurtenance to a caste —ways of dressing and eating, marriage and festival customs. In addition to this they gave them foreign names and encouraged them to eat beef and drink liquor, habits abominable to the caste Hindu.

Because of this habit of drink and the eating of beef, the Europeans—the Feringhees or Pranguis, as they were called —came to be considered as belonging to a low or debased class. The vices and brutality of the rank and file of soldiers, merchants, and adventurers who flocked to India from Portugal increased the hatred of the respectable Indian for the Feringhee. Even the holiness of many of the missionaries and the undoubted intellectual and moral eminence of many of the Portuguese leaders could not appreciably diminish this contempt. To become a Christian meant, in the popular estimation, to become a Feringhee, a man without caste. The missionaries did nothing to counteract this view. In fact they confirmed the Indians in their opinion. The question addressed to a candidate for baptism was not whether he wanted to become a Christian, but, "Do you want to join the caste of the Feringhees?"

Lest this description should seem exaggerated, let me quote the words of the greatest of the later successors of Father de Nobili, St. John de Britto, martyred in the Marava in 1693. In his Annual Letter of 1683 he speaks thus of conditions before Father de Nobili began his apostolate:

" 'When some one is known to have become a Christian, he is at once abhorred as a Pariah, driven away from those of his caste, and forbidden to have his dwelling among them, to enter their houses, to eat with them, or touch their clothes or vessels. To be the disciple of a Feringhee is considered a much greater infamy than to be publicly flogged or branded as a robber. It is no dishonor for them to carry dirt or rubbish, but it is the indelible infamy to receive baptism at the hands of a Feringhee because the terms Feringhee and Pariah are identical.

" 'Again what contributes greatly to confirm those people in their low opinion of the Portuguese is to see them enter their churches with their shoes on, and even burying their dead in them. For Indians this is a worse abomination than for us to see those churches converted into pigsties. Another thing that gives strength to their erroneous beliefs is to know that the Portuguese are cow flesh eaters, which practice is more repugnant to them than is to a European the practice of eating human flesh. For all these reasons and all such silly appreciations the name of Feringhee is much more hateful, vile, and abominable among Indians than is among Europeans the name of public executioner or any other even more infamous.' " (J. Houpert, S.J., *The Madura Catholic Mission*, pp. 38–39.)

Robert de Nobili resolved at all costs to break this tradition of denationalizing the Christian converts. Circumstances helped him in a singular manner. Already in 1595 a part of the mission territory had been detached from the jurisdiction of the Provincial of Goa and created into the Malabar Province. This province had for its territory the interior parts of south India embracing much of what is known as Tamilnad. The Fishery Coast, which is part of the district of Tinnevelly, was also in this province. The Provincial of Malabar, Father Vega, was extremely pessimistic about conversion in these regions where the Portuguese had no political power. He was removed, and an Italian, Father Albert Laerzio, appointed in his place. Father de Nobili applied for and secured admission into the Malabar Province, and he persuaded the Provincial to allow him to found a mission station in Madura, the capital of the most important kingdom of the south. His petition was granted. De Nobili started from Tuticorin and reached Madura in 1607.

From the eleventh century onwards the great Hindu kingdoms of the north had suffered continually from the Moslem invasions, and in the course of a few centuries the Moslems had established successive empires there, humiliating the Hindus by their arrogance and also compelling their submission by the brilliance of their military, political, and artistic achievements. But the south had successfully resisted the Moslem flood, and under the great Empire of Vijayanagar had kept the flag of Hindu supremacy flying through a long period. The Nayak of Madura was one of the Viceroys of the Emperor of Vijayanagar, and he ruled over territory that now comprises the Madura, the Tinnevelly, the Trichinopoly and Salem districts, and part of Travancore. Madura, on the banks of the Vaigai, was a great city, once the capital of the Pandyan Kingdom centuries before, and even now, under the Nayakers, a city of temples and palaces and of Hindu learning. De Nobili was impressed by its beauty and the number of its inhabitants, the houses and gardens clustering around the great towers of the Chokkanatha Temple.

There was a Catholic missionary already in Madura, Father Gonsalvo Fernandes, who had gone there to minister to the Parava Christians of Tuticorin, who went to Madura for trade. But he and they were subject to the same contempt to which the Christians were subjected elsewhere among caste Hindus. So De Nobili determined to go to Madura not as a Feringhee but as a Roman sannyasi who did not share the practices of the Feringhees. He therefore put on the garb of a Hindu sannyasi, the ocher-colored robe, the wooden slippers, the sandalwood paste on his forehead, in hand the staff and water jug customary among the Hindu ascetics. He built a little hut for himself and lived there in utter seclusion, avoiding the company of Fernandes, the Feringhee missionary, and refusing to have anything to do with his Christians. He avoided eating meat and drinking alcohol, and secured the services of a Brahmin servant and cook. This fact made it clear to those who watched him that he was not an outcaste or pariah but a man of superior caste. When questioned about this he said that he was not a Feringhee but a Kshatriya, a member of the warrior caste in his own country. In truth he was not a Feringhee, since this term in the minds of the Indians applied to the Portuguese. Scion of the Roman nobility and son of a Roman general, he was strictly right in claiming to be a Kshatriya in his own land.

In addition to these external ways of life De Nobili set himself to the study of the languages of the country, Tamil and Sanskrit first, and Telugu a little later on. His Pandit in these languages was a devoted man, Sivadaran, who at first sought his acquaintance not to learn but to gain him over to his own Saivite religion. De Nobili was perhaps the first European to master Sanskrit, the study of which was forbidden to those who were not Brahmins, and to give to the scholars of Europe the knowledge of this great Aryan language and thus to supply the foundations for the modern science of Indo-Germanic philology.

The results of this method of apostolate were soon evident. Learned men among the Hindus began to frequent the hut or ashrama of De Nobili, and to discuss religion and theology with him. He was a first-rate dialectician and metaphysician and soon made many conversions. Among them were men of high caste, and of position in the Nayakar court, and the King himself came to visit him. But in admitting his neophytes De Nobili made certain innovations which he deemed essential for the success of the apostolate. He permitted caste observances which he believed were merely civil and not religious, exactly as Ricci had done with reference to Chinese customs. Thus he allowed his converts to keep the tuft on their heads after shaving off part of the hair in front; he allowed them to put sandalwood paste on their foreheads as marks of their caste. He allowed the Brahmins to have their baths and ablutions and to wear the "sacred thread" after blessing the five strands in it as representing the Blessed Trinity and the two natures of Our Lord. With great ingenuity he translated Biblical names into their Tamil and Sanskrit equivalents and gave them to his converts instead of the Portuguese names hitherto imposed on them. Naturally he did not encourage them to drink alcohol or eat beef or dine with people who did not belong to their caste. Finally he introduced two other innovations which were to become the subject of endless controversies after his death. He permitted the dropping of the Ephphetha ceremony in baptism because the application of saliva was abhorrent to the Hindus. He also allotted places in church according to the caste of the converts, and decided that the Viaticum was not to be carried solemnly but discreetly to the dwellings of the low-caste Christians. These points he considered to be equivalent to the distinctions permitted in Europe among the nobles and the commons in regard to seating in the churches and the solemnizing of marriages and funerals.

But these bold innovations did not go unchallenged. First there were the Brahmins who did not naturally welcome one whose teachings, whatever his readiness to accept certain external customs connected with caste, were opposed to their doctrines and to their sacerdotal claims. So they stirred up trouble against him, alleged that his presence in Madura was the cause of the failure of rains, and menaced his disciples so that even his servants abandoned him for the most part. From this persecution De Nobili was rescued by the intervention of some of his friends from among the Setti caste who had authority in the Nayaker court. But the most serious challenge came from his own fellow missionaries, and, above all, from Fernandes, who could not approve of his methods and denounced him to his superiors in India, to the Inquisition in Goa, and to Rome. What were the causes of this opposition?

There were some who were ignorant of the reasons that led Father de Nobili to tolerate some of the caste observances. They thought that he permitted idolatry and superstition. But there were undoubtedly human motives in it too. The priests who worked on the missions among the low castes were hurt by the Father's seclusion and refusal to have dealings with them. Probably there was also wounded national feeling because De Nobili's method seemed to approve the contempt the Indians felt for the Feringhees. Possibly also the prospect of the stern and austere life of the sannyasis, which might become the rule for the missionaries, alarmed them. They therefore complained bitterly to the Provincial and to the Archbishop of Cranganore, Monsignor Francisco Roz, a Spaniard, and a zealous and holy man. Both of them had the fullest confidence in Father de Nobili, who, moreover, had done nothing without the permission of the Provincial. But the force and persistence of the accusations impressed Father Laerzio. He asked Father de Nobili to stop receiving converts until he had time to examine the case himself by a personal visit to the ashrama of De Nobili. This forced interruption of some months enabled the Father to perfect his knowledge of the Indian languages and to complete a course of religious instruction in Tamil, *Gnana Upadesam,* which was a veritable handbook of theology.

Father Laerzio came to Madura in due course, and spent some weeks watching Father de Nobili at work. He was filled with admiration for his virtue, his patience and mortification, the zeal and fervor of his religious life. He understood fully the reasons of his innovations and approved of them. But the Father was not left in peace. After the death of Archbishop Menezes of Goa, who had been a friend of Father de Nobili, Monsignor de Sa was appointed archbishop. He came from Portugal with the avowed purpose of ending the "scandal of Madura." He convoked a synod at Goa at which a Jesuit Visitor, Father Palmiero, also known to be unfriendly to the missionary method of De Nobili, was to be present. De Nobili was summoned to answer his adversaries and defend himself in person. He therefore came to Goa with an apology which he had carefully prepared. His defense was powerful. Many of those who had been opposed to him were convinced of the wisdom of his procedure. Among them was Palmiero, henceforth a defender of De Nobili. Father Robert had no difficulty in proving that the customs which had been incriminated were civil and religious observances. He did this with copious citations from the Hindu books, of which the others were totally ignorant. He clinched the matter by showing that the Church had always followed this method of adaptation in dealing with the culture and customs of the nations it converted. He showed the way the Apostles acted, citing the 15th and 16th chapters of the Acts; he adduced the example of saints like St. Gregory Thaumaturgus. Finally he cited the instruction which St. Gregory the Great sent, through Abbot Mellitus, to St. Augustine of England. This remarkable passage is worth quoting.

"Tell the Most Reverend Bishop Augustine what I, upon mature deliberation of the affairs of the English, have determined upon, namely that the temples of the idols of that nation ought not to be destroyed. Let holy water be made and sprinkled in the said temples; let altars be erected and temples blessed. For if these temples are well built, it is requisite that they be converted from the worship of the devil to the service of the true God, so that the nation seeing that their temples are not destroyed . . . may the more familiarly resort to the places to which they have been accustomed. And because they have been used to slaughter many oxen in the sacrifices to the devils, some solemnity must be exchanged for them on this account. . . . They may build themselves huts from the boughs of trees about those churches which were formerly temples, celebrate the solemnity with religious feasting and, without offering beasts to the devil, kill cattle and praise God while eating them. It is impossible to efface everything at once from their obdurate minds." (Houpert, op. cit., p. 42.)

However, De Nobili's defense did not yet fully satisfy the archbishop. He referred the matter to Rome and sent them a biased account of it. The General of the Society and Cardinal Bellarmine were disturbed, and believed that Father de Nobili had committed serious blunders. But the Grand Inquisitor of Goa, from whom a careful account of the dispute was asked, happened to be a man of judgment and fairness. He sent a favorable report. The representations of Father Laerzio and Archbishop Roz also had their own effect. Above all, the apology of De Nobili was a powerful document. Rome was satisfied, and in 1623 Pope Gregory XV gave a decision in favor of Father de Nobili in the brief *Romanae Sedis Antistes:*

"Taking into consideration human weakness in as much as it is permissible without sin and without scandal, desirous to favor the conversion of these peoples who do not wish to give up the tuft of hair, the cord, the baths, the sandal, which indicated their nobility of caste and office, after diligent study and discussion . . . by Our Apostolic Authority we allow to Brahmins and others to be converted the use of the cord and the tuft of hair. . . . Further the sandal which is an ornament of the body is permitted, and so are the baths for health and cleanliness."

De Nobili had won his cause. Henceforth, secure in the approbation of Rome, he developed his apostolate with ever increasing success. Known as Tattva Bodhakar or the Teacher of Truth, he met the Brahmins and learned Pandits in discussion, and his admittedly keen debating powers gave him an extraordinary ascendant. He no longer confined himself to residence in Madura, but with his disciples and servants traveled throughout the Tamil country making numerous converts and writing and translating books in Tamil and Telugu. He founded flourishing communities of Catholics in Trichinopoly, Salem, Satyamangalam, and other important centers. By 1623 converts of the higher castes numbered three hundred. In 1644 they were more than four thousand. The conversion of the higher castes led to a movement of conversions among other caste people of a lower rank, and Father de Nobili welcomed them. He helped in the creation of a separate group of missionaries, the Pandaraswamis, who were destined to minister both to the higher and to the lower castes.

These continual labors and all the anxieties and struggles through which he had passed undermined his health. His eyesight began to fail. He was then withdrawn from the Madura Mission and sent as Superior of the Ceylon Mission. But this did not improve his sight. He returned to India, though not to his beloved Madura Mission, and spent the last years of his life in Mylapore, almost totally blind and living a life of prayer and austerity. There he died on January 16, 1656.

Robert de Nobili was one of the most remarkable men ever sent out by the Catholic Church as missionary to a foreign country. A man of the highest intellectual gifts, a prodigious memory, and quite exceptional dialectical skill, he was also a man of vision, or the capacity to see through the thick mist of convention and break through the prejudice of centuries. Though he was undoubtedly influenced by the report of what Ricci was doing in China, it was De Nobili's genius that excogitated the unique idea of living as a sannyasi. He was also a religious of great virtue, humble, mortified, and of total contempt for personal ease. He loved the austere ascetic life which his method of adaptation involved; he loved the Indian people and understood and admired their culture. He has been accused of dishonesty by some of the earlier Protestant writers. But Latourette says that his device of calling himself a Roman Rajah and Christian sannyasi though astute was honest. A recent Protestant writer, Mr. P. Thomas, in his *Christians and Christianity in India and Pakistan,* thus sums up his career:

"It should not be imagined that Fr. Robert adopted his way of life out of sheer hypocrisy. He loved it. He was something of an ascetic and believed that a meager vegetarian diet and strictness of personal habits was in conformity with the higher life. He became an Indian to save Indians, even as God became man to save Mankind, and there was nothing demeaning or irreligious about that. While he gave up his nationality for India, De Nobili certainly did not give up his religion. . . . In his deep insight into human nature, in his sympathy with Indian culture and traditions, in his recognition of the prophetic presage of the Indian sages of the coming of the Savior, he stands alone among the Europeans of his time, who were inclined to treat the Hindus as a God-forsaken set of idolaters." (New York, Macmillan, pp. 72, 76.)

Though during his lifetime De Nobili won a victory against his adversaries, students of the history of the missions know that the fight was resumed after his death. Decisions and counterdecisions succeeded one another in the course of a hundred years. The famous Cardinal de Tournon was finally sent as Apostolic Visitor both to India and China. On what is now admitted to have been a very hasty and insufficient study of the question the so-called Malabar and Chinese Rites—many of them referring to practices which neither Ricci nor De Nobili had approved—were condemned. Though the large community of converts made by De Nobili persevered and bore testimony to the success and permanence of his work, the identification of Christianity with Feringheeism gradually returned. Conversions dwindled. Then came the final disaster of the suppression of the Society, first in Portugal by Pombal, then in the rest of Europe. The magnificent work of De Nobili ended in the darkest period of the Catholic missions in the eighteenth century, a period of confusion and lapses from the faith.

But the significance of De Nobili's experiment was not forgotten. In the nineteenth century the Madura Mission was once again entrusted to the Fathers of the Society, this time from the province of Toulouse. They revived the methods of De Nobili with the changes necessary in the new conditions. As in China, so here, the Holy See has permitted most of the rites condemned by De Tournon, in particular the omission of the Ephphetha ceremony in baptism. In St. Joseph's University College in Trichinopoly a remarkable Savoyard, Father Francis Billard, began the work of the conversion of Brahmins and helped them to live in conformity with the customs of their caste in a special colony which he founded for them. Today among the Jesuit Fathers of the Madura Province, the first of the Indian Jesuit Missions to be made an independent province, some of the best known and most active among the Fathers are Brahmin converts or children of converts made by Father Billard. They, too, are the fruits of De Nobili's heroic life. In the Calcutta Mission a Belgian Jesuit, Father Johans, one of the most learned Catholic Sanskritists of modern times, has tried to do for the Vedanta what Ricci did for Confucianism. His most important work, *To Christ through the Vedanta,* is a powerful attempt to establish points of contact between traditional Hindu philosophy and the Catholic faith.

In the vast fields which were opened out by these pioneers, the work was continued by many others—Schall and Verbiest in China, St. John de Britto and Beschi in India,—men of almost as great a stature as the protagonists whose lives we have tried to sketch here briefly. During the 19th and 20th Centuries, after the vicissitudes of the 18th, great numbers of missionaries, Protestant and Catholic, poured into these countries. They went there under the prestige of European dominance in all walks of life, and were helped by the enthusiasm of Asia to copy European ways and imbibe European culture. But that heyday too has ended. There is a nationalist revival in these countries which has shaken off the European yoke in politics, and is mistrustful of European ideals in culture. The need for dissociating Christianity from the accidental trappings of Western civilization remains as acute as ever. In these conditions, the wisdom of Valignano, and the courage and foresight of Ricci and De Nobili, still remain as examples and as guides. Such is the weighty judgment of Arnold Toynbee [*The World and the West*, New York, Oxford University Press, pp. 63–64]:

In China and India, the Jesuits did not make the mistake they had made in Japan of letting their preaching of Christianity fall under the suspicion of being conducted in the political interests of aggressive Western Powers. The Jesuits' approach to their enterprise of propagating Christianity in China was so different and so promising in itself, and it is so much to the point today, that our discussion of the Asian peoples' encounter with the West would be incomplete if we did not take into consideration the line which the Jesuits in India and China opened out. Instead of trying, as we have been trying since their day, to disengage a secular version of Western civilization from Christianity, the Jesuits tried to disengage Christianity from the non-Christian ingredients in the Western Civilization and to present Christianity to the Hindus and the Chinese not as the local religion of the West, but as a universal religion with a message for all mankind. The Jesuits stripped Christianity of its accidental and irrelevant Western accessories, and offered the essence of it to China in a Chinese, and to India in a Hindu, intellectual and literary dress in which there was no incongruous Western embroidery to jar on Asian sensibilities. This experiment miscarried at the first attempt through the fault of domestic feuds within the bosom of the Roman Catholic Church of the day which had nothing to do with Christianity or China or India; but considering that Christianity and China and India are still on the map, we may expect—and hope—to see the experiment tried again.

To the expression of that hope the Catholic reader will say a fervent Amen!

4. Social Missionaries

Gustave Weigel, s.j.

MISSIONARIES always have one eye on eternity and the other on time. It would be much simpler if a person could focus merely on eternity, but this is not possible. The task of the priest is not simply to prepare his charges for death, but also to prepare them for life that they may pass through death to the joys of Christ. Though the value of a life may be summed up at death, that value was achieved through days and years of living. A person may make a great renunciation or decision, may firmly decide to follow Christ, which will determine the way of an individual's career, but that moment of resolve will, normally, take years of patient implementation. The hopelessly poor, or oppressed, or ignorant, or unstable nomad is capable of great decisions, is capable of embracing the vision of Christ—and quite successfully if death should follow immediately. The difficulty arises when life continues. It is in many ways simpler to make a success of one's life through an abrupt martyrdom than it is through following Christ day after day. And it is precisely in the attrition of living that destitution, sickness, oppression, and instability raise almost insurmountable difficulties to a fully Christian life.

For the missionary this means that, if he is practical, he soon realizes that it is not enough to approach a people, give them a vision of Christ and instruction in the truths of religion if the constant conditions of their lives are going to make the following of those truths almost impossible. The missionary with his Christlike charity and his superior training must do what he can to help his people achieve conditions more favorable to a human, Christian life.

In our own day there are more socially minded people and agencies at hand to help the missionary and his flock achieve this. But in the days of the earlier Jesuits this was not so.

The following passage in the *Relations,* which St. Jean de Brébeuf dispatched from the Huron Mission in Canada during 1637, shows one of the problems. "It is not I who speak," said the chieftain. "It is all those whom thou seest sitting there, who have charged me to tell thee that we all desire to believe in God, and that we wish to be helped to till the soil, so as to dwell near thee . . . We wish to settle down, but we cannot build houses like thine unless thou help us." Thus were the Jesuit missionaries importuned, three centuries ago, to anticipate the program of technical assistance even while they preached the Gospel.

It is not possible to recount here the variety and extent of the social works performed by missionaries in answer to the spoken or mute requests of their people. Several typical reactions must serve to point up this aspect of missionary work. Two of them were the work of individuals, the other— the Reductions of South America—an organized effort of many nameless Jesuits, of whom thirty became martyrs of charity.

In distant Japan, not long after the company's formation, the splendor of missionary charity for the material needs of a people shone forth in a simple lay Brother, Luis de Almeida.

He was a Lisbon-born doctor who had come with a dream of fortune to be gained in the East Indies. Twice he journeyed in the company of Jesuit missionaries. He left them to begin work in China. Yet he could not forget their fearless devotion to the contagiously ill, and as a doctor he appreciated its worth. He ended by giving his not inconsiderable property to the company, along with himself—an even more considerable gift. He was very probably the first missionary to set up a real hospital. In 1557 a large building went up. It was divided into two areas: one an isolation ward for lepers, the other for the injured and sick. This last, after the custom of the period, eventually became a shelter for traveling Christians.

In only a few months crowds of people of every class came, sometimes from as far as northern Japan, to Almeida's free clinic. In 1559 they had to build a second hospital of sixteen spacious rooms for "persons of prominence," along with a veranda which served as operating room and a house for lay personnel.

Almeida sent to China, Malacca, India, Portugal for medicines; he also performed operations with great success. In a single summer two hundred cases were cured and sent home from the hospital at Oita. Almeida had the foresight to train assistants to replace him. He put young Brother Paul, a Japanese, in charge of the pharmacy; he taught the European surgical techniques to a Japanese lay doctor; he enlisted other Brothers and laymen, Portuguese and Japanese, as nurses.

Brother Almeida, who a contemporary said was "predestined by God to lay foundations for churches," extended the influence of the hospital by making house visits. He did so well that his superiors, in need of priests, made an unusual decision. They sent him, at the age of fifty-four, to Macao to ordain him priest. But it was too late. Worn out before his time, Almeida died four years later. Nonetheless, his work played a major role. It stood as a living refutation of the calumnies against the missions, and the wealth of charity dispensed at Oita proved the good intentions of the whole apostolic effort. Father Gago, Almeida's first and faithful friend, wrote with justice, "This work is an uninterrupted sermon, whose echo resounds to Miyako where the Japanese King lives, to Sakai which is the Venice of this country, to Bando where the University is, to Hiei-no-yama, which is the chief seat of the bonzes." A wide and wonderful sphere of influence.

The second man to be considered, Peter Claver, eventually became a canonized saint and the patron of all missions to the Negroes.

The field of his activity for about forty years was Cartagena in the Caribbean, to the east of Panama. This was a bustling commercial port in the days of Claver, although its climate was hot and moist, and the whole area was infested with fever-bearing insects from the tropical swamps. Claver arrived around the year 1610, when the port was renowned as the chief center of the slave trade.

Merchants would pick up Negroes at four crowns apiece from the coasts of Guinea or the Congo and sell them for two hundred crowns or more in Cartagena. They thought this a just profit because the trip took about two months and they lost about one third of their passengers en route. But they did succeed in bringing in about ten thousand slaves a year.

Claver with his fellow Jesuits was housed between a slaughterhouse and a tavern, worthy to test any man's recollection of the presence of Christ. But he was close to his work, which was to be the aiding of the newly landed slaves. About their slavery Claver was unable to do anything. But he could help their hunger, their loneliness, lessen their afflictions, care for them when dying, instruct them in the truths of Christianity.

The arrival of another slave ship was the signal for Claver to set to work at full speed. He would be the first man to board the ship. Immediately he set about doing what he could with the small stores he had begged to help the sick and terrified people. To all he gave whatever he had, were it only biscuits, brandy, lemons, or tobacco. "We must," he would say, "speak to them with our hands before we try to speak to them with our lips."

Down into the hold of the ship he would go to aid the sick. Oftentimes there was not much that he could do in a material way for those slumped in the stench and slime of the holds. But he could bring the radiance of Christ's love to them. To bodies still bleeding from the lash and souls still suffering from fear, insults, and contempt he brought the deft touch of skilled hands to ease the tortured bodies and, with his saintly charity, a kiss for their sores, which, without any need of interpreters, made transparent his love for them.

He himself would carry the sick from the ship, try to secure carts to take them to their lodgings, so that they would not be whipped on their way, and never leave them until they had a place of rest. While they were waiting to be sold, he visited them constantly, doing whatever he could to bring a little comfort and cheer into their lives. And all of this amid the most incredible crowding and squalor.

Between ships he spent his time begging supplies for the next one and caring for those in the hospitals and prisons of Cartagena, and tending the outcasts of the tough port city. His hospital work was divided for the most part between St. Sebastian's, a hospital for general cases, and St. Lazarus', for lepers. There was no task in the hospitals too menial or degrading for him. He had the reputation of being able to do the work of forty men. To protect the patients he collected material for mosquito netting, had it stitched into shape, and himself attached it to the beds. Especially to the neglected patients of St. Lazarus he brought whatever he could find in the way of linen, perfume, bandages, or medicines.

Not only did he care for huge numbers, but he showed a steadfast devotion to helpless individuals. One Negro had such a noisome disease that no one could stand his presence. So Claver took him to his own room and made the man use his bed until he was well while Claver slept on the floor. Daily he fed the man, washed him, and dressed his wounds. Another derelict relegated to a hut outside the city was visited by Claver every week for fourteen years. The saint would clean his little place, make his bed, tend his wounds, and bring him food.

Between caring for the sick and oppressed and doing what he could to help them he found time to baptize and instruct thousands. He was no sentimentalist when it came to instructions in Christianity, but insisted that the convert really understand the truth to which he was giving his allegiance. Among both the Negroes and the whites he was a most sought-after confessor, but he insisted on giving precedence to the Negroes. The first thing he did on a typical day was scrub the floor boards of his confessional to protect his people from the dampness and any odors the wood might have picked up. During Lent he would start hearing confessions at three in the morning and spend, if possible, more than twelve hours at this task.

How he accomplished so much and continued it for so many years is truly incredible. His normal diet seems to have been bread and potatoes, and his ordinary amount of sleep not much more than three hours.

His social work was not of a modern, organized type which may change the patterns of a society for the better. It was the continually extended helping hand, which is necessary in any society and which can better the individual in a direct way. This was immediate social action. Not for a dramatic moment or for a short time, but for years. And deliberately so, for after six years of working for the Negroes Claver had bound himself by vow to be for the rest of his life a slave of slaves.

In less direct fashion other Jesuits worked to alleviate the economic status of peoples throughout North and South America. Training centers were set up where people could become farmers and ranchers. Crafts were taught, from furniture making to shipbuilding, from jewelry to ironmongery. Jesuits dug canals for irrigation. They started the production of textiles and clothing. Some of the techniques and crafts which missionaries introduced still affect the economy of Latin America. In Chile, particularly, Jesuits opened pharmacies in all the urban centers.

A special difficulty in South America finally led to the bold social experiment of the Reductions, which was city planning of an extent and success never rivaled before or since.

The missionaries had thought that Indians and Spaniards could form one community. But this assumption was refuted by reality. The Spaniards were anxious to use the Indians for labor in the mines, on the fields, and as domestic servants. They transformed a humane institution invented by the crown into practical slavery. The institution was the *encomienda*. By royal decree a Spanish landowner was to be the guardian of the Indians in his territory, educating them in Catholicism and Spanish ways and defending them from attack. The Indians were charges of the *patrón*, to whom they were "commended." The expenses involved could be covered by some work done by the fosterlings. However, from the beginning the Indians were simply impressed into service and forced to work by coercive, much too often harsh, measures. They lost their freedom and became slaves.

This situation did not meet with the approval of the missionaries. Everywhere they prophetically thundered against the abuse, both in the New World and in reports to Madrid. The outstanding champion of the Indians was the Dominican Friar, Bartolomé de las Casas (1474–1566). This man is a glorious example of the Spanish missionaries. Born in Spain and educated at Salamanca, he came to Santo Domingo to make his fortune. He did so, using the Indians as slaves. He was ordained a secular priest in 1510 at the age of thirty-six. He went to Cuba and underwent a kind of conversion, whereby he saw the evil of the enslavement of the Indians. As a result he returned to Spain to consult with the Prime Minister, Cardinal Jiménez de Cisneros, and was named "Protector of the Indians." Thus armed he returned to Santo Domingo, where his campaign brought about his expulsion. He returned to Madrid in 1517 to obtain the King's aid. He offered solutions for the problems involved in the suppression of the *encomienda* system, and even took a group of Spanish farm laborers to Venezuela. The project failed. Discouraged, Las Casas returned to Santo Domingo and entered the Dominican order in 1520, a man forty-six years old. He later went to what is now Guatemala and tried a campaign of evangelization without conquest. He was made bishop for the purpose and his work was initially successful, though it failed in the long run. Frustrated in America, Las Casas returned to Spain at the age of seventy-two but still a fighter who wielded a mighty pen in defense of his Indians. For twenty years more he fought the fight until death met him at the age of ninety-two.

Las Casas was a noble romantic. His heart was in the right place; he aroused the conscience of the Spanish crown and consolidated the minds of the missionaries in their defense of the Indian neophytes. However, his zeal prevented him from painting an objective picture of the colonial situation, which was bad enough but hardly as black as Las Casas painted it. His reports cannot be taken at face value, though the substantial evil he describes was certainly real.

There was no hope of the Indian leading a full Christian life in the Spanish communities. It never entered the minds of the Spaniards that the Indian would be anything but a member of the third of the three Spanish classes, the class of the laborers organized according to a slightly modified feudal pattern. In the beginning there was some respect shown to the chieftain families, which the Spaniards conceived to be relatively equivalent to their aristocratic first class. However, a *cacique* was hardly a Spanish grandee, and soon sight is lost of the Indian nobility, nor is it later reckoned. But even the incorporation of the Indians into the working class did not succeed, because they were being enslaved. The Indian, in consequence, hated and feared the whites. Such circumstances were not propitious to evangelization by white men. Nor could an Indian community be formed side by side with the Spanish society, although in our time this actually takes place in countries like Bolivia, Ecuador, and Peru. Moreover, the bad example of the Europeans was detrimental to the inculcation of solid Christian virtues.

As a result the missionaries wanted to form Christian Indian communities away from the Spanish cities. The missionary exodus begins about 1525. This inaugurated the long period which represents the fanning out of the preachers into the hinterlands, where they founded new communities.

To appreciate the work of the missionaries we must always bear in mind the immensity of the territory in which they labored. It is true that the population was not dense, but the problem of locomotion was formidable. The west coast of South America is marked by a high mountain range which runs from the extreme north to the extreme south. The towering Andean cordillera with its intermittent plateaus and valleys is a hard terrain to travel. In the tropical zone there is a vast jungle of lush but treacherous verdure, rich in disease and killing elements. The verdant tropics are counterbalanced to the south and north by deserts where not even the cactus grows. St. Paul could travel on the highroad of the Mediterranean or the military highways built by the Pax

Romana, but the South American missionary had to travel mountain trails, forest paths, menacing rivers, and uncharted plains. With no feeling of heroism but with steadfast purpose he moved on foot or in small boats to reach the farthest communities.

This work of penetration was incredible. In Portuguese Brazil the Jesuit Fathers Manoel da Nóbrega (1517-1570) and José de Anchieta (1534-1597) organized and developed what is now the state of São Paulo. The Jesuit, Eusebio Kino (1644-1711), pushed north from the Spanish cities of Mexico to what is today Arizona and moved from there to Baja California, the first to take the overland route. He and his fellow missionaries dotted the frontier with missions, which were communities of Indians under the direction of the Jesuit Fathers.

For Americans the California Franciscan Missions and their great organizer, Junipero Serra (1713-1784), are well known. Yet Fray Junipero came relatively late on the missionary scene. The Jesuits had previously planted similar missions in Lower California, but the Fathers were expelled in 1767, when the Dominicans took over.

Anyone who visits a California Mission can see what it was. It was a walled-in community with a church as its central feature. Often enough there was also a *presidio,* a military quarter. The Indians, at least many of them, lived in the mission. They were being protected and conditioned for Christian life. As California today shows, these missions were the nuclei of future cities.

Perhaps the most effective use of this mission method was manifested in the Jesuit Reducciónes. This word today makes us think of the most famous of them all, the Paraguayan Reductions. Although they are so called, we must not think that they were restricted to the territory of modern Paraguay, for they were typical of the whole La Plata river basin, covering an area today divided up among Argentina, Uruguay, Brazil, and Paraguay. The Jesuit headquarters were in Asunción and from this point the Jesuits moved out in the first years of the sixteen hundreds. Not all the Jesuits were Spaniards, and many of the Brothers were Germans. The really remarkable thing is that this unquestionably great project does not evoke one personal name. It was the order that made it, kept it, and on whose death it also died.

The Paraguayan Reductions had a chance to develop unhampered, and from their final state just before the Jesuits were expelled in 1767, we can see what the missionaries had in mind in their apostolic endeavors.

The Indians involved in the enterprise were different tribes of the Guarani people, whose descendants can still be found in abundance in Paraguay, where their language is the main tongue. In a century and a half the Jesuits founded and evolved thirty Reduction communes, which at their high point were populated by 150,000 Indians. From the reports of the missionaries and a study of the few pitiful ruins which still survive on the old Reduction sites we can understand what life was like in these commonwealths.

All initiative for and in the Reductions was restricted to the Jesuits. They carefully selected the sites, seeking a territory which had beauty, water, and natural defenses. The land was cleared and a little city was constructed. The plan was substantially the same everywhere. The center of the town, the square *plaza*, was a green park whose center was marked by a column on which a statue of Mary was placed. On one side of the square stood the church, a good replica of which can be found in our California Missions. Next to the church was the residence of the Jesuits, two of whom were priests with a lay Brother or two where possible. Other buildings gracing the *plaza* were the school, the asylums for widows and orphans, the workshops and governmental offices. The cemetery, too, bordered on the *plaza*. With the *plaza* as town center the community was divided symmetrically into four sections of stone buildings which were divided up into apartments where the Indian families lived.

The economy of the Reduction was communal and the whole group owned the entire plant, except for plots of family-owned lands. The heart of the community was the church with its functions of cult and instruction. The school was a vocational institution where apprentices in the crafts were formed. Little else was taught, though some of the boys were taught Spanish and, in exceptional cases, Latin. The workshops produced metal products, including all the musical instruments known in Europe. Ceramics and textiles were also manufactured. Wood and leather were worked, and the products highly prized throughout Latin America.

The main economic concern of the missionaries was agriculture, whose fruits maintained the people and offered articles for export, which in turn gave the communities capital for investment. Many Reductions let out money on loan to Spanish communities for their projects.

The attitude of the missionaries to all this economic activity was strictly pragmatic. They wanted the Indians to be an independent, segregated Christian people, and the price of independence was economic self-sufficiency. The agricultural production of the Reductions was rationally organized in terms of the possibilities of the region. The principal products were cotton, sugar, maize, tobacco, *yerba maté,* peppers, beans, and hides, which could not only be used at home but also employed for exchange. The *yerba maté* was something the missionaries "pushed." To this day it is a popular beverage in Brazil, Uruguay, Argentina, and Paraguay. The missionaries favored it because it gave the Indians, prone to intoxicating drinks, a healthy substitute.

The cultivation of these crops took on two forms. Each family had its own plot, but besides there were the commons belonging to the community. All the men were obliged to put a number of days per week to work on "God's land." The income derived financed the asylums, church, school, and government.

The government of the commune was quite schoolmaster-ish. The first and last word was with the Fathers in charge. However, they appointed *alcaldes* (mayors) and other officials who were given signs of office and lesser responsibilities. The different Indian officials held their posts for a year, when they were then succeeded by others. They were adorned with symbols of dignity, so that if their power was small their glory compensated for what they lacked.

The cultural life of the group was simple. Religion was the matrix of every activity, and the days began with chanted prayers in the *plaza* and there was a Mass in the church. The Indian's great capacity for music and the dance was exploited. Each Reduction had its orchestra, numbering anywhere from a few to a hundred musicians. They played all the instruments of Europe and rendered the European classics, neglecting, of course, their own traditions. The dance was given religious meaning, and anything not rigidly formal was ruthlessly excluded. The dances were also marked by colorful costumes worn by the dancers.

Guarani was the language of the community, and the poetic forms proper to the people were retained but given religious content. The preservation of the old pagan sagas and legends was discouraged.

There was no police force. The Fathers were judges and imposed punishment for the violation of laws and statutes. Life on the Reduction was pacific, nor did indocility seem to have been a problem. The only menace was from the Brazilian north, where the Paulistas (men from São Paulo) formed raiding parties looking for Indians to capture and enslave. The Fathers, contrary to their own principles, took the matter into their own hands and armed their Indians. Not only did they arm them, but they trained them in military strategy and maneuver, with the result that the Indians were quite capable of driving off the marauders successfully. In consequence there were peace and plenty within the Reductions and no important threat from without.

In many respects it was an Arcadian existence. That the Indians were better off in the Reductions than in their own perpetually menaced villages is beyond question. The real difficulty was the future of the Reductions. The system was obviously paternal, but paternalism keeps its charges in a retarded infancy. There can be no growth. Every kind of conflict was eliminated, but it is the challenge of conflict which brings about maturity and evolution. In the long run the Reductions might have become a real evil, though as an initial experiment they were blessings indeed. Moreover, we need not worry about the long run because the expulsion of the Jesuits brought about the spontaneous dissolution of the communes. The Indians simply never had enough training in responsibility to run the organization which had been created for them, and when the moment to take over came, they could do nothing to keep the organization alive.

The Reductions were, in a way, the high point of the Latin-American Missions and a good sketch of the missionaries' zeal. They wished to establish the kingdom of heaven as far as the wilds of the New World allowed. Faith, virtue, and peace were to be the life of God's people. Everything else was quite secondary or even unimportant.

The Paraguayan Reductions probably came nearer to the missionary ideal than any other of the missions, but all tended in the same direction. But the missionary work originating in the Iberian Peninsula ended when the American colonies broke away from the European powers. The result was a crisis which has not yet been overcome.

5. Men of Learning

George N. Shuster

DEDICATION to education of every kind, and so also to the school, was an unforgettable part of the fabric of the life of St. Ignatius. It is hardly necessary to recall here that at the age of twenty-nine he insisted upon sitting down on school benches beside young boys so that he might learn the Latin language—a trying ordeal for him—and that subsequently he begged his way across Europe so that he might also have, for the sake of his mission in the service of Christ, the advantages of an education at the University of Paris. His first "company" was one comprised of students, Francis Xavier and the rest, which was no different in character from any that might be recruited on a campus of the present day. St. Ignatius himself derived strength from catching glimpses of Our Lord remarkably like those which had radically altered the life of Paul of Tarsus, stricken by a vision on the way to Damascus. Yet he possessed an extraordinary, and indeed uncannily right, grasp of the fact that education and scholarship would thenceforth determine in very large measure the spiritual and intellectual allegiances of mankind.

The ages coterminous and subsequent to Columbus had not merely discovered new continents. They had also opened up new domains of knowledge together with the appropriate techniques for mastering them. On the one hand antiquity had come to life in many manuscripts, easily or laboriously deciphered, seen for the first time. These had for men of that era all the glamour which prehistoric fossils possess for us. On the other hand men, among whom Francis Bacon no doubt took the first place, had formulated methods of inquiry which, though they seemed unwholesome aberrations to not a few observers, were manifestly destined to bring about tremendous and, at least in part, fruitful changes in the outlook and achievement of mankind.

That these innovations, and others which were implicit in the philosophy of the time, might easily divert the attention of the average man from the things necessary for the salvation of his soul was almost self-evident; but many who were dedicated to the Church failed to understand that it was so. The fault was by no means wholly theirs. They were so absorbed in politics, building, and taking up collections that what was going on in intellectual circles seemed inconsequential. Perhaps for this reason the import of the pre-Reformation's too constant associating of the giving of money with the granting of indulgences was not understood until it was too late.

It is a most remarkable fact that St. Ignatius instinctively foresaw why this was so. He transformed himself into a voluntarily poverty-stricken exemplar of what we should now term an "egghead" because—and this is all anybody can say about the matter—the Lord wanted him to do so in order to stave off what might otherwise have been spiritual disaster.

St. Ignatius is even a greater mystery, it seems to me, than St. Francis of Assisi. It would have made practical sense if a Spanish soldier had turned out to be a person who thought that by organizing a first-class regiment he could proceed to conquer the Holy Land. But, while remaining miles removed from being anything resembling a schoolman, that he should have proceeded to influence education as no one before or after his time has ever influenced it is nothing short of being a staggering miracle.

Of course, education was for him missionary action, and it has so remained for his followers. On this ground critics have often found fault. They have said that the object of scholarship is the discovery of truth and not the placing of whatever is discovered in the service of Christ. Their caveats do not, however, quite strike home. For St. Ignatius, at Manresa and elsewhere, had previously entered a place where Divine Truth was present to his mind. He had not so much first sought out the kingdom of God. It was rather that this kingdom had in the awesome manner of grace singled him out. He was become a knight on the chessboard of Providence. As such he and his followers would challenge kings and queens. But the game was always played for the pawns— for all the innumerable millions of mortal men.

There had been other great missionaries prior to the coming of the Jesuits. Las Casas, for instance, is clearly one of the noblest men in history; and I think we can only deplore the fact that there is no biography of him in English which can kindle the spirit as does, for instance, the one published in Germany not so long ago by Reinhold Schneider. There have been many missioners since. But I think there have been no others who so energetically attacked mankind on every front and flank. One's first impression is of ubiquitous travel and constant searching for understanding. Mention a place, from Timbuktu to Tonkin, and a Jesuit seems somehow identified with it and informed about it.

The missionaries' observations became sources for the history, ethnography, and geography of the new countries. The *Relations*, written by French missionaries in Canada and the United States, are the foremost travelogues of the seventeenth and eighteenth centuries. These reports are but one collection of hundreds of similar documents sent in from every corner of the world. Fathers Paez, D'Almeida, Mendez, and Lobo acquainted Europe with the customs, usages, and traditions of Abyssinia, Sicard with those of Egypt. Letters came flowing back, filled with keen scientific observation from the Azores, the lands of the Tigris, Hindustan, Siam, Cochin China, Mongolia, Korea, and Tibet. Not as well known now but just as important as the *Relations* were the *Mémoires concernant la Chine* and the *Lettres Edifiantes et Curieuses*, which brought knowledge of the Orient. Acosta, Molina, Kino, and Eckart, among others, sent information about Central and South America; Combes about Mindanao and the Philippines.

France and Europe learned how to make Chinese porcelain from the Jesuit Dentrecolles. Even the lowly umbrella was first carried to the West by Jesuits from China. Peruvian bark, rhubarb—unfortunately—and vanilla were brought back by the missionaries. A Jesuit laboring in Luzon, Father Kamel, is forever associated with the waxy camellia blossom, which was named after him (using the Latin form of his name). He first brought it to the attention of Europeans.

Literally no activity of the human mind but was sedulously cultivated by these men. Jesuits were actively concerned with the emerging sciences. They undertook pioneering forays into what we should now term sociology and political science. Father Juan de Mariana and others wrestled with problems of economics. Some of the most genuinely original achievements were in the field of exact sciences. Father Zucchi invented the reflecting telescope; and Father Christoph Scheiner, discoverer of the pantograph, observed spots on the sun.

While Jesuits in Europe were earning renown in mathematics, physics, and astronomy, others were doing so on the missions. Ricci's fifteen volumes, partly mathematical, partly philosophical, written in Chinese, are still held in honor. The astronomical instruments of Jesuits who worked at the ruling court of Peking were to our day one of the sights of the former capital. Father Schall lectured to the Chinese on mathematics and was president of the mathematical tribunal of the imperial court. He was followed in this position by no less than six other missionaries.

In cartography and geography they did an immense and valuable work. Most of it was pioneer work, part of a larger attempt to codify all that could be known about the lands where they and succeeding missionaries would work. Acosta composed a lengthy work on the geography and ethnography of the aborigines of Latin America. Blas Valera did the same for Peru and Du Halde for Mongolia and China. The first map of China for Europeans was the work of Martini, sometimes called the father of Chinese geography. Other Jesuits teamed up to produce a monumental map of China, Tartary, and Tibet. In our own country that remarkable traveler, rancher, and missionary, Father Eusebio Kino, drew the first maps of New Mexico, Arizona, and Lower California. Maps of the Amazon, the Mexican Sierra, and Ethiopia came from these scholarly missionaries. Quite fittingly one of them, Father König, published the first known textbook on geography, his *Institutio Geographiae Elementalis*.

The stamp of genuine humanism was upon anything that Jesuits did. They cultivated and used the arts of music and building. To them, of course, all these things were means to an end. That end was the conversion of the world to Christ and the sanctification of souls. But the means, one hastens to add, were always good—were the best that had been known and thought in the world.

Architecture is as good an illustration as any. There is no "Jesuit style," for the Society merely built whenever it had the opportunity to do so in the manner of the then popular baroque, though if one looks closely one will see that humanistic motifs are specially emphasized in décor and iconography. At least it seems so to me. No doubt it would be interesting to compare what was done in this respect during the Counter Reformation era by the Jesuits and the Benedictines. The second also had a long and illustrious humanist tradition; and when they built nobly in styles which blended Renaissance and baroque, as they did at Melk and Metten, Andechs and Weingarten, they blended classical antiquity and the Christian faith in much the same spirit as is manifest in a Miltonic epic.

But the Jesuits, being missioners, could not keep the wide world out of art. Thus when they caused to be decorated the beautiful church of Maria Victoria in Ingolstadt, where they had established a college, the great ceiling was adorned with a fresco in which a prominent role is given to an American Indian and to the vegetation of the tropics. In this act one may see, if one wishes, a deflection from the treasures of mythology to those of anthropology. This was fitting for men of a society who made quite heroic contributions to the "science of man."

Turning now to the pedagogy of the mission to Paraguay, which Chateaubriand was the first to celebrate in lyric prose, in the *Spirit of Christianity,* one finds that it was music which opened all doors. Here, inspired it may be in part by the sketches of utopia in which the Renaissance scholar delighted, as witness the books of St. Thomas More, Cardinal Nicholas of Cusa, and Dr. Thomas of Campostella, there was established a "kingdom of God on earth," in which the doctrine of the "noble savage" took on tangible form.

The Uruguay River, curving southward to what is now Buenos Aires, flows at one point over a cliff and there foams down in a vast and forbidding cataract that cannot be navigated by boat. Crafty Europeans in search of gold and other valuables accordingly turned back. Jesuit missioners, therefore, resolved not merely to Christianize the region but to keep the traders out. Here utopia was to become reality.

But how to begin? Every time a missionary tried to approach
the natives, they took to their heels. One day some Fathers,
in a boat on the river, were singing a hymn. To their amazement the primitives not only came to listen but leaped into
the water in order to be closer to the source of beautiful
sound. That meanwhile a number of arrows were let loose
seems to have disturbed no one.

Having discovered the uses of melody, the Fathers made
the best possible pedagogical use of it. The people went to
work (which, according to the chroniclers, they detested)
to the strains of music. Popular festivals were arranged, fea-
turing much pageantry and song. Thenceforth the diapason
remained the core of a breath-taking achievement. The missionaries taught not only the Catholic faith, which as always
remained their primary concern, but virtually everything
else as well. They instructed their protégés in the arts and
crafts. The natives were found capable of imitating well-
nigh everything then produced in Europe—lace, silver, even
organs.

In our own day of great linguistic and cultural sophistica-
tion it is still not easy for missionaries to come to know a
people. It was far more difficult for the Jesuits of yesterday
to learn everything about the religious beliefs, moral habits,
and language of their new people. They did not have, for
the most part, any organized body of knowledge to fall back
on. They did not have the dictionaries, grammars, and trea-
tises which would have made understanding so much easier.
And so we must admire the extent of their accomplishments
and the magnitude of their zeal.

The problem is admirably illustrated by St. Francis Xavier's
letter written from Cochin China on January 15, 1544:

"And as I can't understand them, nor they me, because their
native tongue is Malabar and mine Basque, I got together the
most intelligent of them and sought out some persons who knew
both languages. After many meetings, and with some difficulty,

we translated the prayers from Latin into Malabar, beginning with directions as to the manner of blessing oneself, and confessing that the Three Persons are one God, then the creed, the commandments, the Lord's prayer, Ave Maria, Salve Regina, and the general confession. After these had been translated into their language and I had learned them by heart, I went through the village ringing a bell, collecting all the men and boys that I could; and after I had got them together, I gave them a lesson twice every day."

How admirable a scene in the history of popular religious education! That the results were forthcoming is evident from the saint's appended account of the somewhat unrestrained zeal of his younger pupils:

"When they report to me that idolatry is practiced anywhere in the countryside, I collect all the boys and repair with them to the spot; and the dishonor the Devil gets from the boys outweighs the honor he gets from their parents and relatives. For the children take the idols and break them into bits, and spit on them, and trample on them, and do other things that are just as well not named. But it is quite proper for the boys to do them to that Power which was bold enough to persuade their fathers to worship him."

This sort of pedagogical give-and-take was also a staple item of intellectual diet in the North American Missions. The *Relation* written from New France in 1634 by Father Paul le Jeune deals at considerable length with the matter of linguistic communications. After observing that the "language of the Mantagnais savages" has no terms usable by "theologians, philosophers, mathematicians, and physicians," and no vocabulary bearing on "the regulation of a city, province, or empire," he nevertheless finds it perplexingly rich in many ways, each of which he submits to acute analysis. Then he concludes in a mood akin to the despair many of us have felt in alien lands:

"They have so wearisome an abundance that I am almost led to believe that I shall remain poor all my life in their language."

(This and subsequent quotations are taken from *Jesuit Relations,* edited by Edna Kenton, New York, Vanguard Press.)

"When you know all the parts of speech of the languages of our Europe, and know how to combine them, you know the languages; but it is not so concerning the tongue of our Savages. Stock your memory with all the words that stand for each particular thing, learn the knot or Syntax that joins them, and you are still only an ignoramus; with that, you can indeed make yourself understood by the Savages, although not always, but you will not be able to understand them . . . it often happens that I make them laugh in talking, when I try to follow the construction of the Latin or French language, not knowing these words which mean several things at once."

Father le Jeune gave his superiors a very graphic account of what it was like to dwell among his forest flock—the openings in the tepee through which on bitter-cold nights one could study the "stars and the moon as easily as in the open fields, the omnipresent dogs, famished, running to and fro gnawing at everything in the cabin"; the pungent smoke, exposure to which made the psalms of the Breviary seem "written in letters of fire, or of scarlet." But in spite of all this, and of the smoked, dried moose meat, and so forth, one is certain that this worthy missioner's sole insurmountable source of regret was his ignorance of the tongue in which he might have taught and preached effectively.

Writing from a Huron village on April 27, 1639, Father François du Peron was able to point out that his flock, whether baptized or not, was greatly in need of training in the arts of tilling the soil. But his linguistic problems were apparently not so formidable as those of Father le Jeune, for he writes:

"Their language is a regular one, as much as it can be, full of constructions like the Greek; differing from the latter in that the changes of mode and person come at the beginning, the terminations being nearly always the same; an accent changes the meaning of the word. It is not as barbarous as is imagined; the nouns are conjugated as well as the verbs; as to syntax, I cannot see that it is very different from that of the French language."

Father Paul Ragueneau wrote from the Huron country some ten years later, just as the attacks of the Iroquois were mounting to a peak of destructive fury. But his letter is moving in its witnessing to the rewards of the missionary teacher and interesting in its faint adumbration of the concept of the "noble savage"—the primitive man possessing virtues European society no longer practiced:

"Nor are these, albeit barbarians, such Christians as one might be inclined to suppose, ignorant of things divine and not sufficiently qualified for our mysteries. Many indeed understand religion, and that profoundly; and there are some whose virtue, piety and remarkable holiness even the most holy Religious might without sin envy. One who is an eye-witness of these things cannot sufficiently admire the finger of God, and congratulate himself that so fortunate a field of labor, so rich in divine blessing, has fallen to his lot."

But Father Ragueneau also includes an obituary of his colleague, Father Noel Chabanel, who was murdered by a renegade Huron on December 8, 1649. There is a brief, poignant description of a scholar at a loss to deal with his class:

"God had given him a strong vocation for these countries; but once here, he had much to contend with; for, even after three, four, and five years of effort to learn the language of the Savages, he found his progress so slight, that hardly could he make himself understood even in the most ordinary matters. This was no little mortification to a man who burned with desire for the conversion of the Savages, who, in other ways was deficient neither in memory nor mind, and who had made this manifest enough by having for some years successfully taught rhetoric in France."

The attempts of Jesuits to learn the multitude of languages of the various countries in which they worked did at times end in heartbreaking futility, but with renewed zeal they labored on, and over the long span accomplished prodigies.

Philology owes much to these pioneers. They first reduced to written form many of the languages of the aborigines of Asia and the Americas. Grammars and vocabularies were worked out for strange tongues which would facilitate the labors of others.

So much work was done in the study of Chinese speech and literature that one might call Sinology, particularly in the seventeenth and eighteenth centuries, a special province of Jesuit enterprise. Ricci was, of course, the leading scholar. But just a single missionary like Verbiest published about thirty books in Chinese on religion, astronomy, and geography, and found time for grammar and dictionary work. Portuguese fathers in India erected printing presses at Goa and Ambalacatta from which issued a large number of translations and new works on the Bible, Christian doctrine, the life of Our Lord and the saints, as well as grammars and dictionaries. Major languages like Tamil, Konkani, and Sanskrit received special attention, but even the dialects were not neglected.

Among the first Japanese productions was a grammar and lexicon by the lay Brother Fernandez. Others wrote Japanese-Latin-Portuguese lexicons. There was even an attempt made to introduce the Latin script into the writing of Japanese. Tagalog and Visayan in the Philippines were codified, and translations of the psalms were made into these languages. A number of languages of South America received scientific treatment. Perhaps most successful was the work of the press set up by the Jesuits at their university in Juli, on the shores of Lake Titicaca in Peru, which printed many books of help both to the people and the missionaries. In Brazil, Anchieta made a noble attempt to substitute a common new language for the too generously proliferated Indian tongues. Fellow Jesuits helped, and it is thanks to their efforts that today throughout Brazil there is a *lingoa geral* which all the Indians understand and which suffices for travelers throughout this vast country.

Scientific language studies and services were combined with literary works, sometimes of a remarkably high order. These missionaries, with a wisdom which unfortunately was not always emulated in succeeding years, immersed themselves in the culture of their surroundings. Noteworthy are the successes of Thomas Stephens and Constantius Beschi in India. These two Jesuits wrote works of lasting literary value in the Marathi and Tamil languages.

Stephens, a contemporary of Shakespeare, was the first English Jesuit to arrive in India. More than a mere grammarian, he fell in love with the Marathi and Konkani tongues, which are closely related, and fell under the spell of their rhythmic flow. Realizing the grip which song and poetry had over the people, he decided that a song narrating the facts of the Gospel and the Christian religion would ensure the permanence and popularity of the faith. So he wrote his long poem which is called the *Christian Purana* or the *Christian Story,* a historical and didactic work centered about the figure of Christ. It has earned an honored place in the respect and literature of the people. At present a new Devanagari edition of the *Purana* is being prepared by a Protestant Marathi scholar with the help of the Jesuits of the Poona Mission.

Beschi, a Venetian Jesuit who came to India in 1710, achieved even greater success than Stephens. Stephens wrote in a language derived from Sanskrit and therefore cognate with European tongues. Europeans do not normally find excessive difficulty in learning the languages of northern India. But the languages of the south, which belong to the Dravidian family, are quite different in structure and genius. Beschi distinguished himself in Tamil as grammarian, lexicographer, and prose writer. But he earned himself an enviable position by his *Thembavani,* an epic poem on St. Joseph which is one of the recognized classics of the language. This is a poem of over fourteen thousand lines which combines the story of Joseph with the life and teachings of Christ. It is thoroughly Oriental in style and spirit, and ranked by Indian critics with the highest classics. A remarkable achievement for a man who was a very zealous and busy missionary, constantly traveling, preaching, and administering the Sacraments.

As far as the pursuit of formal education goals is concerned, St. Ignatius and his associates planned with masterly care. By a stroke of genius the Collegium Romanum was established in Rome during 1551 as a sort of central experimental educational academy. Ignatius spelled out the plan in meticulous detail. The Collegium was to try out pedagogical methods in order to determine which were the most effective, to draw up courses of study, and to undertake the writing of first-rate textbooks. The results of this research could then be made available, to the fullest extent desirable, to education institutions in other European lands. Since the best students were chosen to study at the Collegium, it was not surprising that in a very short time the intellectual and ecclesiastical leaders of Germany, the Austro-Hungarian Empire, and, to a more limited extent, France and Belgium were its alumni. Indeed, the movement to and from this great institution did not cease. For example, during the nineteenth century the most influential of the Hungarian bishops, Ottokar Prohaszka, lived and worked in its spirit.

Since the missionary countries overseas presented quite different opportunities and problems, a special training center was established at Coimbra. Here, too, a bustling and thriving, a recondite and still remarkably experimental, center was established.

The major European institutions of the early period are relatively well known. They were situated at intellectually strategic points in Central Europe, with notable foundations in cities which in a surprising manner followed the path taken by the Irish monks during the years after Charlemagne came to power. Here the famous educational method of the Ratio Studiorum was developed and refined. Not only was solid training in the classical and modern languages, mathematics and science provided, but the individual student was made the object of wise, flexible, and persistent spiritual counseling. Sometimes young men revolted, as witness Voltaire, but in general the system left an indelible mark on the minds and spirits of those subjected to it.

In every missionary field colleges were established as soon as it was at all possible to do so. The territory of South America was dotted with colleges, some of which have survived until this day. But it was, perhaps, in Mexico that the greatest expansion was achieved. Seventeen years after the death of St. Ignatius, St. Idlefonse College was opened in Mexico City, thus outranking Harvard from the point of seniority by more than half a century. During the hundred years which followed the establishment of the province by Father Pedro Sánchez, thirty-two institutions of higher learning were opened. Efforts to find a foothold in the United States were more difficult, but eventually a school was founded in New Town, Maryland, which during 1789 became Georgetown College. The record in the Orient is a long and glorious tribute to the memory of St. Francis Xavier. St. Paul's College in Goa has functioned uninterruptedly until this very day. In India proper the Society maintained seven seminaries. Japanese Christians revered the schools set up in Arima and Miyako, which of course were victims of the great persecution. That in the end many of the missionaries taught from the crosses of Japan and Tonkin was not in their eyes a tragic ending to a great spiritual adventure.

Round the world this effort for the training of the mind in the spirit of the Church of Christ has been recorded with admiration by friend and foe alike.

Viewed retrospectively, the Ratio Studiorum (the full title is Ratio atque Institutio Studiorum Societatis Jesu), which unified Jesuit education in the missions and at home, remains one of the basic documents of modern pedagogical literature. The object was to train an elite by developing as carefully as possible the intellectually useful powers of the young man. These were linguistic memory, expression, and logical thinking. The terms used were, of course, others, being "Grammar," "Humanities and Rhetoric," and "Dialectics." Perhaps it was only in the third area that the Ratio differed markedly from the pattern followed in the Benedictine schools. For both the pillars of ancient wisdom were Cicero and Vergil, the first revered for his contribution to moral and civic philosophy as well as to oratory, and the second esteemed as the "father of the West" by reason of the beauty and nobility of his verse. The "Dialectics" were taught according to the Scholastic method, which sought to bring arguments to a genuine and effective conclusion. Yet neither the Jesuit nor the Benedictine school was tethered to a given set of conclusions or methods. Committed, of course, to the cultivation of the Catholic faith, they could nevertheless permit a great deal of elbowroom in the discussion of everything else. Ignatius, for example, stipulated that the schools of the Society were to teach the "philosophy of St. Thomas," but this was to be in his thinking always the threshold and never necessarily the house. No doubt there were times when the order's great masters fought too hard against an innovation, on the ground that a tenet of doctrine was threatened, but on the whole their record is one of surprising wisdom and caution.

Modern educational theory, especially in the United States, broke abruptly with the Ratio sometime after the dawn of the twentieth century. This repudiation was in part based on criticism which had been voiced earlier, for example by the French Encyclopedists and the English utilitarians. Notable sources of conflict were the disrepute in which the "psychology of the faculties" (e.g., the imagination and the memory) was held, particularly after the emergence of Pavlov's theory of the conditioned reflex, and the quite natural decline of interest in classical antiquity among peoples outside of Europe. But no doubt the basic reason for the unpopularity of the ratio, apart from the waning of interest in religious motivation, was the development of mass higher education. This, which in essence made utility the basic purpose of the school experience, was diametrically opposed to the Jesuit concept of higher education. But of late more and more voices have been raised in demand of a change. That education in the "liberal arts" is an indispensable preparation for success in any calling demanding the exercise of intelligence has latterly been asserted by a large number of responsible persons.

Their definitions, it is true, usually include only the first two steps on the ladder of the Ratio. That is, they favor what the early Jesuits termed "Grammar" as well as a modification of "Humanities and Rhetoric." I have no doubt that any responsible educator associated with the Society would not in our time insist on a monopoly for Cicero and Vergil, though it would be an error to dispense with them wholly. Today, however, the principal content of a "Humanities" course might well be Dante, Shakespeare, Goethe, Molière, Dostoievski. Far more difficulties surround the introduction of "Dialectics." The aversion of the great majority of Americans to abstract thought, and their anathemas spoken against those who have advocated the cultivation of such thinking, is so pronounced that even an ardent member of the Society might desire to be absent when the vote was taken. But in the end I am persuaded that we shall insist, at least for a carefully selected elite, on this discipline as well. Indeed, it may not be extravagant to say that the future of the Ratio as a theory of right education may depend on its description of what the term "Dialectics" is.

But, looking back, one cannot avoid marveling at the genius of the founders and missionaries of the Society, at the scrupulous care which they expended on every aspect of knowledge and education, and at the hope which they entertained that if the mind of man were enlightened his conduct would improve. We can only regret that their way of dealing with the peoples not indigenous to the European Continent was not adopted as a rule of thumb. Had it been, we should now be living in amity with many people for whom we are oppressors or imperialists. If we are wholly honest we shall confess that the major reason for the "superiority" of the white race in the Americas was the command of gunpowder, which was a Chinese invention. I may be an incorrigible skeptic, but I wonder whether even St. Ignatius, were he amongst us at the moment, could extricate us from the impasse to which colonialism and the assumption of race superiority have brought us.

6. Even in Suffering

Jean Monsterleet, s.j.

THERE is no mission field which has not been watered with the blood of martyrs. A missionary order par excellence, the Society of Jesus, for instance, counts among its members more than a hundred martyrs recognized as such by the Church. If we glance through the Proper of the Saints of the Society of Jesus we shall see before our eyes humble or prodigious names from all the corners of the world: from England and Scotland there are Campion, Southwell, Ogilvie, and so many other victims of the heretics; from France, James Sales, Bonnaud, Du Lau, and their companions, slain by the Huguenots or the revolutionists; from Hungary, Crisini and his companions; from Poland, Andrew Bobola; from Canada and the two Americas, Jogues and Brébeuf, along with Gonzales and the forty missionaries who under the leadership of Azevedo were massacred at sea on their way to Brazil; from India, John de Britto, Rudolph Aquaviva, and his companions; from Japan, Europeans and Japanese united in one common faith, Anthony Ishida, Thomas Tsugi, Paul Miki, Leonard Kimura, Jerome de Angelis, Charles Spinola, Diego Carvalho; from China, the martyrs recently beatified, Mangin and Denn, Iroré and Andlauer. Soon, we may hope, we shall be able to add to this glorious list the names of the victims of communism, Father Pro of Mexico, many Jesuits of Spain, and Father Beda Chang in China.

But we do not wish to present here a bouquet made of all the possible flowers that could be gathered for the honor of the martyrs. In the style of Japanese florists we would like rather to trim the foliage so that only a few chosen flowers stand out in the midst of the leaves and branches. We have therefore chosen the heroes of the persecutions of the Japan of the Shoguns separated by three centuries of time but so like unto those of the China of Mao Tse-tung.

These two great assaults upon the faith are comparable both in their totalitarian character and in their destructive effects. They make one think indeed of the most tragic and critical phases of the persecution of Decius. But whereas the Roman Emperor died before he was able to achieve his wicked objective, in Japan the persecution went on for many decades under successive despots, each of whom outdid his predecessor in shrewdness and ferocity. This religious persecution exterminated (to all appearances at least) the small Christian Church of some three hundred thousand faithful, who were too concentrated in one locality.

Persecution was the lot of the Church in Japan from the beginning. Xavier himself, during the two years he spent among his beloved Japanese, realized that their conversion would be not without suffering. In April 1551 he wrote from Yamaguchi, "If there have not been more Christians it is because the people feared the 'Duke' of Satzuma, who is the lord of the country. The bonzes, his servants, seeing the growth of our Holy Faith, went to him and said that if he allowed his vassals to become Christians, he would lose his domains and the pagodas would be discredited and ruined. More than one bonze had declared himself convinced but the fear of losing the income which they enjoyed and of losing the many children whom they instructed in their monasteries was an obstacle to their conversion."

Shortly afterwards this daimyo decreed the pain of death against those who became Christians.

Ten years after this first wave of hostility we have evidence of the first martyr, that of a woman slave who belonged to one of the leading pagans on the isle of Hirado. When she defied her master and continued to go and pray at the foot of a cross she was threatened with death. She was finally beheaded, the first fruit of the Church of Japan.

From the preceding we can judge what were the main obstacles that stood in the way of the preaching of the Gospel. These were the bonzes and the powerful ones of the land.

The missionaries considered the conversion of the bonzes, and they made some attempts in that direction, not without some results. But in the whole course of the history of the Church in Japan it was always the bonzes who were present to checkmate the efforts of the rival religion. Even under Hideyoshi, himself an enemy of the Buddhist monks, an ex-bonze named Seyakuin Sensô gained the favor of the Prince, and his influence was a continuing menace for the missionaries. Under Ieyasu, a fervent Buddhist, the oppression of the Christians became even severer than under his predecessors, who were at odds with the bonzes. In feudal Japan, as in the China of the Mings and the Ch'ings, the persecution of the Christians took its origin from and was stimulated in part by Buddhist opposition.

Nevertheless, in the final analysis the ultimate fate of Catholicism was to be determined by the attitude of the daimyo and especially of the Shoguns when these had become powerful to the point of unifying the whole country. The missionaries grasped this from the first moment of their arrival. Xavier, as we know, went directly to the capital to win the favor of the Emperor. When he realized that in a feudal system, such as it existed at that time, the local daimyo were the true rulers of the country, he and his successors endeavored to establish themselves in their good graces and, if possible, to convert them. Later, when the feudal lords had been tamed and subjected, when the Shoguns had concentrated supreme power in their own hands, we see the Jesuits striving to have one of their number among the friends of the Prince. Valignano himself, the Visitor of the Japanese Vice-Province, went to the court often as an ambassador and succeeded in softening the rigors of the persecution.

As long as Japan was divided among many feudal fiefs, it was possible for the missionaries, and often their converts as well, to take refuge in the territory of a benevolent lord when one daimyo persecuted the Church. Hounded, the first missionaries fled from one fief to another, from Yamaguchi to Bungo or to Hirado. Later, under the Shoguns, the missionaries and the faithful could still for a certain time find asylum in the domains of Christian or friendly lords in the north. But when the day came that Iemitsu extended his persecution policy to the whole of Japan, it was the death of the flourishing Christianity.

In order to better understand the trials of the Church at the beginning of the seventeenth century, in order to appreciate the strategy of the missionaries and of their methods of the apostolate, as well as their worries and sufferings, we must take into account the way the persecution evolved. For it was sporadic and intermittent up until 1614, following which, under Ieyasu, it was increasingly relentless and sustained, more and more totalitarian. This is the same rhythm noticed in Communist China, where, after the final conquest of the country, there no longer remains any place of refuge and the measures of persecution become more and more complete and total, their object being the definite extinction of the visible Church of Christ.

In Japan, as in today's China for that matter, and in Rome under Decius, the persecution changed its character little by little. It became more and more insidious. The persecutor began to seek not martyrs, but apostates. Those Christians who showed themselves pliant to the government to the point of denying their faith were fully rehabilitated. This objective was aided by the development of more refined forms of torture.

In the last state the persecution becomes so severe, without any escape, that the Christians, deprived of their missionaries, and of their leaders, believe that they can conceal their faith while remaining true to it. In this situation they submit to making some gestures symbolizing apostasy but continue to live secretly as Christians. And so Christianity in Japan lived "underground" for two centuries. Something like this is happening in our own time, when some Chinese, under the severest pressure from all sides, without the guidance of their bishops and priests, believe that they can join the national schismatic Church or pretend to apostatize for the purpose of saving their faith and that of their children.

To develop and preserve the young Church in Japan, where they were at the beginning the only missionaries (after 1592 the Franciscans, Dominicans, and Augustinians joined the missionary effort), the Jesuits had to exercise great prudence not to expose themselves without good reason, for they were not very numerous. At the same time they had to exercise great courage by giving their lives, often under savage torture, when the hour of martyrdom had arrived.

Three Japanese Jesuits were the first to give their lives for Christ. These were the scholastic Paul Miki, the novice John of Goto, and the coadjutor Brother James Kisai, crucified with several Franciscans and with some Christians on February 5, 1597, at Nagasaki. "Paul Miki, student-preacher, some knowledge of Latin"; this is the information we read in the catalogue of the vice-province of Japan for the year

1592. But in the following year this student, little inclined to a studious life, became a catechist and was the companion of the Vice-Provincial. Four years later the opportunity came to him to preach Christ from his own cross by word and blood. Before his death he preached forgiveness of wrongs and asked for prayers for his executioners. As for John of Goto, he was aided in his martyrdom by his own father. This courageous Christian exhorted his son, "Believe me, my son, your mother and I are ready to imitate your example and may it please the Lord that it be so."

Twenty-six crosses had been set up for the heroes of this occasion. At their foot was a crossbar upon which the feet could rest; at the center there was a sort of block on which to sit. The martyrs were bound with ropes in the middle of their bodies, at the feet and at the hands. An iron collar held their necks against the wood. Trussed up in this way, they were raised upright. Among those crucified were two children of twelve and thirteen years of age. Paul Miki was thirty-one, John of Goto eighteen, and James Kisai sixty-four. They were all pierced by the executioner's lance, which, entering at the ribs, came out at the shoulder.

When Toyotomo Hideyoshi died in 1598, the persecution, begun only the year before, ceased and the Church enjoyed relative peace. Many conversions were even made. But the first of the Tokugawa Shoguns, Ieyasu, by an edict of February 14, 1614, exiled all the missionaries and the most influential Christians, such as Takayama Ukon. From that time on the persecution, which resumed with unheard-of violence, was destined to have no pause. As a result of the edict sixty-two Jesuits, including thirty-three priests, had to go to Macao. Twenty-three others, including eight priests, went to Manila while eighteen priests and nine Brothers remained hidden in Japan. Counting the religious of other orders and the secular clergy, there were at least thirty-seven priests who went underground.

Ieyasu sought particularly to eliminate the missionaries in the hope that the new religion would disappear with the departure of its apostles. But his son Hidetada adopted a severer policy and made countless martyrs. It was then, alas, that many Christian daimyo turned against their brethren and began to persecute the Church in order to keep the favor of the all-powerful Shogun.

The second great martyrdom of Nagasaki took place in 1622. At this time Charles Spinola and his Jesuit companions were burned alive. Spinola, born of a noble family in Italy in 1564, had spent most of his youth in Spain. The kind of man he was can be judged from the letter he wrote to his uncle, Cardinal Philip Spinola, on the subject of his vocation:

If your Eminence means to hold me up till my father gives his consent, then I may as well say at once that I consider his permission entirely unnecessary; he will never succeed in shaking my resolution, whether he consents or not. Moreover, it was in no sense because I believed that I needed your permission that I consulted your Eminence about this matter, but merely because good manners and the respect I owe you seemed to require it. Strictly speaking, I need no permission. And hence, if I find my request not granted, I shall assert my rights. . . .

After an initial voyage that saw him forced back to his point of departure, Spinola finally set foot in Japan in 1602. He was occupied as a professor in the minor seminary of Arima, as a worker in new territories, and as mission procurator, this latter a very difficult post in those hard times. After his exile edict of 1614 he lived in the underground but was finally arrested in December 1618. He perished at the stake in September 1622 with twenty-four others.

Some excerpts from Father Spinola's letters may serve to provide an insight into what he had to suffer as well as his peace and joy of heart during his four years in prison:

I have finally been arrested. Bound like a robber I have been

led through the streets amid a great concourse of the people
and thrust into prison. I am cheerful and contented and deeply
grateful to God who has granted me such a great grace.

We are not allowed either to wash our clothes or to dry them
in the sun. The place is therefore filthy in the extreme and since
all other needs of nature must be met within this hut it is always
filled with a pestilential and unbearable stench.

I can assure your Reverence that there is no one among us
who would not prefer a fiery death at the stake if we gave heed
only to our natural inclinations. We are almost entirely naked but
the guards will not permit clothes to be sent to us from Nagasaki
and in spite of the bitter cold they have not allowed us to have a
blanket.

Our life is one long fast. They give us enough food to keep
us alive but not enough to satisfy our hunger. . . . Our daily
food consists of two bowls of cold rice that was boiled in water,
a cup of a bitter beverage that can hardly be swallowed, and
either a small portion of vegetables or two small sardels. Since
Europeans are generally not used to these latter dishes we must
be satisfied with the rice. Hunger is so much of a torture that
when a kindly guard gave us some black and moldy bread some
time ago we ate it as if it were the most delicious delicacy.

In 1621 Spinola was joined in prison by Father Sebastian
Kimura, a fellow Jesuit who was the grandson of a convert
of St. Francis Xavier. He was the first of the Japanese priests
to be ordained (1601) and to die a martyr. By this time
there were thirty-three prisoners detained in a small chamber
sixteen feet in width and twenty-four feet in length. In September 1622 Spinola, Kimura, and twenty other martyrs were
burned at a slow fire. The pyre had been set up twenty-five
feet away from the victims, "in order that death might be
delayed and the bodies of the martyrs might be destroyed
by slow torture, being roasted rather than burned," as Father
Majorica tells us in his account of 1623. Spinola already
weakened, died the first; Kimura was the last to die after
having suffered for nearly two hours. Both were beatified
by Pius IX in 1867.

Shortly after these events, in January 1623, Hidetada retired and confided the government to his son, Iemitsu. This new ruler was not an intruder like his father and grandfather but had been born as the son of the Shogun. Conscious of his place, he made every effort to concentrate even more power in his hands and to impose unquestioned obedience upon the daimyo. In order to strengthen his hold he kept a number of local princes at his court and taught them to follow his own example in their respective fiefs. In the very year of his accession Iemitsu gave to the Catholic daimyo, or protectors of the Catholics, the spectacle of a great martyrdom. This new persecution was to spread throughout all Japan up to the very northernmost regions of the land.

The great martyrdom of Edo (Tokyo) took place on December 4, 1623. Fifty priests and Christians died by fire before the eyes of the tyrant and an immense crowd of onlookers.

Among the victims was Father Jerome de Angelis, reckoned one of the great missioners of Japan in the seventeenth century. Born in Sicily in 1568 and a Jesuit since his eighteenth year, he was one of Charles Spinola's group which left Lisbon in 1596, arriving with him in Japan in 1602. Especially distinguished by his perfect adaptation to the mentality and the customs of the people, he was the first European to penetrate as far as the island of Hokkaido, in the north of Japan. He remained in the north, particularly around Sendai, from 1615 to 1621, when he was helped in his work by the Japanese catechist Simon Jempo, destined to die with him as a Jesuit Brother. Father de Angelis was recalled to Edo by his superiors in 1621, where he was soon denounced and arrested. The Franciscan, James de San Francisco, has given us an account of the prison where these victims were incarcerated. Here are some excerpts written by one who had himself experienced imprisonment in that same place in 1615–1616:

They took us to a place with four prisons, or rather one prison with four separate rooms. Next to this prison there was a sort of stable [jaula], the wallboards of which were so closely fitted together that absolutely no light shone through. This dungeon had only one small opening, through which food could be handed to us; one small pan could fit through it. Practically no light broke in, so that we could scarcely see one another. Our prison was 10 meters long and 4 meters wide, and very low. It was enclosed with a larger prison so that no one could speak to us from the outside. Our guard consisted of the warden and 24 men, who kept shouting day and night to prove they were awake . . .

Through the door, which was so narrow that they had to force us through, they brought us into the dungeon, where there were already 153 prisoners with hardly room to squat. The newcomers were given the worst places, though one of the Christian samurai imprisoned there commanded them to give the Father the best place—which was, to be sure, only 60 centimeters long and 30 centimeters wide. The hovel was divided in two by a heavy beam that ran across the middle from end to end. In each part the prisoners squatted in three rows in such a way that the first and third rows faced each other and the second row sat in the middle. This second row was the worst, for when those of the first or third rows got tired of squatting they stretched their legs against those in the middle row and pressed them down, especially if the latter were sick or weak. However, even in this way those of the first and third row could not stretch out well, so narrow was the room. If anyone wanted to sleep he had to lean against his neighbor. Since they were unable to move for such a long time, they were like men robbed of the use of their limbs.

They had no clothing except a small loincloth. . . . Nor was any medicine allowed, for fear that there might be some poison extracted wherewith one might put an end to the terrible suffering by suicide. . . . The place crawled with vermin. For lack of light the prisoners could not kill them so they increased terribly. . . . The stench was terrible. For there were many sick who could not move and so had to take care of their needs right where they were. And nobody cleaned the place. The sick man's neighbor had to put up with not only the stench but the mess. Sometimes in desperation they would knock the invalid's head against the heavy beam and kill him, or if they could not kill the other, they committed suicide. Sometimes, more than 30 got noth-

ing to eat and died of hunger. For, since they couldn't move because of their illness, others took their food away. Since they
can't move to go to the latrine, it's better you don't eat, said their
neighbors, and so fared the sick. Although many died, the total
still remained the same, since new prisoners were continually
cast in. The thirst, too, was unbearable. For they received only a
bit of water twice a day and the heat was so intense that this
was immediately sweated away. Many, consequently, died of
thirst . . .

What was most unbearable was the corpses. For they could be
removed only with the permission of the warden. Because he was
often slow in granting it, the bodies sometimes lay around for 7
or 8 days. The heat was so intense that they began to corrupt
after 7 hours and the stench was hideous . . .

Such details recall others which have recently been heard
about the prisons in Communist China. This letter of three
centuries ago can be compared with the letter sent by Chinese Christians to Madame Nehru. On the martyrdom itself
this is what we read in the Annual Letters:

Early in December the executioners finally came to carry out
the Shogun's sentence. They entered the dungeon, went first to
Father Jerome and unshackled his feet. Then they threw a heavy
rope about his neck and bound his hands behind his back with it.
Father Francis [Calvez, O.F.M.] and the other Christians were
handled in no more human fashion. . . . Father Jerome, for all
like a captain, was on horseback at the head of the procession:
from his shoulders hung a sign with his name inscribed in large
letters. Behind him walked Simon Jempo . . .

Outside the city, along the road that runs toward Kami, 50
stakes had already been set up on the place of execution. Three
of them, those nearest the city, stood a little apart from the others.
All were heaped around with faggots. The firewood was placed
in such a way that when it burst into flame the fire would blaze
about 45 inches away from the stake. The crowd of onlookers,
who streamed in from all directions, was enormous. The place,
which was of no mean dimensions, and the neighboring mountain
were filled with spectators, among them many nobles and princes
who had assembled in Edo just at that time . . .

Here is how Father Jerome de Angelis dies:

As the fire flared up and began to envelop them the servants of God could be seen through the flames braving the first onslaught of the blaze with surpassing valor. Father Jerome could be seen first turning toward the city praying for it briefly, then turning where the flames, fanned by the wind, attacked him the most fiercely, partly to show that he did not fear, partly to say some last words to the folk who stood there in greater numbers. He remained always the same, ever erect and exhorting the crowds with great zeal, until he succumbed to the might of the fire and rendered his spirit back to his Creator, falling to his knees as he died.

From the great sacrifice of Edo the persecution carried its fury to the north of Japan. In the following year Father Diego Carvalho, S.J., died in the freezing waters of the Hirose River at Sendai. He had long lived the life of a hunted animal, such as that described by a Dutch Protestant in 1629:

"The priests are usually concealed in holes in the earth under the floor boards of the rooms of the houses wherein they lie. These holes are covered over with planks and mats. Others stand all day long in a small space behind the privy, in dirt and filth, wherein one would not expect to find a beast, let alone a man; others conceal themselves between two partitions or behind the wainscoting which appears to be thinner than it really is."

Father Carvalho was arrested in February 1624, brought to Sendai, twice plunged into a pit filled with icy river water within an interval of a few days, ending his life on February 22 after undergoing this kind of torture from noon to midnight.

But these torments were still too merciful. The apostates were too rare. Other trials were excogitated. In 1631 Father Anthony Ishida, S.J., died in the sulphurous waters of Unzen. But the most terrible of the tortures was that known as

Tsurushi, or "torture of the ditch." This was a fearsome test that many could not hold up under. The Christian was fixed to a stake upside down. He was then lowered by a pulley into a pit filled with filth. To make death as slow as possible incisions were made in the temples and at the top of the head through which the blood could escape. In such a position the martyr suffered agonies, his internal organs were forced into his chest. Death was slow in coming. The first one to endure this form of torture was a Japanese; Nicholas Keyan Sukunaga, who had entered the Society in 1588. He died after two days and a half at Yendo on July 31, 1633.

Before passing judgment on the many apostasies that these tortures were effective in bringing about, or, better, not to judge but to lament the victims, we should get a full realization of the horror they faced. Some of the forms of brain-washing used in our own time by the Communists exceed the former tortures in their atrocity. But for the most part there is little that is new. Informers abounded and proved dangerous. Rich rewards were promised to those who turned in a Christian, and particularly a priest. The obligation of reporting each year to the authorities for the purpose of proclaiming one's faith had the result of decimating the Christian community and of driving it underground. For such were the refined tortures that awaited those who avowed their Christianity. It became impossible for the missionaries, whether Europeans or Japanese, to hide themselves. On top of this Japan isolated itself from the outside world so well that all attempts to get into the country and to remain were doomed to failure.

More than two centuries passed before the missionaries could return. The Jesuits themselves came back only in 1908, when St. Pius X asked them to establish Sophia University in Tokyo. In the meantime, however, Father Petitjean of the foreign missions of Paris had discovered the descendants of the old Christians who had remained true to their faith and still knew the essential religious rites. The admiration of St. Francis Xavier for his "beloved Japanese" was justified. There were martyrs among them even in the nineteenth century. In the end the Western powers were able to persuade the Japanese that a great country owed it to itself to grant freedom of religion. And thus ends the persecution of the Church in Japan.

7. *Today*

Clement Armitage, s.j.

Today there are approximately six thousand Jesuits in over seventy missions throughout the world. They are the largest missionary organization which the Church has in the field at the present time.

It is not difficult to understand why this is so. The purpose and nature of the Jesuit order make it an ideal weapon for the hand of the Pope. The unique Jesuit vow, to go wherever the Holy Father may command, further facilitates the use of this weapon. The mission history of the Society of Jesus is simply a mirror of the problems and needs which confronted the Holy See during the last four centuries.

That accounts for the seemingly unbalanced look of a map of Jesuit missions throughout the world today. Three quarters of the missionary personnel are found in Asia while only 16 per cent are laboring in Africa and a mere 9 per cent in the Americas. However, we must remember that we are speaking of mission territories in the accepted sense and excluding former mission regions which have been developed to a higher ecclesiastical plane under their own hierarchy. For instance, it has been only in this twentieth century that the United States has been removed from the list of mission territories subject to the Congregation for the Propagation of the Faith. The same is true of other countries in the Americas where the development of the Church has been rapid. Formerly where mission regions looked to Europe for priests and nuns, now their own sons and daughters have taken over the reins. The Church has come of age in the New World and no longer depends on European help. There are still mission areas, but they are cared for by the Church of the Americas.

There are many misconceptions about missionary work, and it might be useful for the understanding of today's picture to make a brief comparison of the mission history of the Americas and that of other parts of the world. The radically different backgrounds highlight the various techniques, approaches, successes, and failures. The Americas were conquered and colonized by the Christian powers of Europe. Missionary activity began almost at the same moment as that early morning landfall off San Salvador which twisted the European world into a new orbit. The soldier and the missionary marched side by side, but with different motives, into these lands.

The religion of the conqueror always has a natural advantage, but this is heightened when the religious beliefs and customs of the natives border on the primitive. Elsewhere in this volume is a more detailed account of the spread of Christianity in the Americas, especially in Latin America, and it is not difficult to see why these countries are nominally Christian today. Not that the spirits of darkness have been conquered and driven out completely; in a Mayan Indian village near the Guatemala border a Jesuit missionary pointed out to me a thatched hut where he had spent uneasy nights with invisible stone throwers. And deep in the mountains of Jamaica I have heard at night the throb of the drums with their dark echoes of Africa.

So there is a different pattern to missionary work in the

Americas than there is in Asia. On the one hand you have a Christian foundation of sorts while the East presents an entirely different world, time-hardened in its cultures and ways of life. That does not necessarily mean that mission work will be the less difficult in the former case. Is it harder to convert an out-and-out pagan than an uneducated descendant of slaves who has been exposed to half a dozen watered-down versions of Christianity and who doesn't see any difference among them and isn't particularly interested, anyway? Just as long as ignorance and prejudice becloud the ways a single human being walks, then there will be need of the men who bring the Light and Truth of Christ.

The Jesuit missionaries of today in the Americas, among their other works, still care for the Indians. The Rocky Mountains and the Dakota Plains, as well as other reservations in the U.S. and Canada, know the Blackrobes. The heritage of the Jesuit martyrs who died in the wilderness of New York and Canada over three hundred years ago is still being carried on. In fact two full-blooded Indians, one from the Iroquois and one from the Blackfoot tribe, are now Jesuit priests and working among their own people.

The Tarahumare Indians, deep in the Chihuahua mountain district of Mexico, have presented a formidable problem to the missionaries. Still savage and uncivilized, prone to drunkenness and caught in the web of ancient superstitions, they provide a continual heartache for the Jesuits and nuns who have devoted their lives to them. The nature of the people is reflected in the rugged country where they dwell, severely remote from the rest of mankind. A missioner could ride continuously for fifteen days and still not cross the entire territory with its precipices, valleys, and treacherous rivers.

Added to these difficulties are the political ones. In the years the Jesuits have labored in Mexico they have suffered no less than three ejections and three suppressions. They have seen the training schools they had set up for the Indian children, kindergartens in civilization, taken over for soldiers' barracks while they themselves fled to the deeper recesses of the mountains, men with a price on their heads and living in caves.

Farther south, along the mountainous backbone of Central America, the Mayan Indians live. Their various stages of progress are a good yardstick to indicate the influence of the missionary. In the remoter districts, where permanent mission stations have not yet been established due to lack of man power, the people eke out a slender living from milpa farming, chicle bleeding, and mahogany cutting. The faith is a fragile thing, although their ancestors were converted back in the seventeenth century. But without the steadying hand of a priest their religious beliefs and practices are as mixed as the sunlight and shadows on their jungle trails.

However, it is a different story when the missionary is close to his people. For instance, in the small village of San Antonio in the southwest corner of British Honduras a permanent mission residence was established a few years ago. The Jesuit priest is the only non-Indian on the reservation and needed a special government permission to reside there. But under his tutelage the life of the village has changed. He taught the people the value of co-operatives, the only possible way they could escape the economic stranglehold clamped on them by truckers and buyers. He organized them into a communal unit which soon achieved economic independence through its own co-operatives and transportation. A new spirit has transformed the village; the attendance at school is the best in the country and the people themselves have built a gem of a church which is the very heart of their lives. San Antonio could be multiplied a thousand times if there were only a thousand missionaries more!

So the value of the missionary is not in the spiritual realm only. A correspondent for a London newspaper in reporting on conditions in British Guiana bluntly said that if it were not for the Jesuit missions among the ten thousand Indians of the jungle area in that country the aboriginals might have become "an extinct race through starvation and disease." He added that "conditions among the Makusi and more enlightened Wapischanas of the interior savannahs are better, owing to the influence of the Catholic Church there. Almost every Indian in the district has had some kind of schooling and owns at least one head of cattle, some hogs and a few chickens."

It should be remembered that the history of the Indians in Latin America has been similar to that of the Indians in the United States. Pushed steadily into the hinterlands by the advance of civilization, they have tried to keep their identity and way of life. As a result they are the most neglected, the most backward of all the peoples in the Western Hemisphere. So the apostolate to them will have proportionate difficulties and problems. A missionary who dedicates his life to these people is asking for a greater share in the loneliness of Gethsemane and the thirst and failure of Calvary.

Yet Jesuit missionaries still tread the jungle trails of Mato Grosso, the "Green Hell" of Brazil; they fan out to the Nhambiquare Indians of the north, to the Apiacas of the northwest, and to the Pareci and Iranche tribes along the headwaters of the Rio Juruena. In Ecuador they care for the Cayapa and Inter-Andean Indians. In Peru the Jesuits of that country must cover an area of 12,600 square miles in the departmentos of Cajamarca and Amazonas. Yet this is only a small corner, this mission of San Jaiver of Marañón, of the great seventeenth-century mission of the Jesuits to the Mayans.

The same thing is true when you travel the territory where the famous Paraguay Reductions once stood. What once was a rosary of shining achievement is now broken and fragmentary. Now and then a town appears with its long-ago name, but most of the sites of the old Reductions are only landmarks now. One has to stop and collect himself before he remembers that this is holy ground, that here a people lived close to God and knew a peace and tranquillity foreign to the world beyond them, that here men died for the sake of Christ. The glory is of the past, but there are still souls to be saved along the La Plata river basin and the Jesuits of the Argentine now travel these ways, caring for the descendants of the original Reduction inhabitants.

But the missionary work in the Americas is by no means restricted to the Indians. It also embraces the Negroes, whose ancestors were brought from Africa in the slave ships to the islands and lands along the Spanish Main. So, for instance, the largest contingent of Jesuit missionaries in a single field here, over eighty in number, is found on the Caribbean island of Jamaica, which is predominantly colored in population. There are missions among the Caribs of the Central American mainland while the Colombian Jesuits carry on the saintly work of Peter Claver in their fifty-two stations, scattered through the malarial swampland of the Magdalena River Mission.

Another flourishing field which was opened only a generation ago is among the Japanese in Brazil. Back in the late twenties there were about four hundred thousand of these expatriates, all pagans. Then an Italian Jesuit, Father Guido del Toro, got his foot in the door through one of his catechism pupils who brought several Japanese children to class. Seven months later forty-eight of the children were baptized, the first fruits of a harvest that is still continuing. One significant indication of the rapid success of this work is the number of vocations. The Society of Jesus alone has averaged a vocation a year, and the time has come when Japanese Jesuits of Brazil have sailed westward across the Pacific to bring Christ to their motherland.

Asia is a different world. When the first Jesuit missionary, St. Francis Xavier, landed in India he found it was a world grown old with the indifference of the aged. Men had watched the days and seasons pass, the unending recurrence of life and death, and had evolved for themselves a cyclical belief that is the key to the mind of Asia. All things pass, so of what importance is the present time? Why bother to change anything in the outside world since the ceaseless turning of the cycles will eventually restore the original conditions?

It is a world at which thousands of missionaries, men and women, have hammered unceasingly for four centuries and more. The Far East is still the number-one missionary objective of the Church. The majority of its people are not yet Christians; only one country, the Philippines, can be called Catholic. Why have the results not been greater? Why was the steady sweep of Catholicism through the Americas not emulated in the East?

Asia offered a far greater challenge to the ambassadors of Christ. They responded to the best of their ability, and no human judgment can adequately evaluate the courage and patience of those missionaries who threw themselves against the citadel of Asia. They had to battle against terrific odds, handfuls of men laying siege to the fortress of some of the world's oldest cultures and most enduring religions.

They had to fight the caste system in India, the primitive but paralyzing superstitions of Indonesia, the pride of China rooted in antiquity and learning. Buddhism, Hinduism, Confucianism, Islam, Shinto, animism, and paganism stood squarely across the path of these foreigners who preached a strange and hard faith. It is no wonder that that path is red with Christian blood.

It was a challenge that was answered, but never completely and effectively. Only in the Philippines was the conquest a permanent or a lasting one. The countries of the older cultures and more hardened pride were not to be shaken deeply by that first onslaught. The besiegers were too few, their resources too limited. They gained their footholds but they could not overthrow the citadel. And then, as that era of colonization came to a close, the greatest challenge of all the modern world of the West rose to confront it, the challenge of communism.

What is the Jesuit picture today in these lands? As we have mentioned previously, three fourths of the entire Jesuit missionary personnel are strung out across this area. In India alone there are over two thousand men, for this has always been the largest mission field of the Jesuits. In early days India was always the gateway to the other countries and the headquarters for the entire East. The people were inclined to be more open to relations with the West than were the people of the more distant and more secluded lands such as China and Japan.

India is an example of the missionary problem of Asia. Christianity was offered to them by foreigners, and that association in the minds of the people has never been completely dispelled. To understand its importance we must remember that the impact of the foreigner on the Easterner is far different from that on more primitive peoples elsewhere. The man of the East looks down on these Johnnies-come-lately from lands and cultures that were in their infancy when his own were already old. His customs and ways of life have been solidified by centuries, and he looks askance at anyone who would dare to try to shake him out of his established paths.

In the face of such opposition the Jesuits have still managed to win a formidable beachhead. Their work ranges through the various strata of the complicated Indian social scheme from the university lecture hall to the simple catechism classes among the "untouchables." Their missions dot the huge subcontinent from Cape Comorin in the south to the northern Himalayas. A few short years ago they even penetrated the forbidden Kingdom of Nepal and now run two schools there. A correspondent for the New York *Times* managed to secure permission for a visit to this remote kingdom and was dumfounded to hear the Jesuit students lustily singing their school songs to the tunes of the Maine "Stein Song" and the Notre Dame fighting song.

What is of tremendous importance to the Church in India under the present circumstances is the training of an Indian clergy. The major part of this has been in Jesuit hands, and the significance of the work is highlighted by political conditions in the country today. After four centuries and a half of foreign domination India has begun its own life of self-government. It is easy to understand that with that first heady air of freedom the age-old antipathy to the foreigner may be carried somewhat beyond a reasonable limit. So today difficulties have been placed in the way of missionaries entering India from other countries. It may be that foreign missionaries already in India will be expelled. That would mean that the entire fate of the Church would be in the hands of the local clergy. So it is gratifying to note that of the present four thousand-plus priests in India the majority are native-born. But how many practically nameless men and women have labored through the years, in the monsoons, the bitter cold and the scorching heat, to bring the Church to such a degree of preparedness!

The problems in India have been many. The stigma of the foreigner's religion took on a new label when the Christ-bearers offered their message of love to the lowest of India's castes, the untouchables. It then became something unworthy of the higher castes, even though some missionaries always imitated De Nobili and directed their efforts solely towards the Brahmins and leaders. But to become a Christian often meant social ostracism, if not physical harm. All the weight of tradition and custom was against the missionary and his prospective converts. Now nationalism, with some of its more vicious offshoots, has risen as a further obstacle. And always in the background is the threat of communism.

Many of the same problems are encountered in the other Jesuit mission fields of Asia. In Ceylon, where the Italian, French, and American Jesuits have been laboring, the recent independence has been carried to the extreme insofar as there is a strong movement to make Buddhism the state religion. Add to that the same sort of situation which makes India's problems almost insoluble—politics interwoven so closely with religion that the embracing of a new creed means the betrayal of one's entire set of beliefs, religious, social, and political.

The 140 Jesuits who till this island field have had their share of heartaches. God made Ceylon beautiful, so much so that local legend acclaims it as the original Garden of Eden, but the similarity does not extend beyond its physical nature. Once the human factor enters in, so do the problems. The population is a heterogeneous one and the major religions, Buddhism, Hinduism, Islam, would hardly be recognized by their various founders. The million Tamils in Ceylon do not see eye to eye with the five million or so Sinhalese. The majority of the people are very poor, little educated, and suffer from that chronic disease of the tropics, lack of ambition. It takes a tremendous amount of faith for a missionary to face these obstacles and to keep pushing on. But from the outcast leper colony of Mantivu through the jungle village parishes to the higher educational work in the larger cities the Jesuit missionaries carry on the task entrusted to them by the Holy See.

About a century ago the Society of Jesus returned to Indonesia and the treasure islands, the "gold and silver islands" of Ptolemy and the Spice Islands which St. Francis Xavier knew. Then began a harvest of souls which seemed to indicate that one of the most fertile fields in the Far East had been tapped. The long blackout of the Catholic faith under the Dutch Protestants (one of the darkest chapters in so-called Christian annals) had finally come to an end. At the turn of this century other religious orders joined the Jesuits of the Netherlands Province.

Within the last quarter of a century the number of Catholics has increased by 500 per cent—and this is not attributable to the influx of European Catholics, for in that same time their number was halved. One leading factor in that increase was the respect and admiration which the Church won during World War II and the subsequent struggle for Indonesian independence. The people saw clearly during those difficult times that the Church stood above all parties and national differences. It was no longer of the West; it had an independent spiritual mission of its own to fulfill. The day was bright with promise.

The 250 Jesuits of Indonesia know how quickly the clouds of hatred and ancient prejudice can gather. Some of them were still recovering from the rigors of Japanese internment camps when they felt the hostile blast which darkened the future. The majority of the people of Indonesia are Moslem, and as soon as the three-hundred-year rule of the Dutch was ended the anti-West, anti-Christian agitation broke out. Forgotten now was the stand of the Church during the darkest days of the Japanese occupation, when the Catholic party ranked among the first to arouse the country towards total independence.

After World War II the revolt broke out against the Netherlands regime. The guerrillas followed the scorched-earth policy and mission establishments were not spared. Some of the extremists, mostly of the "Hizboullah" (fanatical Moslem troops), massacred priests and burned seminary, college, and mission schools. Most of the property damaged was in the custody of the Jesuits. But the significant thing in the entire affair is the violence of the feeling against the Catholics despite their record of patriotism. It may mean at any time that there will be another eruption in which all foreign missionaries will be expelled or put to death. That would leave the Church in the hands of the Indonesian clergy, still all too few. So, for example, on the main island of Java, not much larger in size than New York State but with fifty million people, the first secular priests were not ordained until the time of the Japanese occupation, the first Javanese priests being nearly all Jesuits.

In Japan the picture is much brighter and the Jesuit activities range from the barren village parish where a priest labored a dozen years among the Buddhists before making his first convert to the university level where the numbers asking for instruction and baptism are high and still increasing. The well-publicized change in the Japanese attitude towards Christianity after Japan's defeat in the war presented an opportunity which called for quick and decisive action. As a result the Society of Jesus departed from its customary modern method of assigning a mission field to an individual province. Japan had been previously staffed by German Jesuits, but the war had decimated the personnel of that province. No other Jesuit province could possibly provide the number of men needed to take full advantage of the opportunity in the Land of the Rising Sun. So a call for volunteers was sent out to the entire Society of Jesus and men were rushed from the countries of Europe, North, Central, and South America. Even the Philippines and South America have contributed their share to the winning to Christ of this nation.

The roster of the more than three hundred and twenty Jesuits in Japan today reads like a United Nations list. Some of the younger men actually fought against each other not so many years ago. But they are working side by side now for a higher cause. A student at Sophia University in Tokyo can pass from class to class and his teacher might be Spanish, German, Japanese, or straight out of Brooklyn. Only one of the many projects is committed to an individual province, a high school in Hiroshima run by California Province Jesuits.

The various works undertaken have been aimed at the facets of Japanese character. The ambition for learning, the instinctive Oriental business sense, the love of the arts, the bruised but still powerful racial pride; all these and more can find their outlet somewhere in the Jesuit system—but each one will also have the overtones of Christ. For these men, a Foreign Legion in the real sense of the term, are missionaries first.

Across the Sea of Japan, in South Korea's capital of Seoul, a handful of Jesuits have recently undertaken a formidable task. It is their job to open up a Catholic university in the war-ravaged city. Such an institution is sorely needed and would be a tremendous boon for the Church here.

One of the big problems is the necessity of learning the Korean tongue, and this onerous task will fall on the shoulders of the American Jesuits of the Wisconsin Province who have been entrusted with this particular field. However, they will be ably assisted by four Korean Jesuits who are members of that same province. To some this undertaking might appear very much of a gamble owing to the unstable political conditions of that region, but when men have the pearl of great price, the spiritual faith of the Son of God to spread, there are times when what is at stake calls for gambling.

All over the Far East falls the shadow of the great cross which today's China is bearing. The story of the Communist persecution there during the last few years need not be repeated. But what it has meant is the ravaging of one of the largest of the Jesuit mission fields. Over seven hundred Jesuits served on the China Mission—Spanish, Irish, Austrian, Portuguese, French, Canadian, Hungarian, and American as well as Chinese. The fate of some of these men is not yet known. The martyrdom and the imprisonment of others are clearly reported on this earth and in heaven. That story is told elsewhere in this book.

There are still close to a hundred Jesuits in those ports of the China mainland such as Hong Kong and Macao. Over six hundred others are ringed around that same mainland. There was a definite policy followed in regard to these men who have been expelled from the various missions in China. The Jesuits have made a point of keeping their men among Chinese-speaking peoples. The motive behind that policy is apparent. These were men who were familiar with the Chinese language, character, and psychology. All of that experience, won sometimes at fearful cost, would have been dissipated in other fields. These men had dedicated their lives to China and there was the hope that they might soon return. So even though they were unwelcome on the mainland they regrouped in Formosa, in the Philippines, and in the countries south and southwest of China proper. In Formosa they are teaching in the government universities; they have penetrated the mountain fastnesses where the aboriginals dwell; they are working among both the Formosans and the mainland exiles throughout the length and breadth of this isle which the Portuguese had named "the beautiful." Here, too, in exile the monumental work of editing a Chinese dictionary in several European languages still goes on. In places like Singapore and Bangkok their first step has been to care for the students attending the government schools. They have been drawn to Indonesia by the number of Chinese whose ties with the homeland make them a ready target for the Communists.

In the barrios of the Philippines they still seek the wandering sheep of China. And under their tutelage Chinese seminarians, secular and Jesuit alike, are being prepared for a priesthood that in itself may be an actual Calvary. But every single one of these dispersed Jesuits remembers hourly those fellow members of the same Society under torture in the prisons of China, helpless in the hands of the greatest evil the Far East has ever known, helpless save for the love of Christ which brought them there.

These are the countries age-becalmed and now suddenly restless with the heady winds of freedom, democracy, and promise. But there is another Jesuit mission field where one comes face to face with the primitive. In the Caroline and Marshall islands of the Pacific a missionary will board ship, usually a copra trader, and disappear beyond the rim of civilization for months at a time. He will sail from island to island, baptizing the new and strengthening the old, trying to draw all further away from the superstitions and primitive practices of their ancestors. Less than fifty Jesuits are asked to cover a watery field of two million square miles of the Pacific.

This is one of the toughest missions there is. Materially there was almost nothing left of church buildings after the Japanese occupation and the American bombardment of World War II. In all the Marshalls only one church was left standing after the cessation of hostilities. Psychologically a missionary is faced with a life of loneliness, apart from both his own and his people, with the unbroken expanse of the Pacific to emphasize his solitude. Living conditions are primitive, the food restricted and monotonous, yet he must maintain his health to endure the rugged grind of island hopping. There the languages differ from atoll to atoll, but even a knowledge of the tongue is not sufficient at times to penetrate the culture and ways of thinking of these peoples.

The Jesuits are thinly spread, almost dangerously so, on account of their fewness; but there has been enough concentration on important islands to set up an educational system of high school level and even to begin a minor seminary. An educated laity can do much to spread Christian ideas (one twenty-year-old catechist converted the entire island of

Murilo), but it may take generations for those ideas to really sink in and permeate the Micronesian way of life.

The Philippine Islands came under the domination of Catholic Spain, and is the only Asiatic country where Europe has made any lasting impression. About two thirds of the people are nominally Catholic but those in the remoter parts of the islands have suffered through the years from the lack of priests. Only in this century, with the return of many of the Spanish clergy to their homeland when the ecclesiastical jurisdiction passed into American hands, was impetus given to the Filipino clergy and religious vocations. Even now there are mountain barrios and sparsely settled areas which a priest can visit only occasionally, sometimes only once a year on the feast of the barrio's patron saint.

The Philippines have always been a major mission field for the Jesuits and over four hundred and thirty of them are scattered from the mountains of northern Luzon to Zamboanga's western tip on the island of Mindanao. Luzon has been principally the scene of their educational work, with the university in Manila itself and other schools in San Pablo, Naga, and Tuguegarao. The famous Manila Observatory, whose weather reports were a "must" for Pacific navigators and which the Japanese sacked and burned during the war is now located at Baguio, in the north. Besides the seminaries for their own members the Jesuits are also entrusted with the training of the diocesan students for the priesthood. Social order work is carried on at a high intellectual level, a vital necessity in the modern Philippines. But one of their proudest works has been their constant care for the lepers on the island of Culion.

On Mindanao, in the province of Cagayan, there are a score of mission stations which dot the country from the Mindanao Sea to the rugged mountain interior. Along the coast of western Zamboanga there are another ten central parishes from which more than fifty other substations in the barrios fan out. There are high schools in both of these provinces in the southern Philippines.

At the opposite end of Asia lies an entirely different world. Call it the Near East or the Levant or the Bible lands. It is the world of the Arab with its almost impenetrable shell of Islam, tougher to crack than the ancient religions of either India or China.

The mission history of the East began in India simply because of this Moslem world which lay athwart the trade routes to the East and had to be circumvented. Back in the days of Xavier the Moslem pincers on North Africa and the Balkans were a constant stranglehold on Europe which forced the trade vessels to sail south around Africa and then on to India, gateway to the Far East.

That world has not changed so much in the last four hundred years. Superficially, in politics, communications, etc., it has softened toward the West. But the one unifying bond of religion still provides the missionary with an insoluble problem. In this part of the earth his success in converting the Moslems is infinitesimal.

There is an explanation for this obduracy but it involves factors which lie outside the scope of this chapter. Islam has to be seen against the background of its origin and history and especially against the psychological make-up of the people among whom it flourished. It never captured the minds of men in the sense that it brought intellectual conviction. It has too many contradictions against the natural law. Islam has never gained a foothold among peoples governed by either intellect or will; it belongs to the people psychologically dominated by emotion. Its strength lies in the weakness of men who are unwilling to labor intellectually or morally. It promises quick results, an easier road, a life without complexity. If we wonder at its success we can remember communism and its superficial attraction in our own days.

It has been difficult to penetrate a world of such a nature, but missionaries have been hammering away on every possible occasion for the last six or seven centuries. It was never a spectacular job, except in its frequent martyrdom; it was only a patient, heartbreaking plugging by almost nameless men and women.

The Jesuits first began their work in what today is Lebanon and Syria in the first part of the seventeenth century. After the restoration of the Society they returned again in 1831 and are still in those regions at the present time. Most of their work, as that of other missionaries in these lands, has been with the Christians, both the Catholics and schismatics, who number about a million and a half in the Near East. These Christians are divided into half a dozen or so different rites, the Catholic section in union with Rome and the dissidents with their roots in the heresies of long ago.

One aim of the missionaries is to bring the latter back into unity again, and across the years the efforts have been quite successful. This work is not to be minimized, for the long history of the Church in the Near East is replete with episodes wherein the chief adversaries to the advance of the faith were themselves Christians. But the growth of the Catholic Rites is due primarily to the work of the missionaries.

The French Jesuits who man the Lebanese and Syrian fields have, in typical fashion, emphasized the intellectual apostolate, but not by any means to the detriment of other work. The influence emanating from the University of St. Joseph in Beirut has been felt not only by the Christians but also among the Moslems. The Jesuits have produced many writings on Islamic themes which the followers of Mohammed have tried to refute, and one Jesuit had the somewhat dubious distinction of being known in the Arab world as "the green scorpion."

At the same time the Jesuits were training the local clergy, traveling the steep mountain trails to the villages whose remoteness has kept them havens for persecuted Christians, sending priests to the Druse tribes, who had, on occasion, slain their fellow missionaries. They provided the higher education on the university level, had charge of the Christian schools in Transjordan, walked the dark bazaars of Damascus, the world's oldest city, and made their contacts quietly and unobtrusively. Their work with the Moslems was necessarily always on a personal basis and no publicity could be given to its outcome. But I remember a convert whom I met once in Damascus who had two passports, one with his original Moslem name and one with his Christian name. He told me that there were quite a few others like himself. For, although the law of apostasy has been publicly stricken from the legal books, a known convert to Christianity must still face social and economic suicide.

Farther east, across the Syrian Desert in the city of Baghdad, the American Jesuits have established a beachhead. Twenty-five years ago the Christian hierarchy asked them to establish a school for Christian youth. In the face of formidable obstacles, prejudice, and hostility, which showed in various ways, they managed to gain a foothold. They hung on through some grim years in which both public opinion and government hostility threatened to close their schools. But with the coming of World War II and the subsequent enrollment of Moslem boys whose higher education could no longer be safely completed outside the confines of Iraq, the tide finally turned. Knowledge and close association broke down the wall of prejudice and misunderstanding. Today, with government help, the Jesuits in Baghdad—fifty in number—have undertaken a further step and erected a university on the higher level.

The French Jesuits who manned the Near East Mission— two hundred in number—have also established themselves in Egypt. One of their particularly successful works was among the Copts of the Upper Nile region. Many of these *fellaheen* have been restored to unity with Rome. Activities similar to those in Lebanon and Syria have been carried on in Egypt, both in regard to school and parish work.

This is the only Jesuit mission in a predominantly Moslem area of the African Continent. The other missions on the Dark Continent are among non-Moslem peoples. There are about nine hundred Jesuits laboring in the entire continent. The oldest mission here is on the island of Madagascar, which was a stopping place for the early missionaries en route to India and where today over three hundred Jesuits of the French Provinces have two large mission fields which they have tilled for well over a century.

The next oldest mission was opened by the Portuguese Jesuits in Zambesi, and shortly afterwards the Belgians concentrated on the Congo. Today this latter mission shows how deeply the spirit of the Church can be implanted among primitive people.

English Jesuits moved into Rhodesia a quarter of a century ago and their work flourished to the extent that it was necessary to call upon the exiled Polish Jesuits to take over part of the territory during World War II.

The French Jesuits, besides their commitments in Syria and Egypt, have also sent men into the region around Lake Chad. And there is another corner of Africa where Jesuits, dressed in lay clothes, conduct one of the leading schools. The laws on the books forbid their presence in the country, but at the request of the ruler they quietly moved in and they go about their business without any fanfare.

Long ago Ignatius Loyola had given them a motto, "For the greater glory of God." On the Alaskan tundra, through steaming jungles and across mountain plateaus, on the banks of the Tigris, the Ganges, the Congo, and a hundred other rivers, that greater glory is reflected in the lives of these men.

8. Social Work on the Missions

Raymond Bernard, s.j.

JESUIT missionaries work in some of the most beautiful countries in the world, the same countries whose exotic sights and charming vistas entice the jaded tourist. But behind the beauty are thousands of people with problems of malnutrition, improper diets, leading to a variety of deficiency diseases, particularly among the children. Illegitimacy rates and infant mortality are oftentimes extraordinarily high. Aboriginal people, especially, are prey to infectious and contagious diseases. There is lack of housing or unhealthy housing. Simple hygienic requirements are not appreciated. Country roads and city streets are filled with large numbers of people suffering skin diseases or infections of the eyes. Curative and preventive medicine is inadequate.

There is lack of work or technical training to plague these people. Not merely one town will be economically depressed, but a whole area. Water will be lacking sometimes for the bare essentials of life. Or the people of a very large area will be entirely dependent upon the success or failure of one crop or industry. Fluctuations in stock markets or one sudden hurricane can leave the natives in wretched conditions for several years. They lack secondary industries; lack initiative or simple knowledge of how to diversify their business life and thus cushion a community against economic disaster.

Besides the health and welfare situation, in which the Jesuit must necessarily interest himself, the cultural and social framework of the people must be understood and respected. Any attempt to force changes on these people leads to problems. The missioner therefore needs to study this aspect of native life and proceed slowly to introduce features of another way of life. He cannot ignore their customs, their language, their mode of life, or their religion if he earnestly wishes to make true Christians of them eventually.

Over the globe today industrialization and economic development programs are accompanied by social problems which the international agencies are studying carefully and on which they are gathering data. The agencies and commissions have recognized that failure to take appropriate action in the health, education, housing, social service, and labor standard fields may impose serious handicaps upon the successful implementation of economic development programs. These situations become the items of agenda for formal meetings long after they are encountered by the missioner, and sometimes, as in the case of the co-operatives, after they have been in some measure greatly ameliorated. Thus it may be said that often the missioner has anticipated the collection of data by some scholarly body and the consequent discussion and programming of activities—he has already seen the whole matter in a small compass and taken action.

The difficulty is that his funds are quite low, his access to the authorities often difficult, his scientific preparation and equipment often inadequate.

The missionary, hardly settling down from his flight or passage, finds himself thrown into activities that vary little in every mission field. There are schools and hospitals, orphanages and credit unions, sick calls and catechist instruction, and many other items. Change the costumes and the language, and the people could be the same all over the world: the poor, the sick, the lame, the needy, the neglected—a tremendous part of the world's population. If all the works and plans of missioners everywhere could be thoroughly described and compared and co-ordinated, probably there would appear a magnificent master plan for the various Point Four suggestions and programs.

The Jesuit missionary—or any other—goes out to aid people to love God and serve God and their neighbors. Sometimes he seems remarkably preoccupied with material concerns. But the people and their neighbors are human beings, made of body and soul, living and working and suffering in a very material world. Therefore the missioner cannot ignore the material world around him, from which the people and himself take their support and their bare existence. The physical world is there, it must be acknowledged and used.

But the primary concern of the missioner is not with the physical world, but with the spiritual life and the practice of virtue among his people. He studies the physical, material surrounding in order to so arrange the elements in it that the people will not have to spend every second of their life in grubbing out their existence. He knows that a hungry person and a sick person will not put much attention on the catechism and Christian virtue.

Such is the missioner's primary concern, his pervading motivation that has led him to this new environment, this unpromising and materially unpleasant commitment.

This is the conviction that has led so many missioners in past centuries to undertake various projects for the economic and social improvement of the lot of their people. It is the same motive that discloses to a Father Marion Ganey the possibilities of credit unions and co-operatives for the improvement of living conditions among the Honduras Indians along the Caribbean coast and suggests that the same aid could be extended to natives five thousand miles away, down in the Fiji Islands. It is the same drive that has led to the establishment of clinics in India, of schools in the Amazon jungles, of some sort of local government among migrant tribes, of organization and instruction of catechists, in the slow formation of labor unions among the Philippine workers and farmers, and it is the same motive that will invent new projects and adapt contemporary institutions in order to enable the people to live good lives.

Today the motivation is stronger, perhaps, than ever. In so many lands agents of communism are feverishly at work to try to win over the leaders and the people, or at least to stir up ferment which would ease the way of conquest, and it so happens that the Communist agents find most promising precisely those areas which the Christian missioners select. These are the underdeveloped areas, generally, the regions in which the United States wisely was once going to apply a Point Four program for reasons which both we and the Communist agents should understand very well. The fact that these two forces are working to improve the material lot of the people should be convincing persuasion of their tremendous needs.

Should one need it, there is a scriptural justification for helping people satisfy their material needs. St. James and St. John say that no one can say to a cold person, "Go and be warmed," and he will thereby be warmed, or "Go and be fed," and expect that his stomach will be filled by mere words and wishes. The implication is that if we love our neighbor and profess this love as a Christian tenet and obligation we need to implement our profession by deeds. The effectiveness of our belief would be proved by our practice. "By their fruits you shall know them."

What are some of these fruits by which men will know that these missioners are true Christians? A whole book could probably be devoted to an account of them, and even this would merely chronicle the items.

For one prime example, the exploits of an Illinois Jesuit who has worked among the Fiji Islanders to establish credit unions at the request of the Governor, Sir Ronald Garvey. After two years of meeting with natives and discussing the idea of setting up a "people's bank" Father Marion Ganey and an associate had established 154 credit unions by the summer of 1956, with more than seventeen and a half thousand members, a truck bank to reach remote villages, and some two hundred thousand dollars in assets. All this in a district where the majority of the islanders are Methodist.

So great has his fame grown that today the natives have composed special ceremonial dances in his honor. The two greatest modern events, in the esteem of the natives, have been the visit of the British Queen and the coming of Father Ganey.

The people themselves could show you what changes the credit unions have brought to them. Villages that formerly used kerosene tins for cooking now employ pots and pans, and coconut shells as crockery have yielded to real, plain but wonderful cups and saucers, the Stone Age equipment in tools has been replaced by axes, shovels, and various tools. Robert C. Miller, a newspaper correspondent, has epitomized it: "Many a Fijian has been married in style, buried in class and kept out of jail for delinquent taxes by his village credit union."

Every Sunday afternoon in the typical South Sea island villages of this group the community conducts elaborate ceremonies during which the bank is opened, deposits are made, loans considered, and the books balanced. Before each business session the traditional making of kava, the local milky liquid, occupies the attention of the crowd and thus provides gallons of refreshment during the course of business transactions of the afternoon.

The only American in the project, Father Ganey has the

technical aid of an Australian bank clerk, Richard Phillips of Dubbo, an Anglican.

Each enterprise is completely of the people and is housed in the village of thatched roofs. The officials of each credit union are chosen by their fellow villagers and have learned a deep sense of responsibility.

Requests for loans do not read like the requests made at Wall Street offices and in the major banks of the world. To begin with, the natives practice their requests and rehearse for hours in order to make their appeals persuasive. They are definitely sincere in their requests, but they want to make sure the treasurer, secretary, and directors of the local union understand their sincerity. The amounts requested are never very high, sometimes reaching twenty-five dollars for house repairs. Generally they are for the purchase of chicken wire (twelve-fifty), payment of taxes (about seven-fifty), radio repairs (ten dollars), a new fish net (ten dollars), or a new gaslight (fifteen dollars). The repayment of the loans extends for a long period and is made in small amounts each week.

Deposits are often made by youngsters while their proud parents watch them set a few pennies before the treasurer—just as in the United States or elsewhere. Thrift is an important lesson in the Fijis and everywhere else. The children and parents are proud of their passbooks and growing accounts, and the whole village treasures the thick ledgers in which columns of figures show the whole series of financial transactions.

To facilitate matters and insure a certain regularity about them the bank truck moves from village to village on a 185-mile circuit on Monday and a 140-mile route on Tuesday as it collects the village deposits. The truck not only collects payments, but it also cashes checks and makes payments. It meets the village treasurers all along the way, waiting with the moneybags in hand, all alert at the sound of the approaching truck's horn. Some village treasurers manage to meet the split-second timetable of the truck only by walking for miles after the conclusion of their Sunday local ceremonial to transact their business at an appointed spot on the road.

Somewhat the same remarkable story had unrolled in British Honduras, where Father Ganey had first been assigned to do missionary work. In the hill villages where the mahogany workers lived and the small farmers, the Jesuit had initiated his career as a credit union builder. The Governor of the British colony there had been impressed by his efforts and sacrifices—and so had many other persons who learned of them and saw the credit unions in operation. Against all sorts of odds Father Ganey had set up a credit union enterprise which is still operating quite successfully. Here again he was an adviser, not a principal participant, and the activity was the people's own, as it was based on their own convictions and staffed by their own elected agents.

Farther to the east across the Caribbean, in Jamaica, Father John Peter Sullivan, S.J., a Bostonian, had earlier toiled to set up credit unions for his people and co-operatives for his fishermen. He is something of a pioneer in the work. He has seen his efforts almost collapse through the sudden destruction of a hurricane, but again and again he has rebuilt. His efforts provided a model and a stirring inspiration to missioners and people in the whole Caribbean area. Again in a democratic process the Jamaican members run the operation. There has been an attraction about this project, so that it drew a very capable Missouri credit union organizer, Lee O'Brien, and his wife to Jamaica for their vacation one summer and benefited from their expert advice and help.

When Father Sullivan took up his work at St. George's College, Kingston, Jamaica, he inherited the directorship of the local boys' sodality. Things went well for a while, but despite the piety and co-operation the boys manifested, Father Sullivan felt that something was missing. Could this group spirit meet the test of outside effort, of working in the market place, of affecting one's neighbor for good? As it was, the boys listened regularly to a series of talks on the Mystical Body of Christ at their meetings, followed the dialogue Mass at the monthly gatherings, but parted at the doors of the college afterwards.

The boys and the director faced it. They selected fourteen fellows who wanted to do something about the situation. For thirteen months these boys continued to meet one evening a week to discuss and investigate the economic conditions of the island and determine the possibilities of some economic uplift movement. They studied in particular the credit union idea.

Soon this corps of would-be economic saviors went out to contact the people and bring them the new tidings. They walked along the beaches, stopped where fishermen sat, and began to talk credit unions. They met the clerks in government offices and talked. They contacted the department store workers and sold them the idea. They went out from the towns to the land, and there they talked with the farmers, always about credit unions. By 1944 over two hundred and twenty-one credit unions had made a start in the island through the efforts of fourteen young men under the guidance of a young priest from Boston.

Meantime the sodality within the college had set up its own credit union as a laboratory for these economic experiments. The external project was put under the wing of the extension department of the college as an educational work.

In 1943 the government showed interest in the new movement, which also had some groups independent of the Catholic leadership. A conference called by all the groups elected a St. George boy as chairman and Father Sullivan as president.

From points all around the West Indies came questions and requests for further information. Barbados, Trinidad, and British Honduras sent appeals. In Trinidad the credit union idea took such firm hold that the meetings were begun in the bishop's palace.

For seventeen years Father Sullivan has been building Jamaican credit unions and co-operatives. In the past seven years more than five hundred co-operatives were formed in British Guiana. Where there had been none when Father Sullivan began his work in Jamaica, March of 1956 saw a week-long meeting sponsored by the Technical UN Food and Agriculture Organization and the Caribbean Commission, with delegates in attendance from eleven countries.

The aims and effects of the credit union movement in the missions were well summed up at this meeting by Father Sullivan:

"Everywhere I have seen that when a co-operative becomes solid in a particular territory, it contributes to economic democracy, and from economic democracy to political democracy—the glorious goal to which so many of our Caribbean people are marching in a march that today can never be stopped.

"I am worried that we are not going fast enough. Some people are willing to go only as fast and as far as they are financially assisted to do by the government. That is not the ideal."

When Caribbean hurricanes destroyed much property along the southern coast of British Honduras in October 1945, it was Father Ganey's St. Peter Claver Credit Union at Punta Gorda which proposed a plan for co-operative rebuilding of homes. Owners of damaged houses would be allowed to borrow from their union the funds needed to pay workmen a dollar a day, on the stipulation that the laborers at once deposit thirty cents of each dollar to their own accounts, in order that the credit union might extend loans to as many of the homeless of the district as possible. This first union to be established in British Honduras thus exercised its initiative in undertaking community self-help some time before the government furnished aid from Belize.

In 1934 missionary Jesuits, hailing chiefly from the New York area, began a Crusade for Social Justice in the Philippines. This has been acknowledged as a profound influence on the Filipino Constitution because of the embodiment there of much of its platform in important social legislation.

For use in Jesuit schools in the islands a catechism of social principles was worked out and adopted widely. Thus for five years before war broke out at Pearl Harbor every student in a Jesuit institution was grounded in social principles and ideas. These social principles went out over the radio, through the press and public forums. Each week an English broadcast was made for an hour, and a broadcast in native dialect for forty-five minutes.

The summer of 1945 (July 2–August 3) saw the first Institute on Social Work in the Mission sponsored by the Institute of Social Sciences (since renamed Institute of Social Order) at St. Louis University. This project was in line with the thought expressed by the Very Reverend J. Moyersoen, then Superior of thirteen hundred Jesuits working at the time in India: "One of the greatest services you can render us in India is to promote the *social training* of young men destined for the missions." The summer institute was a start of exploration towards an eventual program of special studies in missionary preparation.

Next summer the institute was continued. Its courses in the four-week session were especially designed to aid interested missioners to raise the economic level of their people by the use of modern sociological techniques. Classes were held in marketing, credit and distribution, co-operatives, rural life, British colonial policy, United States government aid, and missiology. The faculty included Father Sullivan of Jamaica, Father William Gibbons, S.J., then on the staff of *America*, Miss Mary Dooling of the National Sodality office, Father

Edward Murphy, S.J., the first Doctor of Missiology in this country, Father Leo C. Brown, S.J., director of the Institute of Social Sciences, and Father Bernard W. Dempsey, S.J.

New and perplexing problems were rising in the vast lands in which missionaries worked. How to make contact with the caste peoples of India was a question that plagued many a modern apostle. Father James Creane wandered up and down the Bihari section, clothed in a wanderer's outfit, hoping to make friends of the aboriginal Santals. For years he explored, talked, wandered, sought to win acquaintances among these outcastes, but in the end found that he had made only slight progress. Two other Jesuits made a similar attempt by dressing as sannyasis, or holy men, and wandering among the natives. They were accepted to some degree inasmuch as the people came to look upon them as "men of God," who brought medicines, loving care and friendship, and observed strict fasts and penances. The approach via this native role is, obviously, limited and not yet very fruitful; but the fact that these experiments have been made in our own day indicates that more serious effort and study will be devoted to the matter.

A different approach in India is the instrument of the labor school. In Jamshedpur, a heavily industrialized coal field center which today has a population of over two hundred thousand but in 1911 numbered only seven thousand persons, a labor school experiment has been inaugurated. This city of phenomenal growth draws its lifeblood from the huge Tata Iron Works, in which some seventy thousand men work to produce two million tons of steel a year. Just outside Jamshedpur, however, you find the ancient customs and beliefs of the natives unchanged from antiquity. In Bihar, the province on the Chota Nagpur plateau, approximately one quarter of the 4,400,000 people are aborigines. There are only about ten thousand Catholics, a number of whom work on the great railroad lines and are served by "railroad chaplains" (missioners who move along the main lines).

The director of the labor school there, Father Thomas Q. Enright, S.J., has given great aid to the growth of unions among the impoverished workmen, much to the satisfaction of management. He has sent out at least one of his staff for special studies in the United States. Jamshedpur has, of course, fine Catholic school facilities to which many engineers and professional men send their Hindu children.

These present-day missionaries in India are inspired in their social work by the example of two outstanding men, Fathers Lievens, S.J., and Hoffman, S.J., who preceded them. Probably the most amazing missionary that India has seen since the time of Xavier was Father Constantine Lievens, who worked in the whole of the Chota Nagpur area. The section is as large as his native Belgium. At the age of twenty-nine Lievens went to the mission of Chota Nagpur to care for fifty-six Catholics. When he died in 1893, eight years later, he was a prematurely aged man but he had the consolation of having, in a short time in the mission, personally baptized twenty-five thousand of the aborigines. His organization and example had led to the conversion of close to fifty thousand more. Sixty-five years after he began the work, when the first aboriginal bishop of India, Bishop Kujur, was consecrated in Ranchi, which had been the center from which Lievens worked, there were some four hundred thousand Catholics in the Chota Nagpur area, of whom a quarter of a million belonged to the Ranchi diocese.

It was really through his efforts to obtain justice and security for the aborigines that Father Lievens opened the way for mass conversions among the aboriginal Oraons, Mundas, and Kharias. These aboriginal people, native to India before Aryans entered the country, are a simple shy group. They had for centuries before Lievens' time been at the mercy of police officials, powerful landowners, and moneylenders who, trading on their ignorance, had taken control of much of the aborigines' land and kept them in a perpetual state of debt amounting to serfdom. Lievens set about to correct this situation by becoming an expert in the land law of the area and was soon able to give the people clear advice on their rights and ways of recovering them. After he won, as legal adviser, several cases for his jungle clients in the high court of Ranchi, the news quickly spread that this Father would right their wrongs and the aborigines started swarming in to Lievens for help. He also did what he could in establishing schools and co-operatives and credit societies to stabilize the new-found gains for the people. It was his reputation as a champion of justice and an extraordinarily charitable man which won the hearts of the aborigines and led to their mass conversions.

It might be interesting to note that when men from a new village came to Lievens asking for baptism he would instruct them and then send them back to their own village telling them that he would come to visit them only when they had instructed and prepared for baptism the rest of their native village. In this way, using ready-made catechists, he would find whole villages fairly well prepared for baptism when he found the time to visit them.

Also, incredibly, Father Lievens found time in his short period on the missions before his health broke to translate and write in several native languages short biographies, a history of the Old and New Testaments, catechisms, and parts of Scripture.

His successor, Father J. B. Hoffman, did much to stabilize Lievens' work. Hoffman set up a central Chota Nagpur bank which served as the basis for a credit union which finally was taking care of over five thousand villages. Through its granting of loans for cattle and land development under the direction of local members of the credit union the bank is able to help the aborigines achieve a certain amount of economic security.

In Mexico today the twenty-six Jesuits working among the forty thousand Tarahumare Indians in the northern, desolate area three hundred miles from El Paso follow a comprehensive program ultimately to incorporate the weakened tribe into Western culture by means of schools, factories, and religious instructions.

The Tarahumares wander about with the seasons, from mountaintop to valley, planting just enough corn and other staples to take care of tomorrow. They generally live in a cave or, if fortunate, in a hut of stones and scrap lumber. In 1905 the Jesuits set up a boarding school, by which they hoped to wean the children away from the wandering habits of the tribe and make them over into responsible citizens. Revolution and religious persecution, however, soon interrupted this plan. In 1940 the school property of the Tarahumare Mission was returned by the government to the Jesuits.

As a result of the sporadic and secret work carried on by the Jesuit Brothers during the years of harassment, and the resumed program after the restoration of the property, there has been established at Sisoguichi an "agricultural-industrial colony" of some twenty-two families, alumni and alumnae, each with a house and a field. Jesuit Brothers run the whole operation and have set up facilities for making lumber, dressing leather, making shoes, and providing other basic needs. The town is yet quite simple, but its unique distinction is that its inhabitants come from a nomadic, illiterate people. For the use of these people there have been published a dictionary of the Tarahumare language, textbooks in basic fields, a book of devotions, and a missal.

An alumnus of the Jesuit college at Guadalajara, Dr. Adrian Quiroz, started a hospital there, inducing two or three interns to come each year for their apprenticeship.

Fifty nuns labor in the hospital and in the various schools. Prospects are bright in this first town established for nomads in northern Mexico.

Remote and mountainous Chihuahua, established as a mission in the seventeenth century and more recently revived, has seen the labors of Mexican Jesuits through persecution and peace materialize in a settlement with carpenter shop, shoemaking shop, tannery, school, and other activities.

Such projects, together with Mexico's own "Boys' Town," may indicate that the Jesuit efforts in Central and South America follow the bent of the ancient Reducciónes of Paraguay and Brazil, large communities set up to provide atmosphere for the Christian life of the natives. But this would be a presumptuous generalization, for there are various other social works undertaken in this half hemisphere.

In Cuba's labor circles the outstanding leader is Father Manuel Foyaca, a professor of sociology at Belen College, author and street speaker. Everyone respects the good, spellbinding Padre.

Jesuits from the Spanish province of Leon are actively engaged in various social works in the island of the Dominican Republic.

British Guiana, the long sprawling colony off the northeast coast of South America, has had English Jesuits long absorbed in the co-operative development. There a giant with a soft voice, Father A. V. Ellis, S.J., did some tough organizational work before co-operative credit and marketing were set up.

One could not ignore the outstanding achievements of Father Frank Kempel, S.J., of Akron, Ohio, in the Jamaican social front. Father Kempel was the prime mover in starting the whole egg-marketing co-operative on the island. Most of the members of his organization are Protestant, but they show their esteem and gratitude for his talents by keeping him as president of the federation.

Another Jamaican worker is native-born, Father Charles Judah, S.J., whose efforts have seen a co-operative religious-goods store set up for the islanders.

Thus one social activity after another may spring up once the ground has been broken and the laity are seriously trained in the methods of the apostolate. In Jamaica, besides the egg-marketing co-op and the religious-goods stores already mentioned, there has emerged another plan for better living. The Holy Family Homestead aims to furnish small plain houses for lay families, to keep them from growing up in one room or two, to prevent the resultant health and moral conditions in restricted quarters. In this work the chief mover was Father Raymond R. Sullivan, S.J. Discussing his aims, this missionary briefly put into one sentence the motivation and objective of all missionaries when he said, "Every missionary hopes to place his people in circumstances so that they may grow up in an atmosphere of Christian charity, justice, sacrifice, and selflessness."

Again and again the thought recurs: the human being must live in an environment conducive to human existence and aspiration. Whether he teaches in some high school, in a city, in a mission field, or labors among the Caribs or the Tamils, the Cantonese or the Eskimos, the missioner runs into the identical problem. That undoubtedly is the reason why so many of the remedies proposed in the fields and in institutes and conferences run along economic lines. It is a situation in which the simplicity and strong appeal of the co-operative movement seem to offer a natural solution.

Yet there are other attempts to humanize the living conditions of the missions and increase the effectiveness of the works under way.

A Jesuit agricultural school at Angers, France, now directed by Father H. de Montbrun, S.J., has sought since 1889 to restore agriculture to some healthiness and respect. This group grew and branched out, setting up at least two effective instruction centers in North Africa for agricultural colonists among the Mohammedan Arabs and Berbers.

At Calcutta, for instance, the Belgian Jesuits have, in co-operation with their confreres from Canada, Malta, Yugoslavia, and Sicily, set up an Oriental Institute for the apostolate among the Hindus and the Moslems of India. Thus there is offered an opportunity to study together the cultures and customs and history of various groups and districts, all with the view of co-ordinating the mission work of the present and the future.

A special meeting of mission personnel in the tropics in 1947 stimulated much thought and much activity. Wider participation and leadership by the laity was insisted upon, as the severest problems are those which primarily and continuously concern the laymen and the family: poverty, small farming, fragmentation and inadequacy of land holdings, pauperization and exhaustion of the soil, Communist infiltration, serfdom to immense estates and factories and foreign capital, restoration of confidence and initiative to the mission people themselves. At such a meeting racial differences must be ignored if full effectiveness is sought; language barriers must be overcome by various translation apparatuses; and, most important, the real and present problems must be faced honestly, freely, critically, constructively. It is the growth of the Church everywhere which is at stake, not just one person's sensitivity or another's pride in accomplishment or a third's preferences and dislikes.

A large and important meeting held in the Philippines in 1950, named the "Priests' Institute for Social Action" and organized principally by Father James J. McGinley, S.J., now stationed at Fordham University, may be taken as typical of the more frequent gatherings of priests active in missionary work and in missionary lands. The glimpses which will be given here are drawn from a long private report by Father Catalino Arevalo, S.J., who was present.

The organizers and delegates, gathered from all points in the Philippines, were motivated by one thought: to know and tell about the Catholic social program in a beloved land seriously threatened by both an industrial revolution and a Communist infiltration. They had come by bus, plane, car, ship, train—123 of them, representing fourteen dioceses and archdioceses, one apostolic vicariate, one apostolic prefecture. Twelve religious orders and congregations had sent representatives. Priests had come from twenty-five provinces and ten cities, but the majority were from rural and agricultural districts. There were seventy-five secular priests, forty-eight religious priests. The religious belonged to these bodies: Congregation of the Missions (Vincentians), Congregation of the Immaculate Heart of Mary, Congregation of the Most Holy Redeemer, Mill Hill Missionaries, Missionary Oblates of Mary Immaculate, Order of Discalced Carmelites, Order of Friars Minor Capuchin, Sacred Heart Missionaries, Society of the Divine Word, Society of Foreign Missions of Quebec, Society of Jesus, and Society of St. Columban.

They expected and, as the director promised in a short introductory talk, they received facts, motives, and methods in the social apostolate.

In series the delegates received a picture of the social conditions of the whole area (as distinct from the overwhelming problems each one of them knew in his personal domain). The increase in population is seen as a steadily growing problem (it was estimated at the time that the population would be doubled by 1980). Figures were given on land ownership, widespread tenancy, and the relationship of the Huk disturbance to the extreme poverty. Then the Catholic social program as drawn from documents treating property, the dignity of the individual, and the authority of the Church in social matters was presented in summary, with emphasis that it is not a haphazard accumulation but a real program.

A talk on the role of the family in social reconstruction

followed by the famous John P. Delaney, S.J., who had pioneered in the Cana movement in the United States and
whose death in 1955 was felt as a serious loss by leaders and
masses of the islands. The speaker would have the assembled
priests teach their people the dignity of the family, its importance, and its responsibilities.

Discussion, questions and answers, several brief talks on
the weaknesses of liberal capitalism as the real source of
strength for the Communists, then a doctrinal talk on the
Mystical Body of Christ as related to and affecting daily life,
charity, co-operation between bishops and clergy, secular
and regular priests, clergy and laity—such is the plan as followed the first day of this particular institute.

Next day classes treated the psychological attitudes of
clergy towards the people (of whom 92 per cent are working-
men); the common points in the outstanding social documents of the day, *Rerum Novarum, Quadragesimo Anno,
Statement of the American Hierarchy* (1940), *Statement of
the Philippine Hierarchy* (1949); the necessity of unionism;
the living-wage problem; the actual cost of living in this particular region; the dangers of paternalism; the means of
achieving genuine social justice.

Next the institute considered the need for seeking a solution with the aid of the people who are most interested—responsible labor unions, since the employers had not felt any
particular responsibility so far and the state could not furnish much aid. The means of working out a solution were
explored: Young Christian Workers, Catholic Action, cate-
chetics, street preaching, labor schools, and so on. The Apostolic Delegate visited the gathering and gave a strong
exhortation, and the archbishop had visited briefly on the
opening day; obviously the meeting had the hearty approval
of both dignitaries.

Economic life, domestic life, social life, political life—these
were the facets considered by the assembled delegates anx-

ious to set about a concerted program of social reconstruction in a war-devastated land.

Such realization of the need of more study and social training for missionaries is growing. For it is clear that the man and woman who as missionary priest and Sister will go out one day after a "departure ceremony" to work for religious truth in a foreign land need to be as qualified as the specialist in any other field. He and she need to know the real problems of the people and share them. This was the way of Christ.

9. Missionary Educators

Barry Ulanov

A POPULAR myth of the modern era is the one in which some eternally nameless Jesuit asserts that if he can supervise the education of a child until he is six or seven there is nothing he cannot do with him thereafter. Thus, this persistent fiction goes on, do Jesuits preserve the faith and extend their control over the faithful.

As a reflection of actual Jesuit practice there is almost nothing to commend in this myth except its suggested emphasis upon the importance of knowledge at any age and upon the need of systematic training. Indoctrination, however, has never been an aim of real Jesuits. Rather breadth of knowledge, humanistic wisdom, and formally systematized education have been the treasured values of Jesuits since Ignatius' time, both at home and on the missions.

Modern Jesuits show the same zeal as their predecessors in the pursuit of knowledge and its dissemination. They have distinguished themselves in the natural sciences. Among leading astronomers have been Father Francis de Vico, who discovered forty-six comets and made important studies of the rings of Saturn and Venus, and the great Angelo Secchi, one of the founders of astrophysics as well as one of the first to make observations of the sunspots, inventor of the meteorograph and spectral type of the fixed stars. In seismography American Jesuits were pioneers and hold a pre-eminent position.

On the missions proper Jesuits made the observatory at Zikawei a center of distinguished meteorological study and an invaluable aid for commerce and maritime shipping in the Orient. The same can be said of the Manila Observatory, where Faura and Algué especially did important work. The former invented the cynconoscope, the latter the barocyclonometer.

The historic concern of the Society for languages is reflected by Dahlmann, an outstanding Indianologist; Zimmerman, an authority on Sanskrit; Wieger, who produced twelve volumes on Chinese literature; Boucher and Ralouin, who wrote guides and dictionaries for both classical and dialect Chinese; Desgoding, who is the author of a Tibetan-French-Latin dictionary; Butaye, of a Congolese and a Kicongo-French dictionary; Férard and Barnum, authors of an Ojibway and Innuit dictionary. Valuable work has been accomplished by the various university presses on the missions. Of special importance has been the publications of the press at the Jesuit University of Beirut. They range from translations of the Bible and liturgy to new dictionaries and studies in archaeology and history in more than seven languages. Although modern missionaries cannot match the literary endeavors of men like Stephens and Beschi, they perform a valuable service through periodicals, newspapers, and general books. This past year Jesuits issued about fifteen hundred books, and were editing more than thirteen hundred periodicals and newspapers. A great proportion of them were published in missionary countries. Works of the press are peculiarly emphasized by modern Jesuits both at home and abroad.

Other traditional fields have not been neglected. Father

Rahouis' important *Memoires Concernant l'Histoire Naturelle de l'Empire Chinois,* his ten volumes on the marine shells of Nanking and Central China, besides other works on the Philippines, Indochina, and a complete herbarium of China, are scholarly work reminiscent of the very first Jesuit missionaries. Even the termites of India have been accorded authoritative treatment by Father Assmuth. In cartography a modern general map of China and an atlas of the Upper Yangtze Valley have been published by Chevalier. The Philippines have been rather exhaustively studied by Algué and his fellow Jesuits. They have issued scientific studies of the winds and sea, the magnetic and seismologic conditions of the archipelago, as well as reports on its linguistics and ethnography. The first complete geographical atlas of the Philippines was produced by Algué and his Jesuit associates.

It is true that modern missionaries do not stand out as much for their scientific work as their predecessors. This is because for the most part they are no longer pioneering in the various fields and many other secular scientists are engaged in similar work. But they still display a love of knowledge and an awareness of its usefulness both for the faith and for men.

Of greater importance today is the formal educational work of Jesuit missionaries. This is at once extensive and varied, and at the same time quite unified in its basic aims and approach. For Jesuit education is, in fact, a vast empiricism, a daily compounding of experiences based upon a rationale worked out three and a half centuries ago. A grasp of the Jesuit plan of education makes more intelligible the story of Jesuit schools in the various mission countries.

From its earliest beginnings as a missionary and a teaching order the Society of Jesus has practiced that systematic mixture of the fixed and the fluctuating which primarily led, in the government of souls, to the formulation of the retreat and the formation of the spiritual director and, in the educational field, to the Ratio Studiorum. It ultimately became the ideal of Jesuit life, the ideal of the contemplative in action. St. Francis Xavier and Matthew Ricci were capable of handling the immovable facts of the faith with such a mobility of expression as to make their demonstrations nearly irresistible wherever they went. It is that sort of flexibility which the modern Jesuit must practice as he moves among cultures, speaking the languages and teaching the philosophies at once of permanence and change.

An emphasis on the human marks the Ratio Studiorum as one of the most malleable of educational methods and gives it a special adaptability to the missions in the twentieth century. If reduced to a hard core of prescriptions and proscriptions, in which the teacher is limited to his *praelectio* and the student to an accompanying series of exercises, the Ratio would long ago have died alongside the birch rod and hornbook it did so much to combat. If expanded to the elasticity of that principle of accommodation which is no principle at all but simply a system of self-demand which should be discarded no later than at the time a baby emerges from rompers, the Ratio would be today as worthless as any jungle code must be in a civilized society. It is not in extremes that the Ratio atque Institutio Studiorum Societatis Jesu finds its vitality and its range, but in a reasonable system of checks and balances in which each branch of the governing body is limited by the counsels and commandments of Christianity, and the service to which all are dedicated is defined again and again as human.

Both the Ratio of 1599 and the revised code published in 1832, eighteen years after the restoration of the Society, emphasize the flexibility of the plan: changes can be instituted by Superiors to fit special needs in particular countries. Any number of Generals of the Society have stressed this adaptability of the Ratio Studiorum and some have gone further, insisting that any valid pedagogical method, of any particular epoch, should find expression either in the Ratio itself or in the use to which the Society puts it. Thus, in practice as well as in theory, the Ratio encourages a balance of prescribed studies and of electives; of contests and competitions which crown the victors with special rewards and public recognition, and of discussion groups which take on the nature of a legislative assembly; of courses which develop useful skills of a vocational kind joined in curricula with others quite impractical in one sense, thoroughly liberal in another, and of a considerable humanist inflection in still another sense.

It is neither an empty redundancy to iterate and reiterate the human purpose of the Ratio Studiorum nor an underscoring of the obvious to insist upon its divine sanctions. For it is only with such motivating power that the Society can direct the enormous motions—of such geographical length and of such spiritual depth—of its educational arms across and around the world. Nothing less than the universal is enough to fit all the particular needs and desires of all the places in which the Jesuits today set up school. And nothing less than the riches of the Christian tradition, of every type and kind—the crabbed exercises of a Donatus, which for so long stoked the fires of Latin learning, and the magnificent audacity of an Erasmus, which brought modern scholarship alive; the vision of a Vives, and the orderliness of a Johannes Sturm; the depth of insight of an Augustine, and the prodigious embrace of an Aquinas—all this and more must be sifted and sorted every day by Jesuits teaching somewhere, everywhere, if the work of the Society is to go forward in the spirit and tradition of its founders.

In just the sixteen mission areas in which American Jesuits work some twenty-four languages and countless dialect variations upon them are spoken. To the Philippines, Ceylon, India, Formosa, and Japan; to Korea, Iraq, Alaska, Honduras, and the island of Jamaica; across the two-thousand-mile domain of the Caroline and Marshall Islands and to the hinterlands of the United States, the American Society brings method and purpose and a large catalogue of courses—at the university and college level, the secondary and the elementary school plane—which could not be listed, much less described, in any volume short of encyclopedic dimensions. In this vast realm of the Ratio, American Jesuits administer and teach in some fifteen universities and colleges, twenty-five high schools and five seminaries for the native clergy, in addition to taking part in the operation, maintenance, and direction of several hundred more elementary and high schools.

The figures are impressive; they indicate clearly the boldness and breadth of the business of education in which the Society is engaged. But behind them there is a far more significant and more dramatic story, the story of the many people the Society's teachers are serving, of the vital need they are filling, of the great problems they are facing.

There is, for example, the story of the overcrowded land of Japan, into which the Society's Sophia University graduates must go, even as the graduates of any other Japanese institution of higher learning, and into which they are making their way with a "rate of placement," as the assistant dean puts it, "higher than the national rate in Japan." "We are trying," Father William A. Laney explains, "to prepare the young men to take their place in Japanese society. We wish to give them a solid philosophical background so that they can think for themselves in a changing Japan. They are the ferment for a new citizenry." There are gratifying successes in the placement of graduates. And there are the large-scale problems of any educational institution in Japan: "Communism has infiltrated the Japanese public school system and its tenets are taught by the professors of some of the big universities. The economic problem in an overcrowded land is ever present. Our work is held back by a lack of men and money . . . especially the lack of men with a fluent knowledge of Japanese." In an attempt to remedy this latter defect every newcomer among the priests and scholastics is given a two-year language course.

The Society runs schools which cannot possibly accept all those who apply: of eight hundred applicants for one school 160 were taken; of six hundred for the new secondary school in Hiroshima only 120 could be accepted.

At the first Jesuit high school in Japan, Rokko in Kobe, the problems are those which afflict secondary school education generally in Japan. Great changes have been wrought by the introduction of co-education (the cant phrase is "democratic progressive education"), by the prolongation of compulsory education beyond the primary grades and the broad dissemination of films, magazines, comic books—popular culture at its lowest level—made, poorly made, in America. Discipline is not easy to maintain and, with success dependent upon the record of graduates in the *daigaku nyugaku-shiken*, the college entrance examinations, a "specter," in the words of a priest who teaches at Rokko, "haunts" the school. It is abnormal, Father Robert Flynn admits, "but the abnormal fact is there: a few hundred thousand Japanese high school graduates try every year to get into the universities, and not just any university, but a top-rate one, and there just aren't places for them." The pressure is too much for many; a teacher or spiritual director hesitates to ask for any sacrifice of time for anything else. The way out? Father Flynn answers the question simply: "Success in the entrance exams—there is no other." But at a Jesuit school much more than preparation for college entrance exams must be made and so somehow a delicate balance must be found and kept, that balance which accounts for the fact that of the two hundred Catholic boys at Rokko (of a school population of 870) the vast majority were baptized after entering the school.

In the Hiroshima school the entrance exams for the universities remain, according to a teacher there, a crippling burden. Here, too, the size of the job to be done is staggering: the number of applicants for study at the school is fully five times the number that can be accepted. But there is satisfaction in the fact that conversions are being made and that the undergraduates include the son of a Shinto priest, which indicates the far reach of such education. Another insight into the structure of a Jesuit school six thousand miles away from its home province is provided by a list of the faculty: there are four full-time lay teachers, three of whom are Catholics; three part-time teachers, one of whom is a Catholic; three American Jesuit priests, one German priest, one Japanese Scholastic, and one Brother.

At St. Joseph's College in Trincomalee, Ceylon, a major difficulty is that instruction must be trilingual, in Sinhalese, Tamil, and English. As a priest at the school admits, "Unity suffers" as a consequence of the division of classes into language groups, and the Ratio cannot be followed except in spirit. The recent legislation making Sinhalese the official language of the island will not solve the difficulty, for exceptions are made for the Tamil-speaking districts, of which Trincomalee is one.

Again, at St. Xavier's in Patna, in the state of Bihar in India, the question of languages is a troublesome one. Although the medium of instruction is English, all the students likewise study Hindi, the national language. The rector of the college adds, "Those students whose mother tongue is Urdu or Bengali may take classes in those subjects." One indication of the influence of St. Xavier's is the fact that the graduates, practically to a man, go on to university studies, either in Bihar or elsewhere in India. One of them at the present writing is the Rhodes scholar for 1955 at Oxford in England.

The boys at St. Xavier's are the members of the families of government servants in the capital city of a huge Indian state of well over forty million population or are the sons of university instructors and administrators, of high court justices and lawyers, and of estate owners and landlords. The popularity of the school and the numbers seeking admission have forced the Jesuit administration to adopt a selective policy. The curriculum itself is a fairly rigid one which embraces both arts and sciences, with only one elective allowed, besides the study of Hindi.

Another example of the far-flung educational setup is Baghdad College, in the capital city of Iraq, the venerable metropolis on the Tigris in which American Jesuits must match ancient and modern cultures, join the influences of the East and Near East and West, and make all emerge with something of the serenity and depth of the faith they profess and the rational educational method they pursue. In spite of occasional differences with the country's ruling elite the administrators and instructors at the college have managed to represent the Ratio and the Constitutions of the Society more than adequately, and to confer upon the graduates of their institution that special esteem, as much social as intellectual, that goes by the name of cachet.

At the secondary school in Jamhour in Lebanon the College Notre Dame, "a French school, employing the French system of education slightly modified to meet local Lebanese needs," four American Jesuits, two priests, and two Scholastics teach and ponder the marvels of an order which ranges so far afield and sends Americans trained in the Latin Rite to teach in a French school in Lebanon, where the native language is Arabic and Latin Rite Catholics are outnumbered by those whose rites are Maronite, Greek Orthodox, Greek Catholic, Syrian, Armenian, or Chaldean, not to mention "the considerable portion of the student body" which is Moslem. One reason that may be advanced for the assignment is to bring American Catholic educators into an area traditionally Catholic, in which American Protestant educators have worked long and well. Another is, presumably, the problem of man power, which is universal in the Church and which must be solved by all the missionary societies and orders. And still another, one must assume, is the ingenuity of the American priest, which has met and managed to unravel other educational situations at least as knotty as this one.

If in Jamhour it is a confluence of cultures and languages, religious rites and educational theories that can be upsetting, at the Ateneo de Davao in the Philippines it is the number of levels of education combined in one school. At the Davao Athenaeum the closest thing to cradle-to-the-grave education is offered by the Jesuits: from kindergarten through college nearly every kind of teaching is made available, including four-year courses in education and commerce as well as the liberal arts.

The Davao project is an excellent example of the educational flexibility of the Society, one which makes possible adaptation to the often inflexible rules of the different governments and societies into which American Jesuits go. In the Philippines it is the custom of private schools to offer an education that extends from kindergarten to college, hence the Ateneo's startling program. The government of the islands has been insisting more and more upon vocational instruction; the Society has met these requirements by interpreting "vocational" broadly enough to fit almost any extracurricular activity of a useful sort into the time prescribed for such instruction, and by developing pre-engineering and chemistry programs in the college in spite of the limited training in mathematics of the school's freshmen.

In the Philippines there are two kinds of competition any school which maintains standards—any standards at all—must meet. For one thing, there are the so-called "diploma mills," which practically guarantee a diploma in return for the payment of the required fees. For another, there is the absence of a substantial educational tradition, and of a complementary motivation to broaden the native culture, to deepen the existing knowledge of other cultures, to make the average student in the Philippines more fluent in English and all those things to which a fluency in the language would serve as an introduction.

For all these difficulties, however, and the inevitable financial problems and inadequacy of quarters, the Ateneo has been much praised as the best school in its part of the country. In the eight years of its operation it has assumed a role of sufficient importance to place more of its graduates in positions—positions of some kinds—than those of other schools, an advantage of striking importance in a country which is, according to those who teach at the school, in an economic state "worse than that of the United States in 1932."

The Ateneo de Naga College, in the Philippines, is a remarkable example of the application of the Ratio Studiorum in a modern situation, a situation not at all unlike that which the Davao Ateneo faces. In Naga all the same negative influences prevail, but against these the Society has constructed a curriculum and a campus, a variety of degrees and disciplines, of general extracurricular and special religious activities which compare favorably in number and quality with those of any other institution of the same nature in this country. The courses offered are in the liberal arts, in general education and business administration and commerce; there is a special secretarial training program and there are pre-law and pre-nursing courses. All have as their objective, according to the eloquent words of the Ateneo catalogue, the development of men and women "who are able to take their part in this world without becoming entirely of it. Men and women with an ingrained respect for true values . . . who can think clearly and express themselves effectively . . . Men and women deeply steeped in the rich culture which, by the grace of God, is theirs."

No matter what the program of instruction, the first year at the Ateneo de Naga begins with two semesters of "Moral

Guidance," and those who remain for a full four years must take required courses in "Evidence of Revelation" (one year) and "Lay Theology" (two years). For the rest, apart from vocational emphases, the education is classical, with a substantial administration of philosophical procedure and a variously elastic program of electives, confined to one or another faculty, depending upon the degree for which a student is a candidate. Impressive to an American educator is a system of scholarships which automatically grants a full tuition scholarship for one year to valedictorians from any high school in the country and a one-half tuition scholarship for a year to salutatorians. But more to the point, perhaps, of this system of education is the description, by an American Jesuit, James J. O'Brien, who is a part of it, of "the bright side to the picture that makes it a pleasure to work with Bicolanos," that is, with the natives of this province of the Philippines:

"Their cheerfulness and joy in life. Their devotion and loyalty to their family and friends. Their docility and acceptance of correction. Their quiet acceptance of the Fathers and their appreciation of the work being done for them. Their friendliness that is undemonstrative but lasting. Their generosity. Their respect shown to the Fathers that expresses itself in not questioning or talking back. Their religion which is open and free of self-consciousness: tough guys wear Our Lady's medal on their shirts and stevedores fight for the honor of carrying her statue in the fiesta procession; each street has its intricately decorated May altar and its shrine to the true Cross; every Holy Week has its colorful pageantry and ceremonies participated in by the whole city; each fiesta has its devotion to Mary and the Saints expressed in bright processions watched by the entire town and enlivened by brass bands, fireworks and skyrockets. They are, all in all, a lovable people of a gentle race, and though they have much difficulty before them in the way of virtue and the full life, still their patience and good hearts often, apparently, bring the victory that we all seek."

The two schools run by the American Society in Jamaica,

in the British West Indies, Campion Hall and St. George's College, form an impressive unit together. The first acts as a screening for the second, so satisfactorily in fact that now, after sixteen years, the suburban prep school regularly provides the Kingston boarding school with about one third of its students.

Campion Hall was founded as a result of the crowded conditions in the city schools of Jamaica; out in the foothills that ring the outer stretches of Kingston, it was possible to provide Catholic boys from the age of eight to twelve with an adequate background for the demanding classical curriculum of St. George's. As in so many of these Jesuit schools, the student body presents the faculty with a kaleidoscope of cultures, with a far more than casual introduction to the races of man: almost one third of the students are Chinese; the others are East Indian, Syrian, German, French, Spanish, English, American, "and all the shades of straight Jamaican." And again, as in so many of the schools run by the Society, it offers a service unique in its community: Campion Hall is the only boys' school in its age range on the island, preparing its students for that "thorough education, based upon a careful moral and religious training," which St. George's aims at in order "to mould the lives of young men to noble purposes."

At St. George's College noble purpose is joined to majestic method: "The academic system in use at St. George's," the catalogue solemnly proclaims, "is the 'Ratio Studiorum,' a set of educational principles drawn up by the most eminent Jesuit educators and commonly applied to Jesuit institutions the world over." The Ratio is implemented at the college (which is, of course, a secondary school) by a faculty of thirty, more than half of whom are priests, the rest being Scholastics and laymen. Religious instruction is given daily and supplemented by the religious societies usually sponsored by the Jesuits: the Sodality of Our Lady, the Apostleship of Prayer, and an altar boys' society. The pedagogical language spoken by the faculty of St. George's and faithfully reproduced in the catalogue and other publications is that of the English public school, but the accents are unmistakably Roman.

In Belize, in British Honduras, the American Society conducts another secondary school along the lines of St. George's, St. John's College. Here, however, the solid entry made into the life of British Honduras on every level by the college is far more like an American university's relationship with its community than it is like the reserve which sets a British public school apart from its town. At St. John's the number of school buildings on the new Landivar Campus in the northern suburb of Belize is always increasing, and the courses of study and services to the country grow with them. The college's Extension Department enrolls more than one hundred and fifty adults in courses in economics, public speaking, journalism, law, trade unionism, parliamentary procedure, and the mysteries—simple and complex—of the English language. A study of co-operative housing organized by the college led to the formation of the Harmony Housing Co-operative Society, which in a four-year period was able to build nine low-cost houses and has become an integral part of the economy of British Honduras. In addition St. John's staff members have been "loaned" to the summer convocations of the General Workers Union to organize and conduct seminars on the subject of "Trade Unionism from the Christian Point of View." The teacher-training program at the college is a success; labor union leaders are being turned out not only for the colony but for most of the other Central American states. The ambitious statement contained in a recent issue of the *Alumni News* of St. John's seems more than justified by the extraordinary achievement of this school:

"St. John's College is not and cannot be an 'Ivory Tower' of learning that stands separate and aloof from the everyday life and problems of the people. As a Catholic educational institution SJC must function for the benefit of the people in the community. It must aim and work towards improving the intellectual, moral, social, and economic life of the community. Naturally its principal contribution results from its work of training and educating the youth who will be the teachers, lawyers, doctors, workers, farmers, business men and civic leaders of the future. However, the College does not limit its educational activity to the boys in the classrooms . . ."

How much more can a religious order offer in the way of education? Well, for one thing, it can reach into the obscure shadows that fall across its home territories and attempt to cast some light as it reaches, as the American Society does, for example, in its Holy Rosary Mission School for Sioux Indian children at Pine Ridge, South Dakota. From the reservation, where generations are often separated from each other in culture and interest and concern more sharply than the Indians in general are from white men, the mission school has sent its graduates in large number into colleges and universities all over the United States. The result is excellent for the communities into which the Indian college graduates later move but unfortunate for the Indian reservation, which must necessarily lose its leaders, or potential leaders, this way. Furthermore, distances from one part of the reservation to another are very great and communications, consequently, something less than smooth. Much still remains to be done to acculturate the Indian who stays at home, to give him the motivation to raise his cattle economically, to achieve some balance between his old way of life and the new, to which he must adjust if he is to survive. The Jesuits bring no all-curing nostrums with them to their Indian mission schools, but they do offer the wisdom and knowledge of a great educational tradition and a faith with which to bulwark it. With such tools neither a dying culture nor a feeble system of communications can pose absolutely insurmountable problems.

Extending their resources to the resourceless or discovering residual strength in those who did not themselves know they possessed it is a central procedure of Jesuit missionary education. It is the precise method of operation, really, of the five seminaries for the native clergy which the American Society conducts. At St. Michael's, the minor seminary in Jamaica, for example, an attempt is made "to bridge the gap scholastically between the education a man has when he comes to us to study for the priesthood and the beginning of the philosophy course, and to help ascetically to make the transition from the lay to the clerical state." Studies more or less literary, rhetorical, linguistic often must be imposed upon an inadequate secondary school education. Lectures are delivered and discussions held in quarters designed in 1763 for a large private family but hardly suitable now for a seminary. Funds are low and the faculty and administration too small, but St. Michael's has turned out two graduating classes of five men each and has taken formidable steps in the direction of the establishment of a Jamaican clergy of a size and stature consonant with their own considerable resources and those of the Order now so much concerned with them. And always before it, it has the stirring example of India, where as a result of the application of Jesuit educational methods some nine hundred Jesuits, about 50 per cent of the Society in India, and twenty-eight members of the hierarchy are Indians.

The philosophate the Society runs in the Philippines, at Berchmans College at Cebu City, is, in a manner of speaking, bulging with young Jesuit philosophers, with twelve American Scholastics, and forty-seven Filipinos. The course at Berchmans is "the regular one according to the Ratio Studiorum Superiorum"—that is, the Method of Higher Studies, the adaptation of the Ratio for seminary usage—"but at the same time we cover all government requirements for a B.A. and an M.A. degree, including an M.A. thesis. The Scholastics also take enough courses in education to be able to teach in the schools of the Philippines," the rector explains. The effect of the graduates of the college on their environment is "immense, since our Scholastics spend three years teaching in our seven different Ateneos scattered around the Philippines, or in San Jose Seminary in Manila. During those years of teaching they are constantly in contact with and forming young men of high school and college age."

On and on the seminaries go, farther and farther out they stretch their life lines for the Church. In Ceylon the Society has begun to train young men for the priesthood as secular priests of the Trincomalee diocese. In Hong Kong, Jesuits conduct a regional seminary founded a quarter of a century ago by the Apostolic Delegate and the bishops of South China to supply the two provinces of Kwangtung and Kwangsi with Chinese secular priests. In twenty-five years the seminary has ordained 149 priests who pursued within its walls some or all of their studies. It has been a refuge for many seminarians from other parts of China, and has on several occasions housed entire seminaries in addition to its own staff and students—seminaries escaping, more or less intact, from the Communists. Its present success? Father Rector answers, "Our priests are working in many parts of China, many are in Communist prisons, at least one has been shot by the Reds. Since 1951 it has been impossible to send our priests back to China so they are working in Borneo, Java, Dutch New Guinea, Sarawak, Madagascar, Formosa, Tasmania."

Thus do postage stamps come alive. Thus does a cornucopia of studies, picked and polished, clipped and shaped at the end of the sixteenth century continue to yield its plenty in the middle of the twentieth.

This is Jesuit education, not a myth, not a fiction, but the steady dissemination of sturdy truths; not an inquisition of six-year-old souls nor an indoctrination of seven-year-old minds, but the extension, far and wide, the sharing as fully as possible of the wisdom and grace to which every member of the Society falls heir. In this education, rational and spirited, sane and sweet and comfortable but not undisciplined, and as broad as the faith which inspires it, modern Jesuits emulate the high watchfulness of their Spanish founder. For this, too, is a vigil of arms and a constant dedication of life to the service of God.

10. *Modern Personalities*

Thomas J. M. Burke, s.j.

ONE of the most remarkable differences between Christianity and other religions is the fact that the great mainspring of Christian activity is love. This may at first sight seem like a rather elaborate oversimplification, but actually it does make sense. Certainly no other religion in the long history of mankind has ever presented the astonishing spectacle of thousands upon thousands of people marching determinedly, if not cheerfully, to lay down their lives for their faith.

The history of Christianity, from the days of Stephen in Jerusalem to the latest news from China, is filled with the tales of men, women, and children who were perfectly willing to cast themselves into a fire for the sake of their faith, as if their lives were worth no more to them than a pinch of incense. So much so, in fact, that it seems something of a commonplace. A defection in some particular instance causes Christians, and even non-Christians, to stop for a moment, startled at the astonishing sight of a disciple of Christ drawing back from the sword of the executioner.

The reason for this is perfectly simple. Christianity is a religion whose core and heart is built around a Person. It isn't merely the ideas and ideals expressed by Christ that does it. It isn't the carefully worked out philosophy and theology, the staggeringly solid and unassailable system of thought, the magnificent panoply of ordered concepts marching like an army in battle array to the complete satisfaction of the inquiring mind that made it possible for Lawrence to joke as he broiled on a gridiron and Father Pro to cheer for Christ the King in the face of a firing squad. These things might help. They might bring the awareness of being right to help strengthen the sagging knees and the sinking heart. But they do not explain it. For among the martyrs there are thousands upon thousands who could not read, and thousands upon thousands who never once realized how trenchant and forceful are the intellectual bases of the Christian faith. The thing that makes all this possible is the simple fact that, to martyrs, Christ is not merely a philosopher or theologian or teacher, but simply a Person Whom they love as no other being on earth has ever been loved.

That is the secret of the martyrs. That is the simple answer to the problem of how a persecuted Church, at times ill governed, at times rent by family quarrels and torn apart by schism, could go on and on, still abreast of the day, still enkindling the spark that makes martyrs willing to put down their lives for their Friend. To the true Christian, Christ is not a mere teacher, nor an interesting historical figure, nor even a model man. Christ is Incarnate Love, Love made flesh, virile, attractive, appealing, admirable, arousing a vast, fierce, and almost frantic loyalty. Christ is a Divine Man Who captures the imagination and makes His followers long to be as much like Him as possible. He is, in short, not a being who came and went and is no more, like Buddha and Confucius and Mohammed, but a living and breathing and constantly present Person Who can be, and actually is, loved. It is this which Christians find so satisfactory. For Christians are, after all, human. And human beings have an insatiable hunger for loving and being loved, appetites which no mere ideal nor abstract system of thought and loyalty can possibly satisfy.

It is this Christian love which motivates the missionary and drives him on, as it once drove on St. Paul, to follow the command of Christ and make Him known to the rim of the universe. And just as the complete perfection of Christ makes it impossible for any man to reflect Him perfectly in all His aspects, conversely it makes it possible for any man to reflect Him according to his own personal limitations and capacities. This fact is what makes it possible to succeed as a missionary. It is for this reason that men and women in strange and faraway lands, in the most unlikely places and from the most astonishing backgrounds, suddenly yield to the appeals of a missionary and become followers of Christ.

In their effort to bring Christ to the hearts and lives of people the circumstances under which they toil and their own personal equipment limn the outlines of the missionaries' activity. This is why the activity of Jesuit missionaries today, as in the past, is so bewilderingly varied. For in spite of popular legend Jesuits are about as dissimilar and divergent a group of men as have ever joined in a common cause. At first glance there appears to be no resemblance at all between the work of a Jesuit lecturing on German literature at Sophia University in Tokyo and a Jesuit floundering through the jungles of Ponape to bring the last Sacraments to a dying fisherman. Yet there is a tremendous similarity and it is this: both men are fundamentally motivated by love for Christ. One is bringing up to the face of his listeners the Christ Who talked learnedly about the Scriptures and spoke as one having authority; the other is showing forth the Christ Who walked in the midst of a loud and disorderly mob to bring to life the daughter of Jairus. Both are dedicated to working for Christ. Both are using their talent and their energy to reflect Christ, to make Him known and loved.

The purpose of this chapter is to outline, however rudely,

portraits of a few of these men, and to indicate how their personal equipment and the circumstances in which they labor serve to bring out some facet of the lovable Christ and draw disciples to the feet of the Master.

In Ceylon, for instance, the Superior of the entire mission is a gentle, soft-spoken man named John Lange. His hair has long since thinned out to the point of invisibility. The tropical sun of the hot and lovely island where he works has tanned and toughened his skin to a rich, leathery brown, to such an extent that when his blue eyes twinkle one is faintly surprised that eyes so blue could be looking out of a face so tanned. He speaks softly, in a gentle drawl which he has never lost, yet his laughter is unexpectedly loud and ringing, almost as if he had been speaking behind a door in another room and came in just to laugh. He is a man of scholarly interests, and of scholarly leanings, with a fine reputation among the learned as an authority on the Tamil language and literature. Somebody once came into a room where he was typing with almost painful slowness and twitted him about his awkwardness until he discovered that the typewriter was equipped with Tamil characters and Father Lange was engaged in composing an article for publication in some scholarly periodical in Colombo. It is not very usual to find someone coping successfully with so many problems simultaneously: machine, type, language, and composition.

Outside of this linguistic and literary accomplishment the only impact that Ceylon has made on him is a gustatory one. Years of highly seasoned food has made American cookery insipid to him. The result is the rather disconcerting one of having people at table stare in some amazement as Father Lange shakes the tabasco sauce into his soup while he talks. To sensitive American palates which may have been singed and seared by the fire of tabasco, the sight of twenty-five or thirty dashes of the seasoning going into a bowl of soup is enough to set the teeth on edge. It takes a little while to realize that this is not a careless gesture performed while distracted by his own conversation. Father Lange likes tabasco. He deliberately puts a half teaspoon of red pepper on his potatoes. Ceylonese food, he explains gently, is hot.

It is a delight to talk with and listen to Father Lange. Words fascinate him (this, perhaps, explains how he became an expert on Tamil), and he uses them with great respect and care. His vocabulary is vast and precise. It is pleasant to listen to him select, without hesitation or doubt, the exact combination of words which brings his idea clearly into view and build those words into concise and beautifully polished little paragraphs. He doesn't deal in monosyllabic answers. When asked a question he replies in a short little essay which is a perfect and polished thing, carefully built. Since the range of his interests is quite broad, an evening with Father Lange is a pleasurable and enriching experience.

It comes, therefore, almost as a shock to find that this cultured and scholarly gentleman has not hesitated to put aside erudite pursuits in response to a need. For example, St. Joseph's College in Trincomalee was for years housed in a group of buildings which hardly deserved the name.

"In these circumstances," Father Lange said, "it is next to impossible for us to teach or for the boys to learn. Human dignity is human dignity everywhere, and I couldn't train a horse in those sheds. How could I hope to educate Christian men?"

The problem, as is usual in the missions, was a financial one. It costs money to buy building materials. It costs money to hire masons and carpenters and bricklayers, and all the other workmen whose skills and strength go into the erection of buildings. So Father Lange put aside his books and started to do the whole thing himself. At first glance it seems incongruous that a man who is a scholar, a priest of God, and the Superior of an entire mission territory should begin to mix concrete and, with his own hands, fashion build-

ing blocks and lay them. And yet Father Lange can see nothing really incongruous in it. He has energy and muscles. He
has hands. He has a blueprint and can read it. And wasn't
Christ a carpenter? A building is needed to make Christ
known and loved among the young men in Trincomalee and
among the widening circle of their acquaintances, so why
should the mere fact of a scholarly reputation stand in the
way of that work? Isn't that why John Lange went to Ceylon
in the first place?

Not everyone in the missions, of course, has the energy
and physical strength to go around erecting buildings with
his own hands. Nor, fortunately, is there everywhere need
of such backbreaking activity. The point is that when the
circumstances of his work called for it the man was able,
out of his love for Christ and the people among whom he
worked, to lay aside books and pick up a trowel, and by so
doing present to the people of Ceylon the spectacle of a
disciple doing his utmost to be like his Master.

Other circumstances call for other talents. Pedro Arrupe
is a Basque. He is slender and of medium height, with thinning brown hair and the long, slim hands which are usually
associated with artists. His English is quite good, although
he speaks it with a strange and hybrid sort of accent, part
Spanish, part German, part almost faintly Oriental, like a
Chinese brogue. He came face to face, as a youngster of
fourteen or so, with the hopelessness and indignity of poverty. This is something Americans find a little difficult to understand. American slums are terrible things, of course. But
even so the poverty there is really only relative when compared to the grinding indigence found in less favored lands.
It is not often, for instance, that Americans at home are faced
with the sight of a family of six living in a doorway. This
glimpse of want, seen when he was young and impression-
able, touched in Pedro Arrupe a wellspring of practical
sympathy and a desire to help people which has grown

stronger and richer through the years. His career as a Jesuit has been extraordinary. He studied medicine in Spain, psychology in Germany under the great Dr. Behn, and was all set to work for a degree in psychiatry in the United States when the revolution in Spain cut him off from his native land. So he volunteered for the Japanese Mission. ("I was intrigued," he says, "by the difference in the two civilizations.") He was assigned to Hiroshima.

The story of what happened at Hiroshima on August 6, 1945, is too well known to bear repetition here. What is worth noting is that while he stood in the midst of the dust and smoke churned up by the world's first atom bomb attack, he was capable, quite calmly, of planning the steps which would be necessary to transform the mission house, somehow still miraculously standing, into a rough clinic where the ghastly wounds of the victims might receive attention. And in the nightmare that followed, without sleep, without rest, without adequate bandages or palliatives, the former medical student used his skill and the gentle touch of his slender hands to ease as best he could the agonies of the seared bodies brought to him.

"I remember," he recalled with horror, "a girl about twenty dragging an old man. She had wrapped a skirt or something around his waist and kept pulling and pulling, and biting her lips so she wouldn't scream. I never saw such a mess before. His chest and back were one vast festering wound. And he wasn't old. Only twenty-three. They had been married only a month. And there was nothing, not even a little wine."

It took hours. Hours of smothered gasps and moans that could not be choked back, of gentle hands forced to hurt in order to heal, of clenched teeth and clenched fists and courage that left them all limp and exhausted. Somehow the wounds were cleansed. Somehow, from some deep store of energy, the seared and battered body drew strength to hang grimly on to life. It had been August then: it took eight months before the young man and his bride were able to depart. Now it was April, and Pedro Arrupe was a happy man as he watched the two of them walk hand in hand down the road along which they had dragged themselves into his life.

Much has happened since then. Father Arrupe is now Provincial of all the Jesuits in Japan. The hands that proved so skilled at healing are charged with directing a complex and enormously active missionary endeavor involving parishes, high schools, orphanages, seminaries, and a university in Tokyo. He still goes along quietly, unimpressed by the magnitude of the burden he bears, and somehow finds time for an amazingly active literary career: he has translated into Japanese all the works of St. John of the Cross, and the letters of Francis Xavier. He has written a Japanese biography of Xavier, a four-volume commentary on the Spiritual Exercises of St. Ignatius, and a book on vocations for teenagers. Besides this he also has found time to give a long series of lectures and conferences to the Buddhist monks of Japan. Serenely writing letters and giving talks in English, Spanish, German, and Japanese, Father Arrupe brings to everyone he meets a brief glimpse of that wonderful and lovely thing called dedication.

Father James Thornton of Hsinshu in Formosa, on the other hand, is quite unlike Father Arrupe. He is much taller, for one thing, and his still dark hair curls crisply above his long, craggy face. No one has ever called him handsome, but his eyes are lively and shrewd behind horn-rimmed glasses. Thornton is a tall man, and moves rather awkwardly, like a boy who grew big too quickly and never found precisely what to do with his long arms and legs. His hands are large and square, and they are constantly moving, as if endowed with a life of their own. His voice is faintly hoarse, suggesting that his throat is somewhat raw. His rich brogue is so pervasive that those who know insist it tinges even his Chinese, which he indignantly denies. He, too, is gentle. But his gentleness is not so much in his actions and his words as in his attitudes and his thinking. And he, too, is concerned with poverty. In Hsinshu there is a long row of squatters' shacks called Thornton's Alley. Here live the poorest of the poor, refugees who have escaped from the mainland and have set up against the public wall a couple of partitions made from a packing case or cardboard and an equally rough-and-ready roof. Four feet of public wall, a little cardboard, a board for a bed, and it is home.

Here James Thornton comes daily with his big hand stretched out in friendship to talk and listen. Their problems become his, and by the strange and wonderful alchemy of love that sharing seems to bring some fashion of solution. His words carry comfort and assurance, and he seems to know every available job in the city. There is no effort made here to set up a formal Church. There is no organized charity. There is only the warmth of sympathy, the strength of real friendship, and the example of the great, openhanded love of Christ, which insists on regarding every man, no matter how abandoned and poor, as the child of a Heavenly Father.

The story of how old Ma arrived in Thornton's Alley after his flight from the Red terror in China illustrates the circumstances which drove so many to seek refuge under Father's wing. Ma had been sleeping peacefully one night, he related, with his wife and children, when a loud knocking aroused him. He thought it was the Communist police. It was his brother-in-law.

"The cadres," said he, "will be here in a little while. I have just accused you of being a reactionary and anti-revolutionary." He paused and then added apologetically, "It was either that or lose my skin."

"It was," said Ma judiciously, "rather decent of him to warn me."

Before his bed was cool, Ma was out of there on a south-bound train. He had no money, no ticket, nothing. Yet, with the aid of friends and relatives and strangers who proved surprisingly helpful, he managed to make the five-hundred-mile trip to the coast and smuggle himself into Formosa with a shipment of pigs. He found four feet of wall in Thornton's Alley and promptly settled down. Just as promptly Father Thornton arrived. He knew Ma's town. He had spent time in Communist jails, ten long, grimy months. Of such common interests is friendship born. And friendship led to interest in what made the Father so friendly. After a while, sitting on Ma's bed while his friend ground pepper, the tall priest from California initiated the old man from China into the mysteries of the Catholic faith.

Only once did Ma boggle: "Love your enemies" included Communists, and this was difficult. But here was the tall man with the brogue, unembittered and gentle, with no rancor against his jailers, and Ma understood and acquiesced. A week later he had a newcomer sharing his shack and refused a job at an army camp because Father Thornton would not be there. Ma and Li, the cobbler, and old Wong, who sweeps streets, came into the Church together, with Ma utterly fascinated by the thought of the agility of a risen body. "Fast, man, fast!" is all he can say.

Thus James Thornton carries on his work, patiently, quietly, his sympathy and understanding reflecting the love of Christ in Formosa.

In the same half of the world lives Father Hugh Costigan, at Ponape, in the Caroline Islands. He is a big man, six feet two and muscular, whose brown hair has become gray without thinning, whose face has been seamed by the sun, wind, and long days of toil until he looks older than his forty-two years. It was while he was at Xavier High School in New York, he explains with a perfectly straight face, that he decided to become a missionary. "The boat ride did it," he says.

"I developed a sudden passion for boat trips, and the longest one I could think of for which I didn't have to pay was the one from New York to Manila. So I decided to become a missionary."

This yearning for the sea has been amply satisfied. It is the only way of getting from one place to another in the Carolines. This vast and sprawling mission territory presents a peculiar difficulty. Other lands, as lands, have either actual or potential resources which offer some hope of eventual prosperity. In Alaska, for instance, there are enormous mineral deposits, and lumber and fisheries. India is a subcontinent with a teeming population where practically everything will find a ready market and it, too, is fabulously rich in resources. But the Carolines are dots of islands, scattered over a tremendous area, sparsely populated and out of the shipping lanes. The soil is fertile, true, but it is merely soil: there are no rich mineral deposits, and about the only marketable commodity is copra, something whose future, due to the growing use of chemical detergents, is not entirely unclouded. But the people are a joy—friendly, gay, simple, and entirely winning.

It is the future of the mission that has kept Hugh Costigan awake nights: how to build a church for worship, schools to educate these people, a parish house to foster and Christianize their social life, a pier to make it possible to market the copra crop. The result of his sleeplessness has been startling.

There was abundant sand. So Father contracted with the territory government to make cement blocks for government use. The territory supplies the cement and takes away the blocks. In exchange for the work the mission receives cement and a small amount of steel, saved from Japanese military installations, for its own use. This made it possible to build a permanent pier. Next came a poultry farm, so that everybody would have meat and eggs. Then roads were extended to places in the islands where the Japanese had built fortifications they never used, where there were galvanized iron and tin and zinc and steel which could be stock-piled and used for barter with other islands.

Now a cocoa plantation is coming into being, and as a result of Hugh Costigan's imagination and energy the mission is booming: boys are learning to be mechanics, carpenters, masons. They are finding out about soil and how it is enriched by rotting vegetation, how it will yield other things besides taro and coconuts. They are finding out how pigs and chickens can be kept fat and healthy. They are learning what makes a jeep tick, and how a truck is kept running long after it should have expired along the rugged roads. They are finding out how to put up a pier that will last, and how to make a highway that will not wash away. One man's energy has picked up an island, shaken it by the scruff of its neck, and set it on its feet, alert and alive and looking forward to tomorrow.

As he sits wearily at his desk after a long day writing letters to his friends and his family in distant New York, Father Costigan must wonder, at times, what on earth he ever saw in a boat ride to lead him to this. For the life of a missionary is not without discouragement. But in the morning the children will gather in the church and their voices will rise in song: "Jesus, Jesus, come to me. Oh how much I long for Thee. . . ." And then the loneliness will be bearable, and the breeze cool, and the sun will smile on the orderly acres carved out of a once all-conquering jungle. And there will be no unanswered questions.

A missionary's life is a life of love, and love is the most versatile of all the emotions, not in the sense that it is the most varied, but rather in that it has at its disposal an array of powers upon which to call. Missionaries make it impossible to doubt the rightness of St. Paul when he exulted, "I can do *all* things in Him Who strengthens me!" And a brief catalogue of some of the things done by some of the missionaries of today shows what a bewildering diversity of circumstance and personality mirrors forth the magnetic and lovely image of Christ.

In atom-destroyed Hiroshima in Japan the people at war's end were depressed and drained of enthusiasm for life, perhaps more so than the mass of the Japanese. This spiritual desolation impressed a very vigorous Belgian Jesuit, Father Earnest Goosens, when he returned to Hiroshima after his liberation from wartime imprisonment. He thought that music would be a way to bring new courage and hope to these people, and also would serve as an avenue to the rising intellectuals of Japan (who are going to determine the future of the country). These people are very conscious of culture and read extensively. With very little background to discriminate between truth and misleading philosophies they are becoming victims of Marxism. Father Goosens received a degree in music in New York City and then went back to start a full-fledged music school. It is along the lines of an American conservatory and has around five hundred students at present in all phases of music and composition. The school is besieged with applications for admittance and has received a great deal of publicity throughout Japan. It is now sending out teachers inspired by this priest with a true love of God's beauty as reflected in music. The Japanese, always lovers of classical works, are very impressed with Gregorian chant, whereas jazz developments are not too much to their liking.

Up in Hooper Bay on the Bering Sea there was until a few years ago nothing but a collection of mounds. Each mound was an indication of a dwelling underneath, a dwelling which was ill lighted, constantly damp, and with floors of evil-smelling mud into which had been ground during the course of years grass, seal oil, remains of dried fish, and so many other off products of civilization. As a result of such living conditions the number of babies who died was very little short of the number born. The only pleasant feature of such a situation was the fact that heaven was terribly close to Eskimo babies.

A wonderful transformation has taken place in the last few years, however, at Hooper Bay. There are still a few of the old mounds to be seen but most of these are used as storage houses. The people of the village, for the first time in their history, live in decent homes which are easily kept clean, warm, and dry. The man responsible for this is Father Paul O'Connor, S.J. He had spent more than fifteen years with Eskimos in various parts of Alaska before he was sent to Hooper Bay. The filth and disease were a challenge. He had visited government officials but nothing was done. Then one day there appeared in Washington, D.C., a tall gray-haired priest built like a football player, with facts and figures at his finger tips. He obtained a hearing before the Finance Committee of both House and Senate. He spoke for his people and came back to Alaska with the battle won. Acting as an agent for the government, he went from person to person, explained everything, and made loans to 170 different families. The only security was the word of the borrower. Through other government agencies building supplies were purchased in quantity and shipped by barge. The people of the southern Bering coast went on a building spree. One village after another took on a changed appearance and almost instantly the incidence of disease took a sudden drop.

Father O'Connor, a veteran of over twenty years in Alaska, is happiest when he is celebrating Mass for his people or reciting the Rosary or bringing Christ through the Sacraments into their lives, but the work of being a building administrator was necessary in order to let these people have the fundamentals of a sound human life. He became the Chairman of the Federal Housing Administration in Alaska, a position he still holds. In the spirit of Christ, Who was willing to help a married couple have a wedding feast, he has helped the people of the Bering Sea to secure decent homes.

Before the war in the Philippines it was not uncommon for the captain of a ship lying alongside Manila's famous Pier 7 to regard coldly a white-clothed figure approaching the dock. As soon as the priest introduced himself as Father Doucette of the Manila Observatory, all the coldness vanished and the captain welcomed him warmly. The Jesuit Fathers over a period of eighty years at the observatory were known for their help to seamen and navigators in the prediction of weather and storms and typhoons. Men like Father Doucette, Father Selga, and now Father Depperman, have shown that nothing that is of God is foreign to men of God. If men could be helped through scientific knowledge, if Christ could be made more attractive to certain people through scientifically knowledgeable priests, then they were willing to spend years of labor on the minutiae of science. Father Selga was decorated for his work in meteorology, seismology, hydrography, and astronomy by government after government. Father Doucette, now working with Father Depperman, is studying microseisms to determine the relationship between these and larger quakes which cause typhoons and ocean swells, frequently dangerous in the Pacific. Perhaps recalling that St. Ignatius was fond of looking at the stars, they also look at the skies and study the ionosphere. The ionospheric layers are the ones which make long-distance radio propagation possible. Working with an ionosonde day after day, they gather the information which helps to make the plotting of world charts for radio transmission possible.

Behind all the headlines in various mission countries stand the hundreds of Jesuit scholars working in the field of education, trying in their classroom activities to mirror Him Who is the Word of God. Their works are the slow works, the more tiresome, and the works which are never acclaimed. Important to these people are their fellow Jesuits, who by their quiet example and cheerfulness manage to keep a community encouraged and enthused to go ahead with its day-by-day work. There are many quiet missionary personalities whose greatest contribution perhaps is in the realm of human psychology, helping to keep other men cheerful and courageous enough to face the tedious task of getting out of bed and going about the prayer and the routine of their day.

On the other hand there is a different sort of help which is necessary in carrying out any missionary work. What very few people realize is that missions, for the most part, are almost literally run on a shoestring. There is enormous faith: the picture of a man standing and saying to a mountain, "Move!" is by no means inapplicable to missions and missionaries. But, as St. Theresa very wisely pointed out, it isn't enough merely to stand while issuing the order. It helps if the command is accompanied by a determined push in the right direction. And very few people have pushed with more energy and to better effect than Father John Buchanan.

This is a young man, not very tall, but with the general structure of a good-sized bulldozer. He gives that impression, too. There is an irresistibility to his movements, and the sense that here is a great engine running with great power at full speed. The amount of work done by John Buchanan since he was appointed to Alaska in 1951 is almost unbelievable.

To begin with, he was assigned to cover an area of 74,000 square miles! The Alaska Highway is the main artery of this area, which at its widest point is 234 miles, and here there were no schools, no churches, nothing. And no money for building them, either. He begged a truck. Then he begged for building material, things he could nail and cement together, and hauled them along the big highway. Somehow, too, volunteers would come along to help in the lugging and the building, and chapel after chapel, school after school, the buildings began to dot the vast expanse of his territory: Big Delta, Glennallen, Copper Center . . .

But he saw that isolated small schools were not enough. Somewhere there has to be a big central plant, and at Copper Center, Father Buchanan drew up plans for this: a big plant with wings like the spokes of a wheel, a grammar school, a high school, a convent, a church, and eventually a college. In the States it would cost two million dollars; in Alaska, where the transportation increases the price of everything, it would be much more. So John Buchanan looked at the impossible mountain, climbed into his truck, and said, "Move!"

If the men who drive the screaming diesels on the U.S. highways are a recognizable fraternity, the truckers who ply the frozen and mountainous roads of Alaska are a race apart. Courage, skill, strength, and resourcefulness are required for mere survival. Father Buchanan has become a respected member of this brotherhood. In his twenty-ton Kenworth he is a familiar figure on the treacherous roads from the port cities of Valdez and Anchorage to Copper Center. Most of these trips are made in the winter, with the thermometer at 20 to 30 degrees below zero. "Any Alaska trucker," says the priest, "will tell you that a frozen snow-packed road is better than a soggy one. These huge trucks really have traction."

But there is another reason for this devotion to this winter transportation. Father Buchanan has to spend the short summer months begging for the large tonnage of material which he trucks in the winter to Copper Center. During this period he practically commutes between Alaska and the States. An airline pass takes him to Seattle. And from there he fans out to the chief cities of the country in search of generous business people who will donate, not money, but material to his project at Copper Center. He travels with a companion by pickup truck equipped with a mattress in the back so that his long trips can be made non-stop. In the large industrial concerns throughout the country he is well known, and his requests for building materials are cheerfully honored. His friends have learned that it is not enough to nail a thing down; better to keep it out of sight. Buchanan laughs easily and shakes his head at the wonder of it; the gasoline alone so far for his trucking operation would have cost more than six thousand dollars, and the plant at Copper Center is rising as a monument to the energy and dedication of a man who feels that it isn't too much to dedicate his strength and energy to the Christ Who died for him.

The secret of Father Buchanan's success in stimulating others to generosity can best perhaps be summed up in an incident that occurred last year. He was trucking a load of building material from Valdez to Copper Center in the dead of winter, as usual. He and his companion, another Alaskan missionary who tells the story, left Valdez with a full fuel tank but with only fifteen dollars in cash. Towards evening they stopped for supper at an isolated wayside place. A lone waitress was at the lunch counter.

"How are your hamburgers tonight?" said Father Buchanan.

"The hamburgers are fine, but not for you," replied the woman tartly. "Today is Friday. The cheese on rye is delicious, Father."

After the meal Father Buchanan paid the check and then quietly slipped a ten-dollar bill under his plate. That left less than five dollars to bring them to Copper Center, and they would certainly need more fuel for the rest of the trip. Outside in the cold his companion remonstrated with him.

"Don't worry, man," Father Buchanan replied, "we'll get along all right. I know that woman. She really needs the money. We'll run into someone who will take care of us."

His companion reports that they arrived in Copper Center the next morning with a nearly full tank of fuel and seventy-five dollars in their pockets.

And there was Father Joe Mulry, who died in a concentration camp in the Philippines the night before the American paratroopers came dropping like angels out of the sky to bring the fresh air of freedom to his fellow prisoners. He was an elderly man who always spoke gently and seldom raised his voice. When he felt sick, they took him to the infirmary and left him in care of Dr. Dana Nance and an exhausted nurse, who shared a cup of weak coffee and the last cigarette in the camp before Nance stripped to the waist and began to operate. Only there was nothing they could do, nothing anyone could do. So they closed him up again and just looked at each other, perhaps remembering the many nights when, after the terrible fatigue and drudgery of prison life, they had gathered together and listened to the gentle, stout man talk about Shakespeare. As he discussed Hamlet and Macbeth and Juliet, his rich musical voice rose and fell and worked a magic which transformed the bleak barracks into an enchanted garden in Verona or a magic island filled with sweet airs and haunting melodies. One man's courage and memory, one man's clear voice and steady untroubled vision of the unchangeable things, whose value is precisely the fact that they are unchangeable, one man's generous and openhanded largesse of the wisdom and scholarship and love which he had guarded and cultivated for many years, one man's strength was enough to bring them all peace and courage and hope.

So the doctor and the nurse looked at each other, without words, because words could not awaken the beloved voice, and then they crossed themselves silently and went out of the building to look at the bright skies from which parachutes would drop in the morning.

These are but a few of the many missionaries who are trying in very varied circumstances and within the limitations of their own temperaments and talents to display the faces of Christ to men. Dimly but surely men can catch from them some glimpse of the loveliness of Christ, Who came that men by knowing Him might be drawn to love Him and follow Him back to the beauty and joy of the Father.

11. *Persecution*

Alan Birmingham, s.j.

HONG KONG, which is the ordinary exit from Red China, has welcomed these past seven or eight years more than three thousand missionary priests who have been expelled by the Communists. Recent arrivals are almost always hollow-eyed and tense; they may bear scars left by their manacles. If they have been outside the bamboo curtain for some months they show some hesitation in talking about their time in jail—not from any feeling of shame, but because they know that most of their hearers have heard similar tales times without number. Men who have suffered for the faith are no novelty in Hong Kong (where this is being written).

And yet even now honest but gullible travelers who have visited China on the invitation of that country's present masters return with bright assurances: their late hosts are all for freedom of religion; they themselves have seen Catholic churches open for worship; they have even heard from Catholic priests in China that there is no persecution, that all is well.

Such stories are not mere "travelers' tales." The visitors are telling the truth and nothing but the truth. But they are not telling the whole truth. Far from it! If they but knew,

243

the seemingly edifying experiences which they describe are essential features of probably the most dangerous and the subtlest persecution the Church has ever known. The same persecution, with local modifications but always with the same deceptive façade of toleration and freedom, is raging wherever the Communists now rule. Wherever communism threatens, oppression of this uniform type threatens. It is thus the typical persecution in our Communist-ridden age.

No apology is needed for confining this article to persecution in China. The Communist persecution has spread to neighboring lands: there may be persecution on a smaller scale in other parts of the world. But China is beyond question the most menacing and most typical example our age has to show of persecuted missions. It has not been primarily a bloody persecution. This has proved disconcerting to those who like all far-off persecutions bright with human gore. The clearest statistical indication of the nature of what has been done in China is given in the following figures.

In 1949 there were over three thousand foreign missionary priests in China. Today there are sixteen; about fourteen of them are in prison.

It is known for certain that over two hundred of the two thousand Chinese secular priests are in jail. These priests belong to the comparatively few dioceses from which reliable information is still available. It is morally certain that at least two hundred others are in jail in the more closely shrouded dioceses.

Moreover, the persecution has been bloodier than its general reputation might suggest. In 1953 the *China Mission Bulletin,* most cautious of sources, gave a list of the priests whom since 1940 "God has wished to call to the supreme sacrifice." There are about a hundred and thirty names on the list. Smaller numbers have won other persecutions gory fame. It is then incorrect to say that it has been an unbloody persecution. But it is accurate to say that bloodshed has not been its main characteristic.

When the Red regime was established in Peking, the Jesuit missioners numbered about nine hundred. They had charge of eight dioceses. Two of these, Sienhsien and Kinghsien, are a little south of Peking. Somewhat farther to the south came the diocese of Taming. Still farther south in a large block came the dioceses of Anking, Wuhu, Pengpu, Süchow, and Shanghai, which among them covered most of the provinces of Anhwei and Kiangsu. The combined areas of these dioceses come to about sixty thousand square miles. The pagan population numbered about fifty million, and there were about half a million Catholics. In the south the Portuguese mission of Macao stretches far into China.

In addition more or less large groups of Jesuits were working in Peking, Tientsin, Nanking, Canton, and elsewhere. The eight dioceses named above were entrusted to the care of the Jesuit provinces of Austria, Champagne, Hungary, Leon, eastern Castile, Turin, lower Canada, and Paris, respectively.

Thus the Jesuit missions in China would have provided abundant and varied material for study if no persecution had arisen, and it would have been legitimate to trace out what seemed characteristically Jesuit in their missionary work.

But persecution has arisen. It has not singled out the Jesuits to bear the whole, or the main part, of the burden. It is a persecution of the whole Church. Local variations do not correspond to the variations of missionary organization. The missionaries of China have been sharing an attack which calls forth a uniform resistance and leaves no room for characteristic initiative. In what follows, most of the experiences described will be those of Jesuits; but it would in fact be equally easy to find such experiences in the annals of the Franciscans, the Dominicans, the Fathers of the Paris Foreign Missions, the Milan Foreign Missions, the Maryknoll Fathers, or any of the other missionary groups working in China. It would be easier still to find examples among the Chinese secular clergy, who have had the heaviest burden to bear and have borne it nobly. The Jesuits in China labored and suffered, but they would be the first to deprecate even the faintest suggestion that they suffered alone or that they suffered most. The persecution in China is a persecution of the Church in which the Jesuits have played their part. As such it will be described here.

Even if it were desirable it would be impossible to isolate the Jesuit share of the persecution. Father Alfred Bonningue, S.J., for instance, was one of the most bitterly attacked in 1951. He was attacked in part as the "underling of the imperialist Vienne." This "imperialist" is better known as Monsignor de Vienne, the Vincentian Bishop of Tientsin. There were many similar cases. More significant still was the division of the diocese of Shanghai, till 1949 the Jesuit diocese with the largest Catholic population. Shanghai itself, with a reduced area, was entrusted to the secular clergy. Many Jesuits remained in the new diocese and took part in Shanghai's glorious resistance to Communist persecution; they did so under the inspiring leadership of Bishop Kiong, not a Jesuit, one of the outstanding heroes of the Church in China. The French Jesuits remained responsible for one new prefecture; the Californian Jesuits took over another; the old Shanghai diocese was, like Shanghai itself, handed over to the secular clergy. Thus even when persecution was mounting the Jesuits became more closely bound than ever to the rest of the Church in China. The whole Catholic body was under the general direction of Monsignor Riberi, Internuncio to China. Under him the Catholic Central Bureau, which he had founded, issued the statements and directives that ensured unity of thought and action. The members of that bureau belonged to many different missionary organizations.

It was an apt symbol of the close unity, almost uniformity, necessitated by the perils of the time.

Not for a long time will it be possible to write a definitive history of the Communist persecution in China. It may, indeed, be thought that the time has not yet come for even a tentative essay. Yet several valuable works by exiled missioners have already appeared. (R. W. Greene, M.M., *My Calvary in China;* Remy, *Vu en Chine, Pourpre des Martyrs;* J. Monsterleet, S.J., *Les Martyrs de Chine Parlent;* Monsterleet, *L'Empire de Mao Tse-tung;* J. Lefeuvre, S.J., *Shanghai: les Enfants dans la Ville.*) Thanks, moreover, to the patient, objective, and persevering labors of the editors of the *China Missionary Bulletin* (Shanghai 1948–1949, Hong Kong 1949, and following years; name changed to *Mission Bulletin,* September 1954), a surprising amount of reliable information is already available. Month by month this invaluable journal has given, particularly in its "Mission Chronicle," a brief, well-tested summary of all available information about the different dioceses of China. Most of its information was derived from the accounts given by exiled missionaries who, though they seldom knew what was happening in areas other than their own, were eyewitnesses of much that had happened in their own missions. Almost without exception the facts cited in the following pages are taken from the *China Missionary Bulletin.* That is the guarantee of their accuracy. It is a good guarantee.

So much for the preliminaries.

Like many another country that has fallen under the Communist yoke China has gone through three stages: the preliminary stage, "They will be different here"; the initial stage, "They are different here"; the final stage, "They are the same here as everywhere else."

In the preliminary stage the idyllic propaganda about Yenan was long taken quite seriously, at least in countries which had had no experience of communism in practice. So late as 1949 I myself heard Chinese communism described in terms suggesting that Mao Tse-tung was a twentieth-century Mr. Gladstone, seeing his way to the beginnings of a cautious and long-overdue land reform.

In China this illusion was less common. Communism was active in China.

Missionaries in particular were unlikely to be taken in. The long series of atrocities committed by marauding Communist bands in many missions was fresh in their memories. Father Laflèche, S.J., for instance, lost half of his capacity for cooing over Communist good intentions in a single night. All that night he knelt in the open under the nose of a revolver watching a Communist band burn down the college of which he had been appointed rector a few days earlier. He lost the other half of his capacity for cooing approval a little later when, clothed in anti-religious slogans, he was tried by the same Communists before a howling mob on the charge of having himself burned down the college.

The climax of these horrors came when Communists attacked the Trappists of Yang-Kia-Ping, destroying the monastery and killing, some by ill-treatment, some by straight slaughter, thirty-one monks. After that it was hard to regard the Communists as single-minded land reformers.

Yet even then some retained a vestige of the hope "They will be different here," but they placed their hopes not in the nature of communism, but in the nature of China. The very immensity of China seemed to promise that any political or economic system must suffer dilution as it spread through the country's uncounted hundreds of millions. Then, too, China had a millennial tradition of absorbing her conquerors and arising unchanged from decades of tribulation. Above all, the unwavering devotion to family unity, which has always been the foundation of China's strength, seemed diametrically opposed to the whole practice of communism. Certainly China was the test. If there was any country which would hope to remold communism, China was that country. If China could not do it, no country could do it. Thus with grim foreboding, yet not without all hope, the Church in China watched the unchecked spread of the victorious Communist hosts.

Nineteen hundred and forty-nine saw all China submerged. In January the Communist armies entered Peking. In April they crossed the Yangtze. In May they entered Shanghai. In October they entered Canton. In November they entered Chungking. After that a few mopping-up operations and the job was done. Meanwhile, in March, the Communist central government had been set up in Peking. China was Communist China.

As in Eastern Europe, so also in China, the early days of Communist rule formed a period of bewilderment. The prime task before the new government was the restoration of public order—no mean task after years of war, international and civil. Until that task had been completed, ideological extremism would be out of place. There was much local unpleasantness but, even for the missionaries, there were also local pleasant surprises. The Communist troops were well disciplined beyond all expectation and there was little or no looting or wanton destruction. Officials in newly occupied districts were courteous, sometimes even friendly. For this period, which lasted till well into 1950, the pages of the "Mission Chronicle" (C.M.B.) are a patchwork of conflicting reports. In Süchow, for instance, the bishop and two of his Chinese priests were arrested on a technical point in April 1949. They were quite well treated and were released on June 1. Itinerant mission work was permitted in some parts of his diocese; in other parts it was forbidden "to protect the missionaries against bandits." In the north and northwest of the diocese the Fathers were more or less strictly confined to their residences. In the rest of the diocese no particular hindrance was being put in the way of religious activities.

At about the same time it was reported from Wuhu that the church bells were ringing as of old on Sundays and feast days, and that the priests, both Chinese and foreign, could travel freely on their missionary journeys. Yet almost simultaneously it was reported from Pengpu that two of the three church bells had been taken away, and that in one town the faithful needed special permits to go to Mass.

News from the schools was more alarming. Indoctrination classes had been set up almost at once to train the rising generation in the new orthodoxy. Student councils assumed all authority, and discipline quickly vanished. Some student councils had tried to expel the missionaries. Ridicule was poured on all religion, and so on. Many Superiors had to solve a difficult case of conscience: were they justified in paying the teachers of dialectical materialism who had been forced on them?

Yet even from the schools there was bright news mixed with the dark. In one mission the Fathers received the following note a few days before the Red armies entered the city: "I hope that you, Fathers and Sisters, are not going to leave. I was one of your students and attended your school for years. Now I am afraid you may leave. Please stay. You have nothing to fear. I will help you." Within a few days the writer of that note was chief of the new Communist Education Board, and the school received official recognition without difficulty.

Elsewhere things were not quite so simple, but for a time most of the schools were able to carry on. In Pengpu the Fathers and the Sisters were excluded from their schools and even forbidden to approach the school buildings; but the authorities decided that the students had gone too far, and some improvement followed. One school in Anhwei was left to go ahead in peace, with little trouble from officials or student council. Another in the same mission was closed down and the Fathers were put under house arrest.

Trade schools and charitable institutions—orphanages, dispensaries, hospitals, and the like—fared better than ordinary middle and primary schools. The government recognized that the work being done in them was valuable in itself, and highly appreciated by the people. Too, it knew that no substitutes could be found to run them if the missionaries were expelled. They were heavily taxed, but this was not exceptional; heavy taxes were the order of the day in China. Certain hopes were even held out of a notable reduction in the taxes to be paid by such institutions.

It was very difficult to see any clear plan behind this mixture of vexations and reliefs. The Common Programme was the nearest thing to a constitution then existing in China, and the Common Programme laid it down in Article 5: "That the people of the People's Republic of China shall have liberty of thought, speech, publication, assembly, association, correspondence, person, domicile, movement from place to place, religious belief, and freedom to hold processions and demonstrations." Interpreted in the obvious sense of the words, this article seemed to assure the future of the Church, and for some time the government did nothing to render such hopes impossible. Catholics, lay as well as clerical, found it possible to escape from many a difficult position by appealing to this article.

A constant stream of propaganda was directed over the people to convince them that religion was superstition, that religious observances were a waste of precious time that should have been devoted to productive work. The missionaries were treated as the worst of all time wasters. A very famous list of occupations published towards the end of the period we are considering gave the Communist view of missionaries with startling clarity. Here is the list in order of merit: "Soldiers, laborers, farmers, government workers, artisans, intellectuals (teachers and students), craftsmen, businessmen, prostitutes, *missionaries.*" (There is much in this list that seems designed chiefly to shock: still, it is very shocking.)

For all that, the higher echelons of the government showed themselves capable of a certain capricious helpfulness. When, for instance, the students' council forced the resignation of the Fathers of the Tsinku University, Tientsin, the Mayor of the city and the Military Governor intervened to ensure the Fathers' return. Later on the Military Governor issued an official statement saying, *inter alia,* "Everyone's liberty to search for truth and to embrace religion will be carefully respected. No student shall be obliged to attend lectures on religion, non-believers shall respect the faith of those who have adopted a religion. Insulting language and disturbances will not be tolerated."

More surprisingly still, the government at times insisted on the return of mission property that had been eased away from the Church by local Communist agents. Indeed, there was at one time talk of an official central government decree on this.

Few missionaries had expected even such slight toleration as existed in those early months, and it is easy to sense the air of pleased surprise that pervades reports from many missions. In spite of many difficulties there was an incipient tendency to say, "They are a little different here."

Yet even at that time the difficulties besetting the missionaries were very grave. As soon as the new government felt secure in any district it introduced the land reform. This could have been used directly against the Church, for in most places the Church owned some land. It was so used at times, but the chief difficulty was indirect. During the land reform there was a complete suspension of all rights of free assembly and free movement from place to place. The first of these suspensions involved the forbidding of parish

Masses. The second deprived priests of all liberty to visit districts other than that in which they lived. Churches, moreover, were borrowed for land-reform meetings. When the land reform was completed, the prohibition of assembly lapsed, but few of the churches were restored to the missionaries and travel without a special permit remained difficult or impossible. Thus, without overt, organized persecution, the countryside was largely deprived of the exercise of religion and of the presence of priests. Only in the larger centers was normal Catholic life at all possible. Great damage had already been done. Yet at this stage it was still possible to hope that it had been done inadvertently, as an indirect consequence of actions taken for reasons that were not directly opposed to religion. There was as yet no formal persecution. It was impossible to be sanguine: it was still possible to hope.

One element in this complex situation was full of present glory and of promise for the future: this was the loyal and unhesitating faith of the Catholics. The missionaries had indeed hoped for great things, but the reality surpassed all hopes. This is not surprising: all men, even the holiest, have something human in their judgment; but the strength of the Catholics came from the Holy Ghost, and the gifts of the Holy Ghost always surpass the imagination of men. Even those still outside the Church felt the outpouring of divine grace. From every side reports of conversions came pouring in. This supernatural steadfastness made persecution certain; but, as the future was to show, it would abide under persecution and would make persecution a channel of grace.

What policy did the priests adopt at this time? First they decided to remain in China. A certain number of invalids were sent away; so were a few against whom there was notoriously strong feeling in the Communist hierarchy: all rashness and all seeking for martyrdom were sternly deprecated by responsible Catholic leaders. A few priests left to take charge of Chinese seminaries outside China. The over-whelming majority remained.

So long as this was possible, those who remained carried on all their old work. In addition they made it their business to strengthen the Catholics for the troubles that certainly lay ahead. It was in the course of this work that Father Beda Chang, S.J., began to attract the attention that would ulti-mately win him great suffering and great glory.

Whether they had a little hope of arriving at a permanent *modus vivendi* or no hope at all—the wisest and best in-formed had no hope—all missionaries saw that a clear dis-tinction would have to be made between the essential and the unessential. Old institutions, old habits, old ways should be defended as long as such defense seemed prudent; but with changing circumstances there would be compromise on such matters, or even complete surrender. On all that touched the faith itself there could be nothing but resistance to the end. It is easy to understand and applaud such a pol-icy from far away; it was another thing to prepare to apply it on the spot. The missionaries had to be ready to see the work of generations destroyed in a day: the faithful had to be strengthened in a loyalty that would survive the destruc-tion of all that had constituted the external appeal of the faith.

In Shanghai, Father Chang, rector of St. Ignatius' College and already a prominent leader of the city's Catholic life, was outstanding in his clear recognition of the needs and circumstances of the times, and still more outstanding for his earnest and successful efforts to give the faithful that deep-ened spiritual life which would stand firm against all the power of the world. Someday—please God!—it will be pos-sible to sum up the splendid tragedy of the Church in Com-munist China by writing a full account of this holy priest's labors during life, and of the enduring effects of these labors, and of his memory among the persecuted Catholics of

Shanghai. Father Lefeuvre's magisterial *Les Enfants dans la Ville* has already shown the way to future biographers.

The attack on the Church started from an obscure center in far-off Szechwan with a Three-Autonomy Manifesto. The three autonomies insisted upon for all Chinese churches were self-government, self-support, and self-propagation. The manifesto purported to have been signed by the local parish priest. (The claim seems to have been false. I cannot find any definite information on this point. Szechwan is very far away indeed.) That manifesto was treated as proclaiming the foundation of a new Independent Catholic Church. The fight had started. It is still going on.

Everywhere priests, especially Chinese priests, were urged to join the new movement.

There was as yet no suggestion of a breach with Rome—for a time not even a suggestion of action against the Pope's representative in China. But there was constant pressure on all prominent Catholics, priests especially, to sign a statement which went no further than to say, "We are Catholics, but we are also citizens of China; we love our country and we will exercise intense vigilance against all secret conspiracies of imperialism; we will not allow imperialism to use religion as a means of aggression." In itself this was a harmless declaration and some did sign. The Communist press quickly showed that these signatures were regarded as symbols of adhesion to Yu Yau-tsung's movement. The fatal ambiguity of the word "country" gave a semblance of justice to such an interpretation. An even clearer indication of the true meaning of the declaration was given by the ever more numerous accusations of "imperialism" brought against foreign missionaries. Clearly such declarations could not be signed; the Chinese Catholic leaders had to risk the odium that might well be stirred up by their refusal to sign a document that, on the face of it, was merely a declaration of patriotism. They took the risk. They suffered much in consequences, but they were spared one great sorrow: the Catholic laity understood and remained faithful to their priests. Few nations have had so glorious a page in their history.

Accusations of, and expulsions for, imperialism soon became so common that they ceased to attract the attention of the Catholic press outside China and were ordinarily recorded in a line or two. One such brief description of an early accusation may help us to understand what was going on. Early in 1951 two priests were accused of crimes of imperialism. For a month before the trial of two priests there was constant propaganda against them, with processions, public demonstrations, and caricatures of the two priests vested as if for Mass and holding machine guns. Despite all efforts none of their students at the accusation meeting showed any hostility. The priests were expelled. Even so early a description as this is brief and colorless. Trials were already becoming part of the ordinary missionary's expectations.

About the same time two Fathers, one French, the other Chinese, were forced to leave the Tientsin university, where, a short time before, the government had protected them from the indiscreet zeal of the students. The circumstances of the second expulsion were like those of the first: the teaching body and the students resented their "increasingly reactionary" attitude: two months later three of the French Fathers were arrested. There was no government protection. Times had changed.

In face of the danger the Catholic authorities strove above all to clarify the situation. The Catholic Central Bureau issued clear statements which removed all ambiguity from the three autonomies. A statement of the lawful Catholic interpretation of the autonomies was offered and was greeted with fury. In April, His Excellency Monsignor Riberi, Internuncio to China, wrote to the bishops disassociating himself from a "reformist" meeting which had been held in Nanking, the city of the Internuncio's residence, under, sad to say, the patronage of the unfaithful Vicar-General of the diocese. The Internuncio's letter roused the government's fury and made the writer the main target for Communist attack. They were still unwilling to advocate open schism—they knew what the Catholic response would be. But if the Catholics could be roused, even by fear or by fraud, to attack the Pope's representative, that would obviously be the next best thing to an attack on the Holy Father himself.

The campaign that followed was waged with all fury, and was painfully serious for those involved in it. Yet it had one comic facet. Knowing that many would refuse to attack the Internuncio but would easily enough petition for the expulsion of an unknown foreign "imperialist," they suppressed all reference to His Excellency's office. Monsignor Riberi is a native of Monaco. So China was deluged with attacks on Riberi the imperialist from Monaco. Poor Monaco! Less than one square mile yet apparently accused of imperialist designs on China.

There was, however, no humor in the situation of the Internuncio or of the missionaries who shared with him the burden of the day. Accusation and imprisonment and expulsion became so common that they soon lost news value. Twenty-nine Catholic missionaries were thrust across the Hong Kong border in a single day in April 1951. On the following day six more arrived. There were, in all, about two hundred expulsions in five months of that year. The pace was kept up, with certain tactical variations, till the supply of foreign missionaries ran out. The Chinese priests shared in the accusations and the imprisonment. Only death, it seemed, could bring their travail to an honorable end. Not only did the majority stand firm, but the seminarians stayed on and the seminaries still existed and continued their preparation for a life which promised nothing but misery in this world. There are many glories in the history of China, but there is no glory greater than this.

It may seem astonishing that seminaries should have survived, yet this was in line with the whole policy of the Independent Church. There was freedom of religion. No one was to be hindered from the full practice of his faith. The Internuncio and certain bishops, priests, Brothers, Sisters, and laymen and women had indeed been attacked in the press and at accusation meetings, and many of these had been imprisoned or expelled; but all this had nothing to do with their ecclesiastical positions or affiliations. The masses had risen in just anger against the individual crimes of these people, and the government, with whatever reluctance, had carried out the will of the people. That was all there was to it. Religion was as free as ever.

Despite all efforts very little support could be found for this Independent Church. Committees of "progressive" Catholics were formed, but most of the members were Catholics who had long ceased to practice their religion. A few priests eager to find a *modus vivendi* with the ruling powers did compromise themselves by signing ambiguous documents; the Chinese priests in prison always outnumbered the waverers; and even the waverers objected when they were asked to separate openly from the Holy Father. Given the circumstances, the number of real apostates was astonishingly small. In June, Monsignor Riberi was put under house arrest and the Catholic Central Bureau, which he had founded, was forced to suspend its activities. In September the Internuncio was expelled, with a flourish of much publicized accusations (espionage, "devising" and organizing the Legion of Mary, opposing the People's Government), and the directors of the Catholic Central Bureau were arrested. All through the country the attack went on. Monsignor Fahy, S.J., and all his foreign priests were arrested, most appropriately, on the feast of St. Ignatius. (St.

Ignatius himself was arrested in his day, yet not so gloriously
as this little band of his American sons.) Archbishop Melen-
dro, S.J., and five of his priests were expelled in August when
an attempt to establish the Independent Church in their
diocese, Anking, ended in a fiasco. In the same month Father B. Chang, S.J., was jailed as a "lackey of imperialism."
And so on, and so on, and so on. During 1951 the number of
Jesuits in China dropped by about a hundred and seventy-
five. The number in jail went up. A little bag containing
what they would need in prison became part of the normal
equipment of most priests.

Even a bare list of the imprisoned and the expelled would
fill many pages. It is impossible to give more than a few representative notes here. Father Beda Chang's arrest, however,
calls for more extended treatment.

As was noted above, Father Beda was far from being the
only priest to suffer death. The spread of his fame and the
abiding power of his memory owe as much to his life and
character as to his death. He played a major part in heart-
ening and briefing the Catholic students for a struggle that
stands out even in the heroic history of the past few years.
In the resistance to the Independent Church movement he
showed up the hypocrisy of the ambiguous use of "love of
country." At public meetings he displayed a fervor of true
patriotism such as no Communist orator could rival, and
with a clarity that could not be ignored he pointed out the
compatibility of such patriotism with full loyalty to the
Church. Unsullied loyalty to his faith and unsurpassed
devotion to his country made an intolerable combination.
Clearly the man was rotted with imperialism. Jail for him!

Not much news is heard nowadays of those who disappear
into Chinese jails; but an exception was made in favor of
Father Beda Chang and of Father Joseph Sheng, who had
been arrested about a month after Father Beda. A much
publicized Progressive pamphlet announced that the two

jailed Fathers had joined the Progressives. No one seems to have given much credence to this startling news, and it was soon superseded by the disclosure that Father Beda had joined not the Progressive Church, but the Church Triumphant. On November 11, little more than three months after he had gone, in good health, to prison, Father Beda died in the prison infirmary.

We may acquit his captors of all wish to cause his death. They wanted to break his spirit, to induce him, by any means, to sign a Progressive declaration. A broken-spirited Father Beda Chang would have been an invaluable weapon in the hands of the Progressives. They had done what they could, and they had gone too far. Father Beda, dead for the faith, was to be the hammer of the Progressive Church. True to their invariable policy, "There must be no martyrs," the authorities made every effort to hush up the details of the death. The infirmary doctor would assign no definite cause of death, and insisted that he could certify that it was due neither to violence nor to poison. No such assurance was needed. Enough was known of the methods of brain-washing.

The news spread through the city, and on the thirteenth, three thousand gathered in sorrow, pride, and triumphant joy for the Requiem. On the following day the students for whom he had done so much gathered to honor his memory. On that day the celebrant wore the significant red vestments, and the Mass ended with a Te Deum. Other churches followed with jubilant obsequies, which continued till the authorities took alarm and forbade further demonstrations. Meanwhile the scarcely recognizable body of the dead priest had been buried secretly under police supervision. It was forbidden to put any inscription on the grave other than the words, "Beda Chang, Criminal." The grave in consequence has remained nameless. It has not remained without honor. The thought of that nameless grave has ever since been a rallying point for the dispersed multitude in many places, but most of all in Shanghai.

The virulence of the attacks on Father Beda's memory in the Communist press is a gauge of the devotion of the Catholics, who, as things became harder, turned to that memory with increasing confidence. Ultimately the authorities felt constrained to tell the Bishop of Shanghai that he would be responsible for any miracles worked by Father Beda.

There is no room here for the epic story of the Shanghai students whom Father Beda had helped to train. It is one of the best-known stories of the whole persecution, yet it cannot be told too often. Most English speakers regard students as irresponsible young men, licensed to stretch their intellectual legs for a few years before taking up the serious business of life. Holders of this view are inclined to smile at lands which take students seriously and to regard them as political and social leaders. There is much to be said for the former opinion, yet events in Shanghai suggest that it does not contain the whole truth. These young men trained themselves spiritually and intellectually for the struggle that they knew would someday come.

They made retreats; they learned to pray deeply. Following out an idea presented in one of the late Monsignor R. H. Benson's books, we might say that they made their noviceship for the Order of Christ Crucified. When the hour of tribulation came, they were ready. Their native Chinese wit had been sharpened by their training, and they displayed the subtlest finesse in using the weapon of the official freedom of religion. They fenced with infinite adroitness; but when a crucial point of principle arose, they fenced no longer; they stood firm. Even the complete communizing of the Aurora University did not weaken their skillful and tenacious resistance. In the end the government dispersed them through the country, but wherever they went their gallant, deeply founded loyalty strengthened and comforted their new companions in the faith.

Once Monsignor Riberi had been expelled, the direct attack on the Pope began in earnest. Caricatures with more brutality than words can tell held him up to mockery as a bloody archimperialist whose plans for Americanizing (Yes! Americanizing. This is part of the cant) the world were being foiled by the noble democracy of the People's Republic. Article after article execrated him in the press.

Then in the middle of 1953 there was a change of policy. The leaders admitted that they had been wrong. Their attacks on the Pope had been a mistake. They now wished all Catholics to remain united to His Holiness. Let the Catholics for their part accept this new gesture and, as a sign of unity, sign professions of love of country and admit the Progressives to the Sacraments. (Those, however, who had gone to prison for loyalty to the Pope were not released.)

This change of policy was obviously designed to make the position of the Chinese priests more difficult than before. How could they stand out against the new friendship of their own government? The new policy was presented with the greatest skill, and for the moment a few were deceived; but not for long. Those who had signed were able to make glorious amends by courageously withdrawing their signatures publicly.

The new policy made little difference in the lives of the missionaries. The old squalid farce of accusation and expulsion went on as before. Indeed in Shanghai, hitherto left comparatively peaceful—note "comparatively"—the full fury of persecution was let loose. Quite suddenly most of the most influential priests were swept to prison or into exile, "expelled from China forever," as the very common sentence put it. The bishop himself was left free for two more years, but the hand of the persecutor was heavy on his diocese. In many other dioceses expulsions were becoming rare: there was no one left to expel. "June, 1953, last foreign priest leaves Wuhu. November, 1953, last foreign priest expelled from Pengpu": so run my notes. I am tempted to dwell on this last Father. For two months he lived on the streets as a beggar till the compassion of those round him, Catholic and pagan, forced the government to treat him a little better.

I am tempted to dwell on many another too. But the history of the past six years is so full of suffering and so full of heroism that even the writer of a large book would have to pick and choose. Monsignor Fahy, Monsignor Lischerong, Father de Bascher, Father Martínez, Father Lefebvre (who died owing, it would seem, to the carelessness of his escort, in Canton on the last lap of his journey to exile)—their stories clamor to be told. If they were told, as many more stories would be left clamoring.

All these names are foreign. What of the Chinese sufferers? I do not dare to mention names lest even such slight publicity as that should involve them in greater suffering. They go to jail, these men, men who may be the fine flower of a culture more ancient and more refined than any known in the West. They go to the hardship and the harrying, and the squalor of their jails. We do not hear of them again. "If the hope we have learned to repose in Christ belongs to this world only, then we are unhappy beyond all other end. But no, Christ has risen from the dead, the first fruits of all those who have fallen asleep." (1 Corinthians xv.)

All the time the great exodus of priests was going on—some forced out, some expelled at short notice, some expelled after imprisonment.

At the beginning of 1950 there were, it would seem, about five hundred and eighty Jesuits in China. By the middle of 1953 there were not more than two hundred and fifty. At the beginning of the present (1956) there were only 150, all except eight were Chinese. Forty-eight of the 150 were in prison.

"Being forced out" is not a euphemism for "quitting." It should be taken quite literally. Bishop Zeno Aramburu, S.J., of Wuhu, for instance, might well have sighed for a simple expulsion. He and his priests were concentrated in the central mission house. A handful of Progressives, with police stiffening, tried to make him join the Independent Church. When he refused, he and his priests were moved to a little house near the cathedral. There the Progressives tried again to force him to join them, or at least to say Midnight Mass for them at Christmas. He refused, so they surrounded the house with continuously blaring loud-speakers in an attempt to shout him out, and they tied a huge hog to his door in an attempt to stink him out. The bishop stayed. The Progressives came once more and evicted him from the little house. The bishop tried to move to a hotel, but the police forbade this. He then said that he would build a reed house for himself, but the police reminded him that foreigners were not allowed to build in the People's Republic. After that the bishop applied for an exit permit. The bishop was then seventy-three years old.

Expulsion may be with or without accusation meetings. When preparing the present account I asked a Jesuit who should know if there was any principle behind the division into simple expellees, accusation-meeting expellees, and jailees. He himself was a man whom any self-respecting Communist must have burned to get rid of in some way or other. Yet he had been let work unmolested for a long time, and then expelled after a private grueling, i.e., without public accusation. His answer was illuminating. Since the whole purpose is to bring about the destruction of the Church from within by turning the faithful against the clergy, the principle of discrimination is one of simple utility. If there is some plausible pretext for public accusation, such an accusation is made at once. If there is at the moment no pretext, imprisonment must be considered. Brain-washing and general ill-treatment may induce the prisoner to confess some real or imaginary "crime": then a damaging accusation meeting will follow. Yet this process must not be used too often: even the simplest would smell a rat if it became obvious that nearly all "criminals" had to be imprisoned before their crimes could be discovered. Accordingly, a certain number had to be expelled in informal fashion, with a brief announcement of their crimes. Bishops and other influential clerics were especially likely to suffer imprisonment. The public accusation of such men would be likely to injure the Church. Expelling a priest without a public demonstration was, to the Communist, a sad waste of an opportunity to split the Church; yet it was often preferable to allowing him to continue his work.

The accusation meeting, if it succeeds, is a very terrible weapon. A mob, of Catholics if possible (it is rarely possible), failing that, a pagan mob seasoned with Progressives, is worked up to a frenzy of hatred against the accused. He is allowed to make no defense. This is not a trial. It is simply the masses calling for vengeance on a criminal. The accused suffers: false accusation is always hard to bear, and long-continued insult also is hard to bear. The accusers suffer more deeply: their participation in such a scene tends inevitably to rot their characters and to induce a feeling of helpless, hopeless guilt. To justify themselves against the reproach of their consciences they are likely to harden themselves in evil.

The crimes ordinarily alleged against missionaries are at first sight very curious. The supremely vague charge of "imperialism" usually heads the list. It can mean anything or nothing, but it makes strong appeal to a nationalistic mob. Espionage is used similarly even when the evidence amounts to no more than a report on parochial matters made to a local bishop. Illegal possession and use of a radio transmitter is a strangely common charge—one which does little honor to the efficiency of the local detectors. Hostility to the People's Republic, sabotage of the Independent Church, and support of the hated Legion of Mary are the other main charges. Apart from the radio charge, which is usually too absurd to be taken seriously, the list seems to the outside world vague and largely innocuous. Yet it is consistently chosen. The aim is kept in sight. The accused are to be exposed as enemies of the masses, as inimical to laws that the masses have passed through their instrument, the government. All the charges listed—even the Legion of Mary charge, if we accept the official view of that body—are capable of stirring up the desired resentment. By planting weapons, and so on, a semblance of probability can be given to the charges.

At times the evidence is displayed before the public in organized exhibitions, but without much success. Very often the organizers have been uneducated agents, and the students, the group chiefly aimed at, have been quick to notice such revealing details as inconsistent dates on documents or carelessly rigged apparatus. Bishop Philip Coté, S.J., of Süchow, for instance, was accused of having a radio transmitter. The exhibitors put the incriminated instrument on view. Clearly the greater part of the exhibit was some kind of radio set, and the attached lettered keyboard seemed to prove that the set was constructed to send out written messages. Very inconveniently for the exhibitors, the apparatus was quite familiar to the students, who had often seen it in the room of their science teacher, Father Maurice Garneau, S.J., supposedly the bishop's radio-transmission operator. The students pointed out that the radio was an ordinary receiving set, and that the damning keyboard was an ordinary typewriter, with which they had often played. Despite this disclosure, which ruined the exhibition, the bishop was condemned and, after prolonged imprisonment, expelled. Curiously enough, Father Garneau was left at liberty for another couple of years.

Charges of sexual immorality are added at times, but these seem to be secondary. They stir up hatred against the individual rather than against the Church itself. Still such charges have proved effective, in public accusations and in private calumny, particularly with young hearers. Chinese priests have been the chief, though not the only, victims. The evidence is easily rigged: a few pornographic pictures are slipped into a priest's Breviary after his arrest or just before it, and the trick is done. If necessary, false witness can be supplied. Considerable skill is shown in arranging these affairs: usually the accused, after expulsion, prefer not to discuss the loathsome details of such accusations.

We may be inclined to doubt the efficacy of such accumulations of trumped-up charges, yet it is well to remember the old principle "Throw enough mud and some of it will stick." Deeper doubts are stirred by our habitual good opinion of human nature. We find it hard to believe that any group of men can indulge in perpetual hypocrisy. Here, therefore, it is well to recall the perversion of the very idea of truth which is involved in the principles of communism. The Communist criterion of truth is a statement's aptitude to hasten the approach of the classless society. Conformity with fact is thus an irrelevant consideration. A Communist falsifier can be sincere with his perverted type of sincerity even when he is busy falsifying.

Prison treatment varies a good deal. Solitary confinement, confinement in a packed cell, refusal of leave to lie down, to sleep, to lean against the wall, to talk, to remain silent, and so on. It is the jailers' job to make life unpleasant for their charges; it must be allowed that they do this job thoroughly. In some places the guards allow the prisoners to relieve nature only at fixed, insufficient intervals. The prisoner suffers, and in a degrading manner. Baths are rare. In close confinement and a hot climate the prisoner's body soon stinks, and the skin becomes diseased. Prison is not pleasant.

Much worse, however, are the endless interrogations. Cinematographic and journalistic descriptions have made this a familiar idea, yet cannot convey any real impression of what such questioning can mean when it is continued without mercy for days at a time or day after day for months. That so many have undergone this torment without breaking is matter for wonder.

Mention was made above of the hollow-eyed men who come from the Communist jails. They are hollow-eyed. Yes! But they are not defeated men. Many have to go at once to hospital, but those who can move round almost always clamor for work at once, scarcely realizing how exhausted they are.

Anyone who met such priests in Hong Kong will have special memories—Father Thornton, S.J., for instance. Nature made Father Thornton gaunt; nine or ten months in a Communist jail had made him ghostlike, yet there was nothing thin about the tale he had to tell. As he told it, there were high comedy and farce in the prison cell scenes, tense vigorous drama in the interrogations—O. Henry varied with Perry Mason, all punctuated with expansive gestures from emaciated limbs and a high explosive laugh.

Father Valois was another Jesuit who came laughing. He had every right to laugh, for during an accusation meeting, being tickled by the absurdity of the charges made against him, he laughed so infectiously that the crowd laughed too.

Father Havas of the Hungarian Province of the Society arrived after twenty-one months of imprisonment. Some of these months he spent in solitary confinement; the rest he spent in all too close contact with his examiners. For two months he answered nothing at all, and when he began to speak he was no great comfort to his examiners. Accused of having refused to register with the Hungarian People's Government, Father Havas asked for his leather bag, and produced a photostat copy of the vital document from the lining. To all accusations he replied, "If I am guilty punish me. I admit nothing and I will sign nothing." He kept his word. During examinations he was barred into a low chair in front of the judge, yet no one hearing his tale can doubt that he was the master in all discussions. I have said that expellees are usually hollow-eyed. Father Havas was an exception. After all he had gone through, his eyes were still sparkling with life and fire; but one feels certain that when he left his prison hollow-eyed examiners breathed more freely to see him depart.

Such highhearted gaiety was rare. Most of those who came out were soberer in their triumph. Yet it was triumph. They had been expelled with every outward sign of degradation. They came aged, hobbling, queerly clad, sick. But in the land they had left, the Catholics they had worked for were bearing themselves manfully in the struggle for God's honor and God's glory. No missioner could think that that was his own doing. All could sing joyfully, "How great are the wonders God has worked through my unworthiness!"

12. *Problems of Tomorrow*

Edward L. Murphy, s.j.

BECAUSE of their wide representation on the missions Jesuits are necessarily concerned with the political, economic, and cultural movements which are sweeping the world. They must understand what is taking place in the world in order to offer Catholicism to the vast populations undergoing change. Otherwise they cannot expose the faith as something vital and present and necessary for every people. The changes in human society require changes in emphasis and method in the missionary apostolate. The present situation of the missionary movement of the Church has to be appraised in relation to events in the world. In the light of that appraisal future procedures have to be indicated, but with caution. Prophecy would be dangerous.

The world scene presents a picture of political and economic turmoil and uncertainty. There are no great static masses, especially in those areas where the Church has worked for years, such as Asia and Africa. The old orders are passing or, at least, are seriously challenged, so that some kind of change is universally inevitable. There are few small enclaves of peoples who can remain for the present unaffected by world movements. Few peoples can now withdraw behind a barrier of traditional forms, because there seem to be no barriers entirely impenetrable now. This is true for both the iron curtain and the bamboo curtain. Only in the deepest hinterlands are there small populations still relatively untouched by the world-embracing changes. Presumably they will not long continue in this state.

On the political level the change has already been made in many places from a colonial status to independence. Where the colonial status still exists, there is constant pressure for more self-government. British, French, and Dutch colonialism are passing rapidly. Complete self-government is now exercised in India, Burma, Ceylon, and Pakistan. Vietnam has been divided between the free south and the Communistic north. Indonesia has passed from the tutelage of Holland. The countries of North Africa have achieved independence or are fighting for it. The Sudan, the federation of Northern and Southern Rhodesia and Nyasaland are controlling their own political destinies. Other places, held in trust by some major nations under the United Nations, are assured of development toward self-government. China, North Vietnam, and North Korea have been brought under Communist domination. Japan is undergoing considerable political change. The lives of 1.38 billion people, one half of the world's population, are involved in political change.

Formidable problems often follow in the wake of such political evolution. An upsurge in nationalism results in a hostility to everything foreign, and this opposition is expressed freely, sometimes violently. A renewed pride in national cultural and religious products deepens the resistance and often begets contempt for what is considered foreign. China has expelled the foreigner and shut itself off from the world. Indonesia has laid a heavy hand on the Dutch. India has placed restrictions on foreign missionary personnel, and in some areas Hindus have resorted to violence in spite of the Constitution. Buddhism has become political in Ceylon. The

Bandung Conference of Afro-Asian nations was the forum for a billion and a half people who have common interests. It was clear that these nations were preparing to control their destinies with concerted action and to promote the cause of their area of the world with their eyes on their own advantage. Newly acquired power tends to extend its control over all areas of life, and the non-national is cast in the role of an intruder or, at best, an outsider. The strong Moslem element in the Sudanese Government attempted to nationalize the educational system in southern Sudan, where there is a heavier concentration of Christians. Thus the use of power will at times be arbitrary due to inexperience and lack of security.

Startling advances have been made in the improvement of methods of production, agricultural and industrial, due in large measure to the generosity of the more highly developed nations. Through the activities of United Nations agencies, programs of technical assistance, and the efforts of local government gigantic efforts are being made to improve the economic lot of immense populations. According to the Statistical Yearbook of the United Nations for 1955 almost every country in the world shows increases in the production of all agricultural commodities and livestock. Most nations show a growth in gross food supplies, although the net food supplies for some areas show no increase in the caloric content of daily diet. Transportation facilities have almost doubled in parts of Asia and Africa above the pre-war level. This promises much for the economic elevation of millions, for a higher standard of living and for a longer life tenure. Such a result is certainly desirable when one reflects on the previous precarious existence of millions and their necessary preoccupation with hunger. Such development becomes imperative in the face of the present impossibility of providing for population growths without the use of modern means of production.

Undoubtedly, to meet the economic needs and to guarantee better economic development industrialization and mechanization are necessary. This is not necessarily an unspotted good—especially when it is effected in too great haste. Western society should be able to remember the miseries and degradation induced by the nineteenth-century industrial revolution. It is possible to forget the individual in an unrestrained and narrow-minded haste for economic development.

Today Africa reveals the effects of industrialization and the concentration of unprepared masses in industrial centers. There has been a serious demoralization of many Africans, removed suddenly and completely from the traditional modes of their tribal existence and injected into a milieu of no restraint and no protective social forms. The temptation comes to herd into centers masses of workers who are unaccustomed to the pressures, spiritual and moral, of modern methods of high-power production. Not all who will be seeking to gain new markets and to utilize new sources of available raw materials will be motivated by human concerns.

Due to the international character of so many movements a world-wide organization of workers is taking place. The International Council of Free Trade Unions has certainly extended its activities to Africa and Asia, although the leadership, at times, is seriously colored with Marxist philosophy parading as social democracy. This is frowned upon in some areas as giving too much power into the hands of illiterate and inexperienced masses who may be easily prevailed upon by demagogic leaders. There is danger, then, of the reaction of a stifling paternalism which is unwilling to accept this necessary evolution in human society. These economic changes impose the need for the social development and reorganization of the lives of people to fit them for the changes. The missionary Church has a deep realization of such need.

These political and economic changes cannot leave undisturbed traditional social forms. Changes in social and cultural life are compelled. For example, theoretically the social and political status of sixty million Haridjan has been changed in India. How long it will take to incorporate them into the national scene with a position of dignity and equality, long denied, cannot be predicted. But an assault has been made from within upon the centuries-old social forms. A wedge has been driven into the ancient rigid social exclusiveness. Communism in China is attempting a complete revolution in the life of the nation. It has made a deliberate effort to break with the past. Not only Christianity but Confucianism and Buddhism have been severely attacked. Rapid change carries with it the danger of too suddenly disrupting the old protective norms of society and of thus creating a degree of social chaos until more adequate forces have been developed. For the most part the leaders in this upheaval of the mission world have been the educated classes, especially those educated in the West, where they have absorbed a secularistic outlook on life as well as an admiration for Western techniques of production. This makes them impatient with tradition, which, coupled with the colonialism of the West, is regarded as the cause of present inferiority. Thus there is the internal conflict between using the advances of Western society and not becoming westernized culturally. But withal there is advantage in these aspirations for change—many customs responsible for cultural and social stagnation cannot endure in the presence of such change.

Programs for reducing the rate of illiteracy and the growth of educational opportunities, especially for women, necessarily create a leaven in the ideas of emerging populations. One obvious effect is a change in the philosophy and status of women. The United Nations statistical reports record the increase in publication of books, many of which deal with philosophy, religion, and the social sciences. Exchange programs for students have been continually expanded, so that the advances of the more highly developed nations will gradually be transferred to the less developed peoples. Immense populations are being exposed through increased literacy and the visual media of communication to all kinds of ideas and attitudes. The world-wide extension of such media as radio, moving pictures, and even television add to the published sources of information. Whether people in hitherto undeveloped areas will it or not, their ideas and their lives are being changed. Former patterns of life are disappearing, sometimes perhaps too quickly.

At no time in history has there been such widespread world consciousness or so much organized help for the cultural and economic advance of formerly undeveloped nations. The establishment of the United Nations has encouraged the sense of the world implications of political and economic systems and cultural forms.

One must also take into account the intense competition between communistic and non-communistic nations. It is indeed a strange phenomenon when former colonial empires have withdrawn their control from more than six hundred million and the communistic system has extended its imperialism over almost eight hundred million people. Such a situation creates an atmosphere of international uncertainty and confusion. This distress is manifest in some new nations which try to follow a middle-of-the-road or neutral policy, lest they be crushed between the stones of conflicting political systems. They think it to their advantage to be noncommittal.

So in spite of a genuine spirit of internationalism which has made the majority of nations broaden their horizons to the sweep of one world, one human family, there remains a condition of fear and suspicion which retards the implementation of this recognized solidarity of the nations.

Even though the world is tortured with wars and conflicts and hostilities, an appraisal, warranted by many facts, of the present scene would indicate inevitable evolution in many societies—transition rather than unrelieved chaos and catastrophe. No one can sincerely will to perpetuate the colonial status beyond its time even though it had some immediate and partial advantages for certain phases of the missionary apostolate. The British and the French may feel that the tempo of transition should not be so rapid. But there can be no holding back of the movements. One could not honestly wish to petrify any society in a social and political system just because it seemed easier to work in the relative stability of what was a fixed and undisturbed context. Historically social and political transition have generally taken place with some kind of violence, confusion, perhaps even temporary chaos. One need but recall the chaos consequent upon the decay of the Roman Empire and the violence in the spread of the Moslem empire. The Western world itself in its own immediate history gives more than ample evidence of this fact in the spread of communism, fascism, and nazism. Extremism seems to be unavoidable, because goals are not clearly defined and the vision of leaders is often clouded by excessive emotionalism. Africa and Asia could no more remain in a state of political and social suspension than Europe and America. The parentage of these new societies is not entirely Asian or African. The political, economic, and cultural ideas of the West have been in gestation for years in those parts of the world. Evidently the ideas are now coming to term and the birth process of a newer world is accompanied by some violent convulsion, anguish, and uncertainty. It is folly to wish it otherwise. The West has sown, almost in spite of itself, the seeds of change; we cannot stifle the harvest in spite of the weeds.

It should not be presumed that only a monster can issue forth from this labor. Already truly human features are discernible: growth in the dignity and self-respect of peoples; increase in a sense of social responsibility; the will to improve the material conditions of life; the desire to take a place of honor and equality in the family of nations. The present aspirations for one world would be an idle dream unless undeveloped nations were brought to the full status of nations. The truth of human solidarity is translated into political and social action. This is much better than the earlier paternalism which too often was content to perpetuate the political and cultural infancy of vast numbers of people.

The horrors of the present need not be minimized in order to pursue the idea of transition. Communism is certainly a present menace and an actual tyranny. But complete chaos can be prophesied only if the Providence of God and the presence of the Church in the midst of peoples are canceled out. Just because the fodder for communism is present in social and economic inferiority, the prophecy that communism will dominate emerging populations is not warranted. The Bandung Conference was as severe in its strictures against communism as it was in its resentment against colonialism. Other forces are at work to counteract the drive of atheistic materialism. Among such forces is the missionary Church, which should not be discounted in a true appraisal of world conditions.

Everywhere the Church is in the midst of these problems and changes. In some places the changes seem to have destroyed the efforts of several centuries, as in China. In other places the Church is bracketed with an undesirable Westernism or with former colonial powers. As a result missionary activity is suspect and the attempt is even made to confine, if not to eliminate, it. The Church does not operate in a vacuum, nor does she try to create a vacuum. "She is not, because of her supra-national character, placed aloft as though suspended in an inaccessible and untangible isolation above the nations; for just as Christ was in the midst of men, so too the Church in which He continues to live is placed in the midst of people." (Pope Pius XII, Christmas Message, 1945.)

The Church extends herself among human beings who live in definite, concrete circumstances, are subject to definite influences—political, economic, social—and aspire to definite objectives. None of these factors can be ignored by the Church if she wishes to be realistic and to belong to a people.

The countries of Latin America present a problem for the Church which is different from the problems in non-Christian nations. Nominally the vast majority of these people are Catholic. But the content of their faith is limited. The growth of the Church was arrested for several reasons. A spirit of political and ecclesiastical paternalism endured for too long. The movements for independence from Spain were founded upon the philosophy of the French Revolution with its well-known anticlericalism and even anti-Christian spirit. In its name the Church was attacked and abused and dispossessed as well as the colonial government. The ranks of the priesthood and religious life were decimated by expulsion and the failure to develop adequately a local priesthood. The Church was blamed for the sins of the powerful and the wealthy, who too often were not distinguished for any Christian social spirit. The arrested growth poses the problem of developing the life of the Church and carrying it to maturity. The instruments for renewed growth will be the expansion of local responsibility for priestly and religious life, the development of a stronger and a better-instructed Catholicism, and the formation of a vigorous and apostolic laity which will translate into national life and action the comprehensive teaching of the Church. The fire of Catholic faith that lies smoldering in the souls of millions must be fed with knowledge, conviction, and a sense of personal responsibility.

Has the Church been taken unprepared for the challenge in the missionary world? A superficial glance might lead the unknowing to conclude that the Church has outlived her usefulness. There is resistance, persecution, restriction, almost annihilation in some places. But immediate approval and acceptance are not the sole measure of the value of Catholicism. If it were, one might say that the Church is not even pertinent to the Western scene because much of her teaching is not approved. Disapproval does not of necessity imply lack of value.

If the preparedness of the Church for situations is to be fairly judged, then the thinking of the Church on events and movements should be studied. The Church reveals her vitality by her perpetual presentness, and that presentness is discovered in her teaching. The execution of her teaching does not always depend upon the vitality of the Church. Often it may depend upon the readiness of society to accept her advanced thought. Actually Western society has not been willing or ready to profit by the pertinent teaching of the Church.

Essentially the pertinence of the Church to our times is the pertinence of spiritual and moral values to every age. It is no valid charge against the Church that people resist her spiritual and moral teaching. It is a more valid charge against society itself, which is always unrealistic when it seeks to order the life of man without such values in the forefront of its designs. The concern of the Church is always the proclamation of the spiritual and moral implications of all human activity. While it is not the function of the Church to direct and control these areas of life, it is her function to give the moral principles which should be the foundation and the goal of such development. Any familiarity with the teaching of the Church during the last quarter of a century reveals the universality as well as the precision of the Church's thought and interest concerning all the problems of this age. With limited personnel and resources the missionary Church has been reducing this teaching to practice, especially in the cultural and social spheres.

A cursory survey of the problems which have been confronted by the Church in this one generation makes clear the presentness of the Church to our times. On the political level much thought has been given to the international community of nations and the political conditions for peace. The philosophy of the functions of the modern state, its purposes, rights, obligations, and dangers, has been constantly expressed in terms of the political forms of our times. The nature of true democracy, the duties of citizenship, the relation of government to the other areas of life, the true objective of colonial power, the responsibility of the developed nations toward the undeveloped have been clearly presented. Undergirding all teaching concerning the international community is the idea of human solidarity. Basic to the conduct of national life is the principle of subsidiarity upon which the Church has constantly insisted.

In the economic sphere the Church has been at pains to call to the mind of the world the divine design for the development of the potential of the material world, the divine purposes which should dictate the use of resources that owe their origin to a creating God. The social doctrine of the Church as it looks toward economic development has been greatly refined by the world's experience during the last half century. A staunch defense has been made of the right of private property as fundamental to any healthy economic and human order. At the same time the social obligations of ownership have been declared. The teaching of the Church on the condition of the working classes and what is demanded in justice for the improvement of such people has been one of her foremost contributions to social thinking in our times. The value of technology and the threat of a technological spirit have been analyzed. The place of government in the economic development of a nation has been measured and not at all infected with the extremism which is characteristic of so much thought in the economic field. The moral principles involved favor neither an economic utopia achievable by rugged individualism and untouchable private enterprise nor one achievable by the collectivistic dream of communism. There has been a strong preoccupation in the Church's thinking with the development of social justice and the primacy of the spiritual and the human in the field of economic development. No one has been more consistent and constant than the Church in speaking of the rights and obligations both of ownership and labor.

The Church has been fearless in her insistence on the place of religion in individual, national, and international life. A constant cause of concern in modern society which has elicited very much teaching by the Church is the status of the family, its spiritual ideals and its centrality in community thinking and planning. The Church has spoken on the objectives of education, the morality of human relations in every sphere, the moral responsibility to the common good of the media of communication, the ideals of the arts and the sciences.

This list could be multiplied considerably, but the summary of the Church's thought should be more than enough to show the realism of the Church and her sensitivity to the movements of the times. Honesty would dictate the judgment that the Church is ready to assist in the clarification and realization of the legitimate aspirations and goals of modern man. Her very involvement in the human scene has called forth emphases, dogmatic and practical, which are a proof of her grasp of the problems and the needs of society. The translation of this teaching into action is not the direct function of the Church in many spheres of national and international life. Especially in the political arena the philosophy of government can influence courses of action only through the Catholic people engaged in government. But the sympathy of the Church with national aspirations to independence has been manifest. To show her readiness to meet these aspirations the Church has increased the native hierarchy in India, Africa, Japan, the Philippines. The record of

Catholics in contributing to the political aspirations of their people is clear in India, Vietnam, Indonesia, and the emerging countries of Africa. There is a less emphasized and perhaps a less obvious contribution by missions to the achievement of legitimate goals. It is the patient formation of people through religion and education with a sense of personal dignity and social responsibility. This is a fact which by its very nature prepares a people to undertake political processes with understanding and restraint.

In the area of economic development and material advance the Church has often been ahead of governments in informing peoples with a measure of self-reliance and self-sufficiency. Missionaries have taken the lead in the establishment of credit union and co-operative movements which have given to their participants a degree of material security that they had never known. By these means people have been freed from the vicious system of moneylenders which kept them in perpetual dependence and poverty. Agricultural and trade schools have prepared leaders and skilled workers for the field of production, and methods have been improved. Experimentation with cattle and crops for the better living of people has been carried on in a number of centers. Catholic Institutes of Social Order have been established for the development of leadership in the social field and for extending the influence of Christian attitudes in the economic and social fields. In some countries missionaries themselves have had to initiate movements for the organization of workers who are trained to assume the guidance of their own destinies according to Christian concepts of social justice. Missionaries have even inaugurated decent housing programs. While the development of better economic and social conditions is not the direct function of the Church, she has generously engaged in such activity with great sacrifice where governments have been delinquent.

In many countries the Church was first in undertaking

the education of illiterate and undeveloped peoples, and thereby has been responsible for their cultural elevation far beyond our power to calculate. This magnificent mission of education continues with even greater energy. The number of schools from the elementary to the university level con-ducted by the missionary Church proves the Church's sensi-tivity to the cultural needs of emerging populations. These schools also testify to the generosity and sacrifice of the Church in meeting such needs. It is painful to read the ad-verse comments by certain visiting commissions on the in-adequacy of mission schools for the needs of our times. Long before the nations of the mid-twentieth century or their com-missions were interested in the cultural development of these people, the Church was hard at work in order to pre-pare them to take their place with honor both in the interna-tional community and in the Church Universal. It is even more painful to have these commissions deliberately ignore the cultural efforts of the Church. One may be sure that they themselves could never do as well with the limited resources on which the Church has to rely. After all, the Church could not in the past nor can she now call upon the millions in money which are at the disposal of the United Nations and governments and foundations. Surely harsh criticism which shows no knowledge of the facts comes with poor grace from people who have never made any sacrifices for the cultural development of underprivileged peoples.

The Church is second to none in the contribution she is making to the cultural elevation of millions of people in mis-sion lands. At the present time she is expanding her pro-grams of education and social works. There is some difficulty in meeting the somewhat arbitrary demands of officialdom. There is the distress of being judged by purely political agen-cies which show too little sensitivity to the religious factors which are a primary concern of the Church. Even more un-realistic are official reports which pretend to offer competent surveys of the cultural, social, and economic conditions of emerging populations and maintain an incomprehensible silence about the instrumentality of the Church in the lives of these people. However, only the unwilling or the uninformed can accuse the Church of being out of touch with the cultural and social needs of people.

The establishment of a mature Church is always the objective of the missionary. This maturity requires the ability of a people to assume the responsibility of Catholic life. In recent years the Church has increased the responsibility of the local Churches by the appointment of so many local bishops. Very serious attention and effort are given to the formation of the local clergy and to the development of religious orders for men and women. Vocations to the priesthood and to religious life are multiplying all over the mission world. There is no stronger argument to combat a charge of foreignness against the Church than a priesthood and religious societies drawn from the very life of a nation. The foreign missionary has never been considered a permanent institution in any mission land. He does not make a place for himself, but for the Church. The backbone of the Church's life in any nation is the clergy, and this foundation is being firmly established in all mission lands.

The missionary of the mid-twentieth century works in a society which differs in so many aspects from society half a century ago. Because this is a period of world-wide transition, he is immersed in populations seething with unrest and new aspirations. It might be said that the service given by the missionary Church for several centuries is bearing its fruit in the awakening of peoples to exciting visions of freedom, self-respect, and self-reliance. But no advance is ever without difficulty and challenge. The missionary finds himself cast in a somewhat new role. Formerly in many parts of the world his character and value were accepted because the ruling colonial powers accepted him—England, France, Holland, Belgium. His efforts to spread Christianity were more or less approved. Now new and independent nations have to be convinced of his worth, because naturally they tend to identify him with the former ruling powers which sponsored or protected or guaranteed his presence. His Occidental origins and the memory of colonialism are not in his favor. He is on his own without the questionable value of Western or colonial support.

This change in his position has been emphasized in the Church by the insistence on the supra-national, almost supra-cultural character of the missionary. He is constantly reminded that he represents no race, no nation, no culture, but only Christ and His Church. It is to his advantage to be dissociated from the purely Western elements of his culture, from the incubus of colonialism and from the misrepresentation of Christianity by so-called Christian nations.

The missionary cannot, however, assume that he will be acceptable to these nations on the basis of his purely religious character. In fact his religious efforts are circumscribed in some places and rejected in others. His cultural and social efforts on behalf of peoples are acceptable while his religious objective is frowned upon by some groups. So he is constrained to preserve his presence and to continue to penetrate the lives of people with different approaches.

This difference of approach and contact has been recognized by the Church in her teaching and directives for the modern missionary. It is evident, first of all, in the kind of training which is given to the missionary. In addition to philosophy and theology his preparation includes such things as the basic principles of cultural anthropology and sociology, an orientation in the economic factors in modern society, a more alert attention to the movements which are affecting the whole world. Thus he is prepared for a better understanding of peoples in their own milieu. He is enabled to offer clearer guidance and help to peoples undergoing the bewilderment of sudden change. Missionary congresses are conducted to investigate the changes in atmosphere and the changes in methods required to meet new situations. Mission institutes have been formed which offer to missionaries more scientific and specialized training for their areas. Missionary writing and research have increased startlingly in the last decade. The science of missiology has taken on new stature and significance.

Very prominent in the principles which guide modern missionary activity is the principle of accommodation or adaptation. This principle proceeds from a profound knowledge of local life and its expression in social, cultural, and religious forms. It is predicated on the fact of elements of goodness and truth in every civilization, high or low. These elements of goodness and truth are the missionary's points of contact with civilizations; upon the foundation of them he builds the new supernatural society of the faith. His mission is not a mission of destruction and condemnation, but a mission of elevation and enrichment. This attitude is especially true of the modern missionary, and it is shown particularly in the linguistic and artistic adaptations which have been made. The primary concern of the missionary is to reveal the universality of the Church and her right to belong to the life of every nation.

During the last quarter of a century the role of the laity in the activity of the Church has assumed a place of central importance. It is clear that the modern error of the secularization of most areas of society can be successfully withstood only when the laity assumes its responsibility for the preservation of Christian principles and spirit in society. This situation is being met by the formation of lay apostles and leaders. The value of this development is deeply impressed when one realizes that the survival of the Church in China now depends upon an enlightened and apostolic laity and that the laity are rising magnificently to the challenge.

Already groups have been formed in Europe and the United States to further the idea of the lay missionary. These lay missionaries are men and women who have special professions and skills which they dedicate to the Church in foreign lands. As laity they are able to live a life that is closer to and more deeply involved in the lives of people; this the missionary priest or religious cannot do. They are more at home in works of the social and economic order than the priest or the religious. By their activity they reveal to people the value of temporal things for a Christian life. From their efforts one may justly expect a richer development of local lay leadership in fulfillment of the Church's emphasis on the role of the laity universally.

The Jesuits' part in this vigorous and alert missionary apostolate is evident from the preceding essays. The Jesuits have played an important role in the development of mission science. They have borne a large share of the work in perfecting the methods of preparation for mission work. The Semaine de Missiologie of Louvain was inaugurated by Pierre Charles, S.J. Each year this congress of missionaries and missiologists meets to discuss specific problems of the apostolate. In this country the Jesuits have participated largely in the annual Missionary Experts Conference, held at Fordham University. They have taken the responsibility for the conduct of the Institute of Mission Studies at Fordham University, which offers to missionaries specialized courses in missiology, cultural anthropology, linguistics, area studies, and modern techniques and methods. At the Gregorian University in Rome the Jesuits conduct graduate courses in missiology for the doctoral degree in the science.

Ordinarily one would hesitate to venture an opinion about the future, especially in view of the experience of the Church in China, North Korea, and Vietnam under the oppression and suppression of communism. However, there are cogent reasons for echoing the judgment of Pope Pius XII that the Church is about to move into the most remarkable period of her long missionary history. Never has the whole Church been so sensitive to the vast missionary enterprise. The Church is on the crest of the most intense missionary movement in her history—a movement that began to accumulate force during the last century, has continued to increase up to our time, and shows no signs of diminishing. Her geographical expansion is the most complete it has ever been. The numerical strength of her missionary forces is the largest in history. The ranks of native bishops, priests, and religious have grown extraordinarily during the last quarter century. The training of her missionary personnel has become more specialized and comprehensive than it has been since the beginning.

History offers encouraging thoughts. It took the Church almost a thousand years to reach the ends of the small continent of Europe. The full concrete vision of her world apostolate was not presented to the Church until the discoveries of the sixteenth century. It is only four centuries since the Church began her expansion into those vast territories which are the mission lands of our times. So the Church is still very young in many places. One does not expect the strength and vitality of maturity, but there has been continuous growth and coverage of the world of souls. For all these reasons there is strong hope, one might almost say breathless expectancy, in the Church as she advances with our times into the new world that is a-borning.